Software Patents

NEW HORIZONS IN INTELLECTUAL PROPERTY

Series Editors: Christine Greenhalgh, Robert Pitkethly and Michael Spence, *Senior Research Associates, Oxford Intellectual Property Research Centre, St Peter's College, Oxford, UK*

In an increasingly virtual world, where information is more freely accessible, protection of intellectual property rights is facing a new set of challenges and raising new issues. This exciting new series is designed to provide a unique interdisciplinary forum for high quality works of scholarship on all aspects of intellectual property, drawing from the fields of economics, management and law.

The focus of the series is on the development of original thinking in intellectual property, with topics ranging from copyright to patents, from trademarks to confidentiality and from trade-related intellectual property agreements to competition policy and antitrust. Innovative theoretical and empirical work will be encouraged from both established authors and the new generation of scholars.

Titles in the series include:

The International Political Economy of Intellectual Property Rights
Meir Perez Pugatch

Software Patents
Economic Impacts and Policy Implications
Edited by Knut Blind, Jakob Edler and Michael Friedewald

The Management of Intellectual Property
Edited by Derek Bosworth and Elizabeth Webster

Software Patents
Economic Impacts and Policy Implications

Knut Blind

Senior Researcher and Deputy Head of the Department of Innovation Systems and Policy, Fraunhofer Institute for Systems and Innovation Research, Karlsruhe, and Reader, Faculty of Economics, University of Kassel, Germany

Jakob Edler

Senior Researcher and Deputy Head of the Department of Innovation Systems and Policy, Fraunhofer Institute for Systems and Innovation Research, Karlsruhe, Germany

Michael Friedewald

Senior Researcher, Department of Emerging Technologies, Fraunhofer Institute for Systems and Innovation Research, Karlsruhe, Germany

NEW HORIZONS IN INTELLECTUAL PROPERTY

Edward Elgar
Cheltenham, UK • Northampton, MA, USA

Published by
Edward Elgar Publishing Limited
Glensanda House
Montpellier Parade
Cheltenham
Glos GL50 1UA
UK

Edward Elgar Publishing, Inc.
136 West Street
Suite 202
Northampton
Massachusetts 01060
USA

A catalogue record for this book
is available from the British Library

ISBN 1 84542 488 3

Printed and bound in Great Britain by MPG Books Ltd, Bodmin, Cornwall

Contents

Figures

Tables

Foreword

This book investigates empirically the economic implications of the patenting of software-related inventions. It evolved from two studies conducted in the years 2001 until 2003 on behalf of the German Federal Ministry for Economics and Labour (BMWA) (formerly the Federal Ministry for Economics and Technology, BMWi). The studies are based upon a written survey of software-producing enterprises as well as a number of concrete individual case studies. The first of these two studies comprised, besides the economic analysis of the Fraunhofer Institute for Systems and Innovation Research (Fraunhofer ISI), Karlsruhe, a comparative legal analysis, which was carried out by Ralph Nack and Joseph Straus from the Max Planck Institute (MPI) for Intellectual Property, Competition and Tax Law. However, the present publication limits itself to the empirical evidence of the economic aspects. Moreover, it does not claim to take all the literature on this subject published since 2002 into account. However, a screening of more recent literature revealed only modifications of existing arguments and a confirmation of our empirical evidence. Nevertheless, this publication would not have been possible in this form without the insights and analyses by the colleagues of the Max Planck Institute. For this reason, our sincerest thanks go to Ralph Nack and Joseph Straus. We thank also Wolfgang Knappe from the Fraunhofer Patent Office for German Research, who unstintingly provided his practical expertise.

Sincere thanks also go to our colleagues at the Fraunhofer Institute for Systems and Innovation Research. Rainer Frietsch supplied indispensable statistical analyses, Ulrich Schmoch his many years of experience with the practices and snares of patenting, Chris Mahler-Johnston translated the manuscript from German into English. Thanks also go to Renate Klein and Sabine Wurst, who with style and élan took pains to achieve editorial clarity, and Jan Mueller, whose pragmatism and dedication made possible the practical realization of the details of the empirical survey.

The Federal Ministry for Economics and Labour as sponsor gave the impulse for this work. A special share in the success of the studies belongs to Ms Weber-Cludius, the responsible expert in the Ministry, for her many suggestions and forthcoming management style, for which we would like to express hearty thanks here. Thanks also go to the organizers and participants of a workshop in the Federal Ministry for Economics and Labour, during which the results of the written survey were presented and discussed.

Karlsruhe, August 2005

1. Introduction

1.1 MOTIVATION

In February 2002 the European Commission presented a new draft guideline which should regulate the patentability of software-related inventions in Europe (Commission of the European Communities 2002). This draft was fiercely debated. Not only the EU Council of Ministers, but also the EU Parliament proposed a number of changes in the year 2003. The question of the patentability of software-related inventions also sparked off heated and in part very controversial discussions among the software-producing and software-utilizing industry, as well as further interest groups, in particular the so-called 'independent developers' of software. The draft guideline is based among others on Europe-wide exploratory feelers which the Commission itself stretched out in October 2000 (Commission of the European Communities 2000) and in which not only governments, but also the interested community were integrated. Parallel to these consultations, the Member States of the European Patent Agreement had already consulted with the European Patent Office about changes relating to the possibilities of patenting software-related inventions. The entire discussion process was difficult and showed just how disputed the question of property rights in the software field is.

The main question is whether software-related inventions should in future be more easily accessible to patent protection in Europe – like the model of the United States of America – or whether, in view of assumed idiosyncrasies in the development and economic utilization of software, patents for software should be awarded more restrictively. The background to the discussions is the fear that the lack of uniform legal regulation Europe-wide could hinder the competitiveness of the software sector and thus also the economic growth of the European Union as a whole. The proposal of the Commission was a new milestone on the way to consolidate the property rights regime in Europe and adapt to new requirements. Its basic thrust was finally to standardize the practice of insidiously extending software patentability through the patent offices in Europe. The European Parliament (European Parliament 2003) has conversely much more restrictive ideas, while the Council of Ministers has adopted a mediating position (Council of the European Union 2002). Meanwhile the European Commission and the Council of Ministers (Council of the European Union 2004) have published a common proposal for a new directive, which still has to be approved by the European Parliament. However, the controversial discussion which preceded the Commission's proposal and is still continuing has made only too evident that this adaptation process will be fraught with difficulties.[1]

The controversy broke out in part because the view was advanced that patents for computer software could promote innovations, as in other technology fields, as they could offer the respective owner an appropriate protection for their innovations, so that greater incentives would arise for further investments in the development of high-performance software. The opposite position, which is formulated above all by the so-called 'open source' movement,[2] refers to the fact that patents undermine fair competition by facilitating the creation of monopolies and thereby hindering innovations.

Independent of the positions in the debate on principles, the present legal situation is unsatisfactory, because there is a lack of clarity and legal certainty in the area of patenting software-based inventions.[3] 'Programs for data processing systems', that is, computer programs as such, removed from their technical base, are not patentable inventions. However, not only the national patent offices in Europe, but also the European Patent Office have awarded patents for technical inventions in which a computer program is used. Furthermore, a software algorithm can be patented in connection with the computer on which the software runs. Software patenting is more easily possible in the United States; the patent classes are also more strongly oriented towards software-related inventions. There is even a patent class in the American Patent Office USPTO for electronic data processing supported business processes (705), which experienced a strong upsurge of patent awards between the mid-1990s and the year 2000, though the patent applications of European firms have not grown beyond an insignificant level (Blind et al. 2003c).

Against the backdrop of legal uncertainties, economic controversy and the European fear of losing out on competitiveness in the software industry to the United States, various studies were carried out. In 1999, the European Commission commissioned a study on the economic impact dimensions of the patentability of computer programs. However, Hart et al. (2000) merely depicted the current legal situation in Europe, the USA and Japan and presented

---

[1] In August 2005, the revised proposal for the new directive was rejected.

[2] The term 'open source movement' describes all those developers of software, who make the source code of their developments – on condition of reciprocity – generally accessible and see themselves greatly handicapped by the patentability of software. See Chapter 2, Section 2.3 for more details on this.

[3] For these statements on the legal situation we have to thank Ralph Nack from the Max Planck Institute (MPI) for Intellectual Property, Competition and Tax Law to a large extent.

economic arguments for and against a patentability of software on a qualitative level, without validating or quantifying this empirically. In the same manner, Lutterbeck et al. (2000) discuss in their study, on behalf of the German Federal Ministry for Economics and Technology, patent law in the most important economic areas, the legal implications of software patents for open source software development and derive therefrom recommendations for action for future patent policy. One of the central conclusions of the investigation conducted by Lutterbeck et al. (2000) is to establish the economic facts and the current developments in the relevant court decisions empirically, before taking a final decision.

This book takes up this recommendation. It intends to contribute to the current process information in the form of empirical analyses from the economic perspective covering the period of transition from the old to the new and still unclear patent regime and sees itself as a contribution to the scientific support and objectification of the debate. The goal was to formulate economic policy recommendations for shaping the future patent regime in the area of software innovations.

This work is based on two separate studies. First of all, by means of a broadly based, empirical representative survey performed in the year 2001, the actual situation and opinions of the software industry regarding the subject of software patents were sounded out.[4] Thus a valid data basis was created, unlike for example the consultative procedure via the Internet, conducted by the European Commission (PbT Consultants 2001) or the British government.[5]

But even such a broadly based survey naturally leaves gaps in the analysis and judgement of economic policy implications of changes in the patent regime. By means of the survey alone, for instance, it is not possible to clarify adequately which mechanisms in the respective companies lead to positive or negative economic consequences of a certain regulation of the patent regime. At the same time, it became clear in the written survey that the majority of the firms want neither an extension of patenting nor an exclusion of software-based inventions from patenting. Still in this grey area of diffuse agreement, dissatisfaction with or fears relating to the existing system became apparent. This dissatisfaction of the majority of firms could only be understood after conducting detailed case studies and analyzing the concrete experiences made by the enterprises.

For these reasons, the second study[6] took into consideration the concrete contexts of the companies in 22 individual case studies mainly drawn from the respondents to the written survey. The aim of these case studies performed

---

[4]   The German version of the first study can be found in Blind et al. (2003b).
[5]   See Webb (2001) as well as UK Patent Office (2001).
[6]   The full German version of this second study was published as Blind et al. (2003a).

in 2002 and 2003 was to present the concrete impacts of existing property law regulations in the software sector on innovation behavior and competitive strategies, and to evaluate their possible advantages and disadvantages for the individual enterprise, or for types of enterprises. The main emphasis thereby, as in the analysis of the survey, was clearly placed on patenting possibilities. The in-depth and differentiated insights made possible a better and sounder assessment of the current empirical data from the representative company survey. Furthermore, they contributed to a confirmation or further precision of the conclusions and recommendations for action derived from the survey.

1.2   INVESTIGATION TARGETS

The targets of the two research projects can be specified as follows:

- to identify appropriate protection forms for intellectual property in the Internet-based knowledge and information society from the micro- and the macroeconomic perspective;
- to evaluate the present patent protection of software innovations regarding innovation and growth impacts against the background of origin, diffusion and application forms of software products and different contexts of companies;
- to formulate recommendations to policy-makers on designing legal protection, in particular patent protection, of the intellectual property contained in software innovations.

1.3   INVESTIGATION STEPS

In order to achieve the above formulated targets, the following steps were undertaken in the investigation:

- evaluation of available literature on the economic effects of protection laws in the area of software-based inventions;
- conduct and analysis of the representative survey of innovation behavior, as well as the market, competitive and protection strategies of German and European enterprises in the various fields of the software sector, taking into consideration proprietary or free software products;
- conduct and analysis of 22 individual case studies in software-producing enterprises;
- formulation of recommendations based on the results of the two empirical studies.

The results and conclusions of both studies are integrated in this book. It is divided into four main parts. First of all, in Chapter 2 an overview is given of the relevant literature in economics on the subject of patent protection in general and software patents in particular, which leads to the structuring of the empirical search and the elaboration of the questionnaire. Chapter 3 presents the results of the written survey. Thereafter, in Chapter 4 the analyses on the basis of the 22 case studies follow, which are presented grouped according to 'patenting types'. Instead of a separate summary of the case studies in Chapter 4, in Chapter 5 the analytical summary of the case study results will be joined directly to the important results of the written survey, thus qualifying the written survey and placing it in context. On this basis then in Chapter 6 a number of recommendations are also formulated for the further development of the regulations for patenting software-based inventions in the future.

1.4   DEFINITION OF TERMS USED

Concepts are often differently defined, not only in the area of property laws, but also in the software sector. For this reason, we provide our definition of the crucial terms used before the literature review.

In Europe, patents have in general only been awarded to inventions in the software area if they have a technical character, that is, in simple language, if they fulfill a function by means of a technical apparatus, if they are based on technical considerations, if they cause a technical effect or if they influence a physical characteristic of an apparatus. When we talk of patents on software- and computer-related inventions, then those inventions patentable in actual practice are meant. By contrast, patents on 'software as such' ('software patents') are in general not awarded in Europe because of the patent laws and court decisions, that is, program codes alone *de jure* cannot be patented without their technical-functional link, that is, only as a mathematical algorithm. Many kinds of computer programs are therefore not patentable in Europe, unlike in the USA. If we mean patenting relevant for software-developing actors in general, without an exact legal reference, then we talk of patents in the software area.

By software development we understand the new or further development, as well as adaptation, of computer programs with the aid of a programming language. It does not include any activities which are within the framework of utilizing software, for example producing Word macros or HTML pages.

The survey and the case studies not only cover companies and independent software developers from the software sector, but also contain enterprises from selected sectors of manufacturing industry, inasmuch as they develop

software themselves for their 'hardware'. Software, which is irrevocably integrated in hardware components and can only function in conjunction with
them, such as for example specific control software in mechanical engineering or vehicle construction, we refer to as embedded software.

A special problem with regard to intellectual property rights exists in the
software sector due to the existence of so-called open source software (OSS).
By OSS is meant that the source code of an application has to be made available (via the Internet) and not only in a compiled form as a software as such.
Moreover anybody is denied the right of exclusive exploitation of a work (St
Laurent 2004). This offers the opportunity to develop the program further
and adapt it to the needs of the individual users. According to the widely
spread Gnu Public License (GPL), OSS is to provided free of charge and
along with the complete source code of the application, even though a reproduction cost or service cost may be charged. Regarding patents, the GPL is
very explicit:

> Finally, any free program is threatened constantly by software patents. We wish to
> avoid the danger that redistributors of a free program will individually obtain pat-
> ent licenses, in effect making the program proprietary. To prevent this, we have
> made it clear that any patent must be licensed for everyone's free use or not li-
> censed at all. (Free Software Foundation 1991)

We refer to those rights which protect intellectual property ('intellectual
objects'/immaterial goods) as intellectual property rights. Third parties may
use these immaterial goods for commercial purposes only with the agreement
of the owner of the right. Among these rights are counted patents, design
patents (petty patents) and trade marks. In contrast to patents, trade marks
and design patents, copyrights cannot be formally applied for in Europe; they
originate automatically with the work. Third parties may exploit for private
purposes a work protected by copyright only with the agreement of the
originator. On the whole, the focus in the discussion about intellectual property rights – if not explicitly further differentiated – is directed above all to
patent protection.

2. Literature Survey

The objective in compiling the literature survey was, on the one hand, to form an overview of the relevant literature available in the year 2001. Further, in a second step, hypotheses were derived which were to be tested in the empirical survey. The literature overview resumes in the first section the fundamental economic arguments in favor of and against intellectual protection rights, respectively patents. The second section is devoted to the central theme of the study, software and intellectual protection rights, whereby firstly the idiosyncrasies of software and their impacts on the effective and efficient design of intellectual protection rights are explored. The second subsection deals with empirical surveys of the patenting behavior of enterprises in general and of software enterprises in particular. In the third subsection, the interdependencies between software patenting and the activities of the open source developers discussed in the literature are sketched. The literature overview concludes with a summary of the arguments for and against patenting software.

2.1 ECONOMIC FUNCTIONS OF INTELLECTUAL PROPERTY RIGHTS

2.1.1 Microeconomic Perspective

The fundamental goal of the protection of intellectual property consists in creating incentives which maximize the difference between the value of the intellectual property that was created and utilized, and the costs of its creation, including the costs for administering the system (Besen and Raskind 1991, p. 5).

Private producers have an incentive to invest in innovation activities only if they obtain a reasonable return from them. Whether the producers have adequate incentives depends on their ability to appropriate at least a part of the estimated value of their innovation from the users. If potential innovators are limited in their ability to grasp this value, then they have only insufficient incentives to invest the socially optimal amount of resources in innovation activities. This is especially the case when other producers can easily copy the products (Arrow 1962), when private users can easily copy the products,

or when the legal framework permits innovations which are in a close sub-
stitution relationship to the original innovation.

A patent gives the holder a temporary, limited monopoly. This allows the
innovator to ask a price for his innovative product which is above the competition price (Scherer and Ross 1990). These above-average returns compensate him for the expenditure invested in innovation activities and for the risk
he took. Consequently, the possibility to patent 'software as such' has positive effects on dynamics and growth of the software sector, because the incentives for spending on development activities increase, and simultaneously
more information about new developments are released (H36).[1] From the
economic perspective, the challenge consists in designing the intellectual protection rights in such a manner that the incentives to innovate that they generate are maximized, and welfare losses caused by the granting of a monopoly
are minimized. Further, it must be considered that the patent system as a
winner-takes-all system in the competition for the patent and thus for a certain control over following innovations does not stimulate an excessive investment of resources. The sum of the expenditures of two firms that want to
win the same patentable invention in a so-called patent race can therefore not
only be higher than those of a single firm, but also higher than is socially desirable (Dasgupta and Stiglitz 1980; Loury 1979). Finally, in designing the
protective rights system, the administrative costs not only of the state institutions but also of the companies and private inventors must be taken into
account.

In return for granting the monopoly, it is argued that certain regulations of
intellectual property rights can also lower the costs for subsequent innovators, in that the copyright registration and the patent application force the
authors and innovators to disclose details of their innovations. This disclosure
may supply subsequent innovators with information which can lower their
own innovation costs. Furthermore, copyrights and patents are not awarded
in all areas, for example the 'discovery' of natural laws. If in addition an
efficient and friction-free market for licenses is assumed, then it can be pre-
sumed that subsequent innovators can efficiently buy these licenses and
profit from the precursor's work (Ordover 1991).

The last decisive question is whether the system of intellectual property
rights can contribute to a reasonable balance between the production and the
diffusion of intellectual property. The creation of incentives to create new
works and inventions leads to resources being spent on innovation activities.
If innovations however are not widely used, then the system is possibly less
efficient than an alternative one which admittedly offers less incentive for

---

[1]   The number in brackets refers to the hypothesis listed in the Appendices.

creative activities, but permits a wider diffusion of new ideas. In this context, the work of Nordhaus (1969) on the length of patent protection and the analyses of the trade-off between length and breadth of patent protection should be mentioned (Gilbert and Shapiro 1990; Klemperer 1990). In case a successful innovation activity depends only to a limited degree on the invested resources and financial incentives, the less a strong protection of intellectual property rights is justified. Despite a long-standing tradition of economic research, there is no consensus about the impact of patent protection on technical change (Kitch 1977), on the optimal length of patent protection (McFetridge and Rafiquzzaman 1986) and on the question as to whether patents have facilitated the formation of cartels (Hall 1986).

2.1.2 Macroeconomic Perspective

Derived from micro-economic considerations, intellectual protection rights also have a macroeconomic significance. Here two dimensions can be basically differentiated. On the one hand, especially in the growth theory literature, the implications of intellectual property rights for the growth of the economy as a whole are discussed. On the other hand, the literature on foreign trade expounds the problems which the impact of different protection regimes create for trade flows and direct investments. The latest investigations into these two areas and their results will be presented below shortly.

In growth literature, most recently since Romer's revolutionary work (1990) on endogenous growth theory, the elementary significance of the factor of knowledge or technical progress has been recognized. Regarding intellectual property rights, the question is now posed whether stronger protective rights create stronger incentives to create more innovations, which again broaden the knowledge bases of the whole economy and thus increase economic growth. For it is conversely argued in the meantime, among others by Jaffe (1999) and Thumm (2000b), that protection rights can also be employed by competitive enterprises to block innovation activities, so that the patent system can be a zero-sumgame or even a game with negative net effect, which may even lead to serious impairment of innovation dynamics for the sector as a whole (H33).[2] Jaffe (1999) also finds no empirical evidence that the system of intellectual protection rights positively influences innovation behavior. Kortum and Lerner (1997) underline his estimation, for they show in their investigations that the most recent increase in patent applications in the United States extended to all technology areas, but can be traced

---

[2] A pronounced form of this strategy is the targeted patenting of components which the competitor has not patented, but which are essential for his product. Rivette and Kline (2000) describe this as 'bracketing'.

back above all to an altered innovation management tending towards a stronger application orientation, and is not founded on an increased innovation potential. The rise in R&D expenditures have rather receded since the beginning of the 1990s. Empirical studies by Gould and Gruben (1996) show, however, that intellectual property rights, especially in open economies, positively influence growth. Thompson and Rushing (1999) also find that patent protection and total factor productivity are in a positive correlation in prosperous economies and thereby favor the growth rate. A positive connection between the intensity of patent protection and real per capita income is empirically underpinned by Maskus (1998).

Keely and Quah (1998) criticize the focus of empirical growth literature on R&D expenditures as input indicators and intellectual property rights, in particular patents, as output indicators in the growth debate, because they refer above all to innovation processes in firms, and the knowledge generated by universities and other state institutions is undervalued because of measurement problems. The high significance of freely accessible knowledge for economic growth, by comparison with proprietary knowledge, was quantified by Jungmittag et al. (1999), who show that for Germany the stock of technical standards and rules has a greater influence on economic growth than the patent stocks. This study points clearly to the ambivalence of intellectual property rights between a positive incentive function for innovators and restriction of technology diffusion, also on a macroeconomic level. For innovations are only a necessary, but not an adequate condition for sustainable growth for the whole economy. Only the broad diffusion of the innovations due to the market introduction of new products or by means of specification of new technical norms or standards raises overall economic production (Blind and Grupp 2000). Transferring this argument to the software sector leads to the following reasoning. Enterprises disclose the source codes of their different software products under certain conditions, and deliver their software free of charge, so that formal protection mechanisms are not necessary. By extending patenting in the field of software- and computer-related inventions, counter-productive effects for the economy as a whole could be triggered off if know-how diffusion is restricted (H16).

If the macroeconomic impact dimensions of intellectual property rights are extended from a closed to an open economy, then the areas of foreign trade and direct investments must also be discussed (Thumm 2000a). Grossman and Helpman (1991) developed the first theoretical models of these strategies from endogenous growth theory, which are not only complementary but also in a substitutive relationship to each other. Due to the complexity of the models, no unambiguous statements can be made on the causality between intellectual property rights, direct investments and foreign trade. For this reason we shall restrict our overview to the empirical investigations.

Not only foreign trade, but also direct investments are influenced by the intellectual property rights regime in the target country. Maskus (1998) finds signs that exporting to countries with strict patent protection is more highly developed. This can be explained by the fact that there is less danger of product imitation here. The case is similar with direct investments. Direct investments are also lower in the countries with weakly developed property rights for the above-mentioned reason. These findings confirm the results of Lee and Mansfield (1996), who determine a positive relation between the direct investment behavior of over 100 US enterprises in developing countries and the functioning of the systems of intellectual property protection there. International technology transfer is also closely related to direct investments. However, no empirical investigations on the relationship between the intensity of intellectual property rights and the extent of technology transfer are available. Extending this argument to the software sector, an expansion of the patent protection for software may increase the incentive for direct investments from abroad, because the foreign investors can better appropriate the profits from their investments in software development (H32).

Follow-up studies by Maskus and Penubarti (1998) and Smith (1999) differentiate the results of Maskus (1998) with reference to foreign trade. For weak patent protection in the importing country only presents a trade barrier for exporters if at the same time the danger of imitation is high. If, on the other hand, patent protection in the importing country is highly developed, then the threat of product imitation lessens, but simultaneously the competitiveness of the local producers is strengthened, if they can achieve a certain monopolistic position through patent protection and can thus withstand the competition from imports.

2.2 SOFTWARE AND INTELLECTUAL PROPERTY RIGHTS

2.2.1 The Significance of the Idiosyncrasies of Software for Intellectual Property Rights

The transition from an industrial economy to a services- and knowledge-based economy also calls the system of intellectual property rights into question. For patent protection in particular, which was tried and tested in the industrial age, can only conditionally be transferred to services or knowledge-intensive markets. The customer-oriented development and the marketing of knowledge-intensive 'complex product' software exhibit a number of characteristics which make it necessary to specify the general function of intellectual property rights (Bessen 2001; Kash and Kingston 2001; Smets-Solanes

2000).[3] Therefore, the central initial presumption upon which the survey is based is that software and its distinct characteristics and functions will influence the significance of property rights. The literature is also largely in agreement about the most important idiosyncrasies of software and the innovation processes in the software area. The following literature review will not so much discuss the existence of these three particular characteristics; this is one central subject of the empirical investigation. It concentrates rather on the relationship of these particular characteristics to intellectual property rights, especially patents.

Some authors question the functionality of patents in the software sector in general, because of numerous idiosyncrasies of software. Due to these idiosyncrasies, patenting does not play a large role; there is neither a broad awareness nor any perception of need. The need for protection is met by other strategic tools (H23). On the one hand, the speed of innovation is extremely fast: by the time a patent is awarded, 'inventions' have changed again or have been replaced by own or above all competitors' further developments (Jaffe 1999; Murillo 1998; Nalley 2000) (H9). In addition, complexity and confusion abound. Software developments are for the most part the result of the compilation of various inputs from different sources. In many cases, the contribution of the individual inventors cannot even be exactly defined, because software developments are frequently the product of complementary activities (Kash and Kingston 2001). The interoperability of the various components and the sequentiality of the innovation process are of great significance in the software area. Both aspects may be hampered by extended patenting possibilities (H10). Furthermore, the effect of patents in the area of software- and computer-related inventions on the innovation activity of enterprises which reuse their own code to a great extent may be positive, because additional incentives for development investments are created (H13a). The effect may also be negative, because complete product lines can be thus protected and monopolies which are difficult to contest are thereby created (H13b). Moreover, often very similar developments are being worked on simultaneously in many locations. This contributes to a special problem of the software sector, which is that today already in many cases the 'state of the art' cannot be reconstructed by the individual inventors and possibly cannot be adequately investigated. For this reason, so argues for example Smets-Solanes (2001), software inventors see themselves exposed to possible patent infringements without being able to gauge this danger

---

[3] There are few authors in the literature who completely deny the particularities of the software sector. One of the rare examples is Heckel (1996), who interprets all arguments against patenting in the software sector as arguments against patents per se and cannot discover any specifics at all which necessitate special regulations for patents.

adequately. This can either be due to the fact that individual inventors do not have the possibility to carry out patent searches for every detail of their programs, or that the inventions on which their own activities are based are not sufficiently documented. The alternatives in these cases consist in either possible patent infringement or the decision not to exploit a development commercially (Smets-Solanes 2001, p. 75). Establishing the 'state of the art' as well as obtaining a cheap, comprehensive overview of possible patent infringements are more difficult, the more generously patents are awarded for software and individually functional, broadly applicable program parts (Bessen 2001; Dam 1995; Gerwinski 2000; Kash and Kingston 2001; Smets-Solanes 2001, p. 75). But it is exactly the complexity and confusion in the software area which leads to patents being awarded for inventions whose level of invention is frequently very low (Académie des Technologies 2001); in other words, it is not unusual that patents are applied for and awarded for usual concepts in software development (trivial patents, see Sietmann 2001 and Garfinkel et al. 1996). The innovation-hampering effect of this dilemma appears obvious in this perspective.

Besen and Raskind (1991) see patent protection in the software sector as less significant because an effective price differentiation allows the producers of innovative products to appropriate a larger part of the returns on innovations even without formal property rights. For example, pioneering enterprises that introduce market novelties have a 'first-mover advantage' and are therefore not so much forced to rely on patents (H8a). In the software sector, it is possible that the price for software licenses is determined depending on the number of users, among other factors. Further, so-called embedded software (software implemented in hardware) can be indirectly protected by the patent protection applicable to the hardware, so that patents in the area of software- and computer-related inventions are of less importance by comparison with independent (stand-alone) software (H2). In an unfavorable case, a monopoly in a hardware market can thus be transferred to complementary software markets (Farrell and Saloner 1992).

A focal question for Besen and Raskind (1991) is whether intellectual property rights, and especially patents, represent the most efficient form of protection, also in the software sector. The costs of creating new ideas in the software sector often depend on the extent to which the innovators are able to have recourse to earlier work, that is, the development of different types of software products depends very much on the input of other developers or firms. Furthermore, the interoperability of the various components and the sequentiality of the innovation process are of great significance in the software area. Both might be hampered by extended patenting possibilities (H10). In addition, the innovation process in software development is characterized by incremental improvements, which to a large extent have recourse to already existing own or foreign code (H12). On the one hand, the effect of patents in the area of software- and computer-related inventions on the innovation activity of enterprises which reuse their own code to a great extent might be positive, because additional incentives for development investments are created (H13a). On the other hand, the effect of patents in the area of software- and computer-related inventions on the innovation activity of other firms which reuse their own code to a large extent might be negative, because complete product lines can thus be protected and monopolies which are difficult to contest are created thereby (H13b). Patent and copyright protection, however, tend to limit recourse to already existing ideas, by giving the creator the right not only to his or her own creation, but also to derivative works, so that the costs for succeeding innovators increase.[4]

A counter argument is quoted (Besen and Raskind 1991) that certain regulations of intellectual property rights can also lower the costs for subsequent innovators, because the copyright registration and the patent application force the author and innovators to disclose details of their innovations. This disclosure may supply succeeding innovators with information which lowers their own innovation costs; sequentiality is thus increased.

Applied to the innovation process in the software industry, two general chains of cause and effect regarding innovation costs can be perceived which are decisive for the efficiency of intellectual property rights. If the software on which the subsequent developments are based is freeware and shareware, then the innovation costs incurred are correspondingly low. It can be derived from this that the economic risk of an innovation process remains manageable and thus the justification for a strong protection of intellectual property is limited. If the exploitation of existing software elements is not possible due to formal and informal protection strategies, or is very expensive, then the innovation costs increase also, and the innovation risk for software development rises sharply. In order to guarantee sufficient innovation incentives despite a correspondingly increased innovation risk, an innovator will take advantage of comprehensive formal protection (H10; H12; H13).

Besides the question of costs, the question of returns on software innovations also presents a special feature. Due to the high innovation dynamic in the software sector which leads to the situation where an innovative product can be replaced within a relatively short space of time by a further developed competitive product, the period in which monopoly rents can be appropriated is extremely limited. By means of intellectual property

---

[4]   In addition, the direct costs of patenting must be reckoned with, which increase the often relatively low development costs by a considerable factor, which is a great strain cost-wise on the many small or one-man enterprises and could make their innovations unusually expensive (Smets-Solanes 2000).

rights, an artificial extension of this period can be achieved, so that the incentives to innovate are sufficiently large. It must however also be considered that through so-called network effects on the demand side, the willingness to pay for the software product increases with an increasing number of users, and the willingness to change to another product decreases (Shapiro and Varian 1999). Intellectual property rights can reinforce these software-immanent appropriation mechanisms to such an extent that lasting monopoly positions are formed. On the other hand, these mechanisms possibly also create incentives to market proprietary products at a below-cost price or even for free, if by this means the demand for complementary products is increased (Shapiro and Varian 1999).[5] For the same reason Shy and Thisse (1999) see a decreasing propensity to patent in the software area. Many enterprises have recognized that without the obstacle of patents – for instance, via imitators – or complementary products, better interoperability and more network effects are engendered and thus more demand is generated for the original product. Their theory is therefore that the stronger the network effects, the lower the propensity to patent (H19; H20). However, the interoperability of products and systems might decrease as a result of stronger patent protection (H34).

In a contrast typical of the subject for intellectual property rights in the software sector, we find an opposite conclusion derived from empirical investigations. Stolpe (2000) perceives, in the areas in which network effects are becoming important, an increased propensity to utilize property rights which would make it possible to internalize positive externalities and rapidly achieve a high market penetration without product piracy and imitation. Simultaneously, he also sees the dangers of too strong a protection in the areas with high network effects through creating a lasting monopoly. He therefore calls for a protective mechanism which differentiates according to software types and individual market segments, and takes into account the different cost sensibilities and benefit expectations (network effects) with reference to protection rights in the software area (H19).

After the observations on the role of sequentiality on software development and the influence of patents, the significant role played by network effects, the necessary standardization, and in a further step the interactions with intellectual property rights must be dealt with. Computer users profit from standardized interfaces in multiple ways (Farrell and Saloner 1985; Katz and Shapiro 1985). The greater the interoperability, or degree of standardization, the greater too is the diversity of complementary inputs

---

[5]   In his theoretical model, Takeyama (1994) even finds evidence that illegal copying of intellectual property rights in view of demand-induced network effects increases not only enterprise profits but also overall economic welfare.

(software, repairs), which are at the user's disposal and the easier the change from one system to another.[6] Patenting may limit interoperability (H19).

Standards have two opposite consequences. On the one hand, they possibly prevent radical innovations up to a new basic standard by fostering lock-ins and reduce first of all the variety of products. At the same time, though, standards ensure compatibility between the products fulfilling the standard; a 'compatible system' evolves. One effect of this compatibility consists in increasing the combination possibilities of products, and hence indirectly the application variety and product utility are strengthened. Because in such a system only new components and not the entire system must be newly developed, the incentive to innovate is increased and therefore also the competitive intensity and the speed of innovation.

Small firms above all see advantages in standards, as they, unlike large enterprises, cannot form their own internal enterprise networks, which build on works standards. The non-existence of a standard can lead to a lock-in of old customers and thus to a monopoly, because the costs of changing are correspondingly high. Sellers prefer incompatibility under certain circumstances because this generates significant switching costs for the customers. New customers can possibly prefer incompatibility, if this triggers off an intensive price competition, so that in this case the sellers prefer possible compatibility.

Farrell (1989) was the first to analyze the influence of intellectual property rights on the standardization in industries, for which compatibility is of crucial significance.[7] The computer and software industries belong to this group. Accordingly, compatibility aspects must be taken into especial consideration when deciding on the design of intellectual property rights, because interoperability is strongly influenced by formal and informal protective mechanisms (H1). This applies not only for the extent, but also for the type of protection. Mazzoleni and Nelson (1998) argue in favor of rethinking the present patent protection, especially for so-called system technologies, whose functioning depends largely on compatible components.

In a regime with weak protection rights, a successful innovation will rapidly attract numerous rival imitators, who will push forward onto the market with similar and compatible products. This will lead to a competitive situation within the compatible and as-standard accepted specification. As the users do not see themselves in a monopoly situation or in danger of a lock-in, the standard will be further diffused and so produce further positive feedback loops. In a so-called open standard, not protected by property rights,

---

[6]   So a frequent argument against patenting is that the common establishment of interoperability between new software developments would be crucially hampered (see also Smets-Solanes 2000).

[7]   Similar statements can be found in Farrell (1995) and in Farrell and Katz (1998).

enterprises compete on the parameters of price, performance and additional product characteristics.

In a regime with strict protection rights, compatibility between the solutions of the different suppliers is made more difficult and competition within a standard less probable. Logically, there is more competition between incompatible products, so that no common specification is crystallized as *de facto* standard, network effects are not possible, and the market becomes fragmented.

Thoughts on competition expressed by Katz and Shapiro (1986) concentrate on a model with two technologies. In the competition of two open, that is, non-protected technologies for market shares, one technology will prevail as the *de facto* standard. We will observe no penetration pricing, that is, prices far below the average cost during the product introduction phase, because the losses in the market penetration phase cannot be compensated for in a consolidated market. The price therefore in all market phases reflects the costs and the benefits with respect to the willingness to pay of the users and customers. Without possibilities of protection, no penetration pricing strategy is pursued, so that a product will not prevail because of initial costs which are higher than the utility for the early adopters, and the expectation regarding the future market penetration will decrease, negatively affecting the adoption behavior (Shapiro and Varian 1999).

On the contrary, in a competition between proprietary technologies, a penetration pricing strategy is possible. In the case of two proprietary standards, in the long term the better one will prevail, so that a market advantage which is bought at the cost of quality reduction does not pay off. However, in a competitive situation with one proprietary and an open standard, an inferior proprietary standard can win the upper hand against a better open standard because of the possibility of pursuing a penetration pricing strategy.

Proceeding from this theoretically based analysis, it can be derived that intellectual property rights make the pursuit of a penetration pricing strategy possible. This means, on the one hand, that the suppliers of products which must first reach a critical mass, have a greater probability to achieve a successful market introduction. On the other hand, in competition, the qualitatively better technology is more liable to triumph. Seen as a whole, intellectual property rights thus contribute to an increase of total welfare, seen from an economic perspective.

If network effects are present on the demand side, as is usually the case with software, then these conclusions must be modified (Farrell 1989). These effects also enable the suppliers to apply a penetration pricing strategy,[8] so

---

[8] A certain cost level is estimated here for costs ensuing from a switch from one system to another.

that the additional award of intellectual property rights is of advantage for the individual enterprise; however in combination, the network effects and switching costs can very easily lead to a monopoly formation, which causes economic welfare losses, not only in a static but also in a dynamic regard (Church and Ware 1998, p. 243; Jaffe 1999) (H5).

One result from the literature survey is therefore that a balanced design of intellectual property rights in industries with network effects should aim on the one hand that economically desirable innovations be stimulated, and on the other hand, however, that the network externalities be extensively realized. In the case of software, a useful innovation should enjoy a certain protection in the sense of a trade-off between a reasonable fee for the inventor and an adequate diffusion. In order to ensure the latter, the user interfaces, the storage and transmission format should be standardized, in order to retain compatibility effects, and not be protected so that other software developers are encouraged to accept these standards and to manufacture compatible products. By disclosing code, enterprises try to establish their products and programs as standard software. However, patenting involves extensive licensing negotiations which in turn lead to higher costs for formal standardization (H18).

Bessen and Maskin (2000) arrive at a similar result in their model of sequential innovation processes, whereby they do not take the network effects on the demand side characteristic for software into account. As they lay particular stress on the already mentioned sequentiality which is an essential feature of innovation in the software sector and is directly influenced by property rights, this model will be discussed in somewhat more depth here. Bessen and Maskin argue that an enterprise which protects its new products by patents could prevent competitors from further developing their products in the software industry with its sequential and complementary innovation processes. For example, due to sequential innovation cycles, patents on operating systems and components of operating systems can lead to a slowing down of technical progress more seriously than patents on application software, which is developed parallel for various areas of application (H3). In general, the interoperability of the various components and the sequentiality of the innovation process are of great significance in the software sector. Both are hampered by extended patenting possibilities (H10). However, the effect of patents in the area of software- and computer-related inventions on the innovation activity of enterprises which reuse their own code to a great extent might be positive, because additional incentives for development investments are created. In contrast, the effect of patents in the area of software- and computer-related inventions on the innovation activity of other firms which reuse their own code to a large extent might also be negative, because complete product lines can thus be protected and monopolies which are difficult to contest are thereby created (H13). As competitors might possibly have ideas which the original inventor did not have, patenting can put a brake on innovation speed in the software industry (see also Kash and Kingston 2001). Licensing would admittedly be possible, but that creates a higher competitive or price pressure which eats up the profits. Therefore the patent-holders have no interest in granting licenses.[9] Jaffe (1999) cites as a counter-argument against patent protection for software that developers must procure the necessary licenses for the various software fragments, which leads not only to considerable administrative efforts, but also to financial costs. In such a constellation large enterprises are at an advantage as they can invest in a comprehensive patent portfolio and thereby be in a good position for negotiating cross-licenses. The dynamic of the software industry is however mainly borne by small software firms whose hands are tied by excessive patenting and who thus can no longer guarantee the innovation dynamic of the entire sector, because they have neither the awareness nor the resources to make effective use of patenting (H39). In addition, enterprises conduct software development in co-operation. Property rights have here under certain circumstances a reverse meaning: on the one hand, they increase the legal security and create clarity in co-operation agreements, on the other hand, however, they erect entry barriers, if firms without a property rights portfolio are refused access to co-operations. Further, they are then unnecessary if a controlled exchange of code and know-how takes place in existing co-operations (H40).

In a model without patent protection, the basic assumption is that an easy imitation of innovations can reduce the innovators' profits, but at the same time make new innovations possible, which again open up new opportunities for follow-up innovations for the originally innovating company. For this reason also, incentives to invest in R&D are higher in a regime without patent protection than in a system with patent protection.

The empirical evidence for the sequential innovation model presented by Bessen and Maskin refers above all to the decline in R&D investments and productivity in the American software sector after the explicit introduction of software patents at the beginning of the 1980s. However, besides these data aggregated on the sector level they do not have enterprise data in their model-theoretically derived causality. Based on the deductions from their theoretical model, they recommend a patenting policy which although restricting the simple copying and imitation of innovative products, allows competitors to make

[9] Ordover (1991) therefore suggests complementing a regime of strict intellectual property rights by a liberal licensing practice. Church and Ware (1998) go a step further and propose a mandatory licensing after a relatively short exclusive exploitation period. As a counter example to a functioning licensing practice, Jaffe (1999) cites the semiconductor industry, where small start-up companies have specialized in developing new chips and have them patented for mass production, but willingly sell the necessary license to large enterprises.

valuable complementary innovations. In this sense, to them copyright protection seems more appropriate to create this balance than patent protection. Further, they argue in favor of a restriction of the breadth of patent protection.

Farrell (1989), on the other hand, views copyright critically too, especially when he refers to arbitrarily designed interfaces. For while the copyright for traditional creative work does not hamper follow-up innovations, in network systems subsequent innovators can be considerably hindered by the protection of arbitrary design aspects. The award of copyright to user interfaces, and to the 'look and feel' of programs, brings unusually large profits for the owner. Competition is not completely prevented by this; but for incompatible solutions a situation with monopolistic competition with greatly reduced price and quality competition can emerge. Simultaneously he cites that through a distinctive protection of intellectual property, such as with patents, the innovation scene is directed away from marginal to radical innovations, which is of economic advantage as long as the resource input is not extended unduly. In order to limit the protection of arbitrary and less innovative specifications and to promote radical innovations, copyright on software should be cut back, and at the same time patent protection which demands a certain level of innovation should be extended.

This different estimation of the meaning of intellectual property rights in general for innovation in the software industry, but also the assessment of the interplay between copyright and patent protection, can be explained by two differing assumptions. Bessen and Maskin (2000) assume in their model exclusively sequentiality and complementarity in the software innovation process. Farrell (1989; 1995) and Farrell and Katz (1998) differentiate on the other hand between incremental innovations, on which Bessen and Maskin concentrate, and radical innovations. Logically, they prefer copyright on principle for the first innovation type and patent protection for the last innovation type. In addition, they assume like Messerschmitt and Szyperski (2001) strong network effects on the demand side, which Bessen and Maskin (2000) fade out in their model. This leads to Farrell also adopting a critical position regarding the copyright referring to interfaces or standard programs used by many economic units, because thereby economically desirable network effects can only be inadequately exploited. On the other hand these network effects form obstacles to radical innovations because they limit the willingness of the users to switch to a new product. Therefore Farrell argues at the same time for patent protection for radical innovations which makes it possible for the innovators to build up a critical mass of users for their innovative products through intelligent price strategies. Without patent protection this venture has a low probability of success.

In the end, in the reality of software development, not only incremental but also radical innovations are basically of elementary significance.

However, there is no empirical evidence as to which innovation type is now dominant and to what extent the network effects quoted by many authors are actually to be observed in software products and programs.

Besides the idiosyncrasies of the innovation process, the marketing channels of the software firms also influence the property rights discussion. For in the meantime software, like so many other digital goods, is marketed via the medium of the Internet. Emery (1996) therefore emphasizes that for digital goods which are placed at the customers' disposal via information and communication networks; especially strict and worldwide enforceable protection right regimes should apply. Technical protective mechanisms such as encoding techniques do not suffice.

Finally, some authors stress that in view of the partly relativized classical functionality of patents in the software sector, the strategic functionality of patents for enterprises has developed particularly strongly and that an additional macroeconomic function lies herein. This means that patents for complex products no longer serve only as actual protection from imitation and thus the appropriation of innovation profits, but are used in the market for multiple purposes (Cohen et al. 2000). Patent portfolios are built up in order that companies are in a position to offer cross-licenses in negotiations with competitors. Together with the prospect of licensing income, this can *de facto* lead to a transfer of knowledge between competitors, which without patenting practice (confidentiality) would not be possible in this manner (see also Smets-Solanes 2000). Patents thus serve increasingly as bargaining chips in strategic alliances (Kash and Kingston 2001) and meanwhile contribute in the market for enterprises (mergers and acquisitions) as well as in the capital market for enterprises (Richardson 1997) to the functioning of the market, by sinking transaction costs and reducing uncertainties (similarly Académie des Technologies 2001). This applies to a number of sectors, but in the knowledge-intensive software industry this function plays a particular role, which in view of an aggressive global competition over future-oriented enterprises and the dominance of the patent-intensive US market will tend to increase (H24).

What impact this development will have for legal certainty and the costs for the legal system is controversial. Whereas property rights tend to eliminate lack of clarity in markets, in the case of the complex and incrementally worked out software developments they could possibly lead to an increase in litigation, with the associated costs (Horns 2000, Para 62 ff). However, legal actions in the area of software- and computer-related patents are still very rare in Europe. German firms are also very rarely the plaintiffs. Nevertheless, the number of legal conflicts might correlate with the activities abroad and company size, respectively market structure (H29).

Numerous authors see the additional danger that if large companies increasingly build up patent portfolios, in order to survive the 'portfolio war' with large internal patent organizations and aggressive patent strategies, patents will turn from being a passive protective mechanism into an active strategic means with the side-effect that development activities are hampered by ever more patents, which in the real sense do not serve the direct need to protect their holders (for example Smets-Solanes 2000; 2001).

2.2.2   Enterprise-Specific Reasons for Using Intellectual Protection Rights

The utilization of intellectual protection rights discussed in the previous section must be regarded in the whole context of the formal and informal protection strategies at the disposal of enterprises. Machlup (1958) questioned the relevance in particular of patent protection for the incentives of enterprises to engage in research and development. In the following, the most important empirical studies published up to the year 2001 on the use of patent protection and other formal and informal protective strategies by companies will be presented, first of all from a general perspective, then specified to companies in the software sector.

In the 1980s, Mansfield (1986) and Levin et al. (1987) conducted investigations among firms with R&D activities. They can essentially confirm Machlup's claim; in most sectors of manufacturing industry, patents are estimated neither as effective nor as necessary in their function as a protective mechanism to appropriate the returns of their R&D activities (H7). Also, the empirical data collected in the 1990s on patenting behavior in the United States (Cohen et al. 2000), in Europe (Arundel and Kabla 1998; Brouwer and Kleinknecht 1999) and Germany (Blind 2003; ifo Institut 1998) document that with the exception of the chemical or the pharmaceutical industries, patents are merely of secondary significance as protective mechanisms. Whereas according to Mansfield (1986) over two-thirds, and according to Cohen et al. (2000) around half of product innovations are patented by firms, according to Arundel and Kabla (1998) only approximately one-third apply for patents. In pharmaceuticals, chemicals, mechanical engineering and for precision instruments, on the other hand, more than half apply.

Apart from the sector-dependent differences, various company characteristics also play an important role in patenting behavior.[10] According to Arundel and Kabla (1998), the tendency to patent increases with the enterprise size (see

---

[10] While the reasons for the patenting propensity have long been empirically investigated, this applies only conditionally for other protective mechanisms. Allegrezza and Guard-Rauchs (1999) found a positive relationship between the application for trade marks and the R&D intensity for firms in the Benelux area. Blind et al. (2003c) further find a positive correlation between patent and trade mark applications for a sample of European companies.

also Brouwer and Kleinknecht 1999). Surprisingly, in contrast to Acs and Audretsch (1989), they could not determine a positive correlation between the R&D intensity and the propensity to patent (H7). Based on data from the European Innovation Survey (CIS), Brouwer and Kleinknecht (1999) can confirm the importance of patents for companies which participate in R&D co-operations (H40). Patents serve here to formalize the technology transfer and to secure own R&D knowledge vis-à-vis the co-operation partners.

It is criticized that in these studies established and rather large enterprises were questioned as a rule. Small and newly founded companies however have a greater need of patent protection, especially in order to gain time to set up their own production capacities, to realize effects of scale or generate license income. Further, patents constitute securities for the process technologies used and products manufactured by small and medium-sized enterprises, which facilitate their access to the capital market (H31). Furthermore, property rights secure the amortization of high development costs on the part of pioneering companies. These firms might support and make more use of patents (H8).

Common to all studies mentioned, however, is that secrecy and time-leadership in the market introduction represent much more significant protection strategies (H8). Due to the idiosyncrasies of the software field, patenting will even play a minor role; there is neither a broad awareness nor any perception of need. The need of protection is met by other strategic tools (H23). However, Cohen et al. (2000), the ifo Institut (1998) and recently Blind et al. (2004) point out that besides the protection motive, a number of other reasons cause firms to apply for patent protection. As the most important motives, they cite that firms attempt to block the innovation activities of competitors by means of patents, and want to protect themselves preemptively against patent infringement lawsuits. In the area of software- and computer-related inventions the significance of the reasons which stand in the way of a patent depends on the various types of software products (H26) The patenting activities of companies also producing hardware follow the example of their general patenting activities in the traditional product field.

The cited studies refer essentially to sectors in manufacturing industry. For the service sector, we can only point to the second Innovation Survey in Europe (Eurostat 2000), the work of Djellal and Gallouj (2001) and Blind et al. (2003c). Not only the survey results of Eurostat (2000) and Djellal and Gallouj (2001), but also the analysis of Blind et al. (2003c), which referred to the actual patent applications, make clear that patents for service enterprises are considered to be less effective in their protective function and used accordingly. There are numerous theoretical studies for the software sector, but very few empirical data on the utilization of various mechanisms. No systematic studies are available for Europe at all.

Only very few specific investigations of the importance of company characteristics for patenting in the software sector exist. They all concentrate on the kind of software produced and do not consider other characteristics such as company size, market form or general innovation strategies. A somewhat older study by Samuelson et al. (1992) makes clear that the majority of software firms do not protect their products or modules, but if they do, then this is mainly via copyright. Copyright is used in particular to protect source code (in 91 per cent of the cases), whereas patents, if used at all, especially protect individual algorithms (in only 9 per cent of the cases). A more recent study by Oz (1998) differentiates according to the type of software developed by the company. He concludes that software enterprises favor copyrights as protective mechanisms much more than patents. If patents are favored, then this is mainly to protect algorithms (by 43 per cent of the firms questioned), while support of patent protection for source codes and modular designs amounts to approximately 25 per cent, and patents are almost completely rejected for all other software types.[11] Derived from these findings, we postulate the following hypotheses. Due to sequential innovation cycles, patents on operating systems and components of operating systems can lead rather to a slowing down of technical progress than patents on application software, which is developed in parallel for various areas of application (H3). In addition, in the area of software- and computer-related inventions the significance of the reasons which stand in the way of a patent depends on the various types of software products (H26). For bespoke software the necessary protection can be achieved by bilateral contracts between producer and client. Consequently, patents might lose (some of) their meaning (H4).

Stolpe (2000) analyzed the willingness and propensity of software companies in the software sector in Germany to invest in protecting their products. However, he did not inquire about intellectual protection rights, but about using certain hardware devices, so-called 'dongles', to secure software. He too concludes that the tendency to take security precautions is generally very weak (only 29 per cent of the firms utilize dongles) and in general the sensitivity to costs for protection measures is high. Again, due to the idiosyncrasies of the software field, patenting does not play a large role; there is neither a broad awareness nor any perception of need. The need of protection is obviously met by other strategic tools (H23).

Up till now there were no empirical data on the extent to which the degree of interoperability of a firm's own products with the products and systems of other firms influence the protection practice and attitude to patenting in companies. The literature supposes, for obvious reasons, a negative correlation:

[11] Oz questioned patent attorneys and software firms, and it is revealing that they speak much more strongly in defense of patents than the software firms themselves (Oz 1998, p. 167).

the more the products of a company depend on interoperability, the less they will be in favor of patents (H19). Conversely, the more patenting is accepted, the less the products on the software market will be interoperable (Murillo 1998) (H34).

To what extent the willingness to secure software is correlated with the size – or even with the age – of the enterprise, has not yet been empirically investigated. The literature assumes almost unanimously, however, that here, even more than for manufacturing industry, SMEs – the following applies implicitly also for young enterprises – are at a disadvantage.[12] The basic problem of many SMEs is that they do not have the resources, knowledge and willingness to make adequate use of patenting (Dam 1995; Hart et al. 2000; O'Reilly 2000) (H22, H39, H41). Furthermore, SMEs conduct fewer searches in patent databases for cost reasons (H27). In addition, the number of legal proceedings correlates with the activities abroad, company size and market structure (H29). On the one hand, this means that SMEs do not patent enough or do not patent at all. According to Murillo (1998), one-product companies in particular endanger their very existence, as they need patents not only for so-called signaling (demonstration of innovative ability), but also to protect their real assets – knowledge (Murillo 1998). SMEs are less able than large enterprises to perceive the direct strategic potentials of patents, although these would provide SMEs with important opportunities (Gerwinski 2000; ifo Institut 1998). Patents have a very broad strategic significance, which extends beyond the mere protection from imitation. This strategic meaning correlates positively with the enterprise size or the market structure and with activities abroad (H25). Through a more efficient portfolio management, large enterprises can establish an efficient portfolio balance in software development projects, so that they are less dependent on a temporary monopoly generated by patents (H37). On the other hand, and here many independent developers see the main problem (see Section 2.2.3), they run a greater danger of unknowingly infringing the patents of other parties. While these special problems are regarded by SMEs on the one hand as a structural problem that cannot be removed (Gerwinski 2000; O'Reilly 2000; Sietmann 2001; see also Section 2.2.3 in this volume), others see the possibility to increase the ability and willingness of SMEs to patent systematically (Académie des Technologies 2001; Hart et al. 2000).

At that time, most authors who express their views on this complex subject see in the particular problems of SMEs (and even more so of independent developers) a central problem, not only for the individual enterprises, but for the dynamics and variety of the whole software sector. Thus for example

---

[12] Over all patent classes, more than half of all applications are lodged by 2.4 per cent of applicants, all of them large enterprises (Sietmann 2001).

Kash and Kingston (2001), Lea (2000) and Smets-Solanes (2000) unanimously point out that in the software sector the great number of SMEs contribute most to innovation, and see the danger that because of these structural problems large enterprises would tend to gain advantages over the more innovative and dynamic SMEs, by increasing their patenting. If these assumptions are correct, then an increase in patenting practice in the software sector would decidedly put a brake on innovation dynamics. Company characteristics and their impacts on innovation and protection behavior is therefore a central dimension in the empirical survey of this study.

2.2.3   The Special Problems of Open Source Development

The practice of patenting software which has increased in recent years has led to opposition, especially in the open source movement.[13]

But besides the protagonists of open source themselves, a number of scientists have also highlighted the significance of the open source movement for economic and technological development in the software sector, and the majority of authors see in the trend to patenting, or possibly new, patent-friendly codifications, a problem for the work of numerous open source developers.

In the following are brought together the most important arguments which are being expressed about the significance of open source development, and the potential dangers or rather chances presented by patenting. It must be stated, however, that till now no broadly based investigations have existed which validly quantify the economic significance of the open source movement.[14] For this reason, the importance of the open source community must be estimated from its wide-spread diffusion and from the theoretically derivable economic and technological functionality.

A first indicator of the economic meaning of the open source-based software is simply its diffusion and the trend with which this diffusion develops.[15] The number of users of the Linux operating system, based on open source, is continually increasing worldwide.[16] According to statistics of the

[13]   The heated debate mainly conducted via the Internet in the open source community about 'software patents' need not be reproduced here in detail; but see as an introduction for example the petition by Eurolinux on the exploratory paper of the European Commission (http://petition. eurolinux.org/consultation/index_html?LANG=en) or the discussion forums of the German Linux community (http://swpat.ffii.org/).

[14]   Nüttgens and Tesei analyze and explain the fundamental concept and the institutional structure (2000a), the production, organization and diffusion (2000c), as well as the market models and economic rationality of networks (2000b). However, even these helpful studies supply only few empirical data on the economic significance of open source development.

[15]   The development and use of open source products is very differentiated; for a detailed analysis see Dempsey et al. (1999) and Nüttgens and Tesei (2000a; 2000b; 2000c).

[16]   The quoted figures are based on chance registrations by the users themselves and the

market research company IDC, 27 per cent of all Internet pages are based on the Linux operating system,[17] meaning the system is the number two in this market behind Windows (41 per cent), whereby the growth rates of the Linux system exceed those of Windows.[18] Worldwide, the Apache server based on open source occupies almost two-thirds of the market for Web servers.[19] Also, the diffusion of open source programs, as well as the practice of disclosing the source codes in enterprises, has greatly increased in the last few years. In Germany the share of software-developing companies, which (also) use open source, lies according to a survey by iX magazine at approximately 70 per cent and thus above the level in the USA (Lutterbeck et al. 2000). Open source development is not, as often assumed, a domain of independent developers and small software companies, but also increasingly plays a role for large, established hardware enterprises. This is seen for example in the announcement by IBM that will invest US$200 million in the development of open source centers in Europe from 2000 till 2005.[20] Brügge et al. (2004) provide a recent overview on studies on the implementation of open source, which confirm the variety of approaches and results.

What are the reasons for the economic benefits of open source development? The economic significance of open source development results basically from the fact that private or also industrial actors produce public goods and place them completely at the disposal of the public, free of charge, without property rights (Bessen 2001). This contradicts the generally held economic basic assumptions, according to which as a rule there is an undersupply of public goods, as their producers cannot appropriate positive externalities (free rider problem) (Arrow 1962). However, the open source developers are acting rationally. They benefit on the one hand from the personal profile in open, transparent development forms, whereby the attractiveness for and the flexibility in the job market are increased. For the appropriated knowledge is not only visible to all, but also relatively easy to apply in other

---

estimates of the actual total number of users fluctuate clearly (http://counter.li.org/trends. html, accessed 23 April 2001).

[17] The organizers of the 'Linux Counter', an Internet page on which Linux users can register themselves, amounted in April 2001 to more than 175 000 registrations, estimate the total number of users at up to 17 million. For Germany, a study by the firm iku-netz comes to the conclusion that 44 per cent of all computers hooked up to the Internet use the Linux operating system http://www.iku-netz.de/netscan/, accessed 21 April 2001.

[18] See FAZ (Frankfurter Allgemeine Zeitung) of 16 August 2001, p. 18 and Computerwoche No. 10 of 9 March 2001, p. 14. This corresponds with a survey from 1999, which revealed approximately 30 per cent of all Internet pages are based on the Linux system (1999). The market research institute IDC assumes an annual growth rate for the Linux operating system of 25 per cent (http://www.heise.de/newsticker/data/cp-03.07.01-000, accessed 23 June 2001).

[19] http://www.netcraft.com/survey/, accessed 23 April 2001.

[20] http://www.linux-community.de/Neues/story?storyid=72, accessed 8 February 2001.

enterprises (Lerner and Tirole 2000). On the other hand, open source developers generate their profit frequently in novel business models, no longer by selling the produced software, but with product-related services (Gross 2001).

The macroeconomic additional benefit from this diffusion of open source development is based in principle on typical interactive and incremental development processes which, rather than closed developments, are better able to work the complexity of software products which must provide a multiplicity of applications adapted for various users. Again, the innovation process in software development is characterized by incremental improvements, which to a large extent have recourse to already existing own or foreign code (H12). The interoperability of the various components and the sequentiality of the innovation process are of great significance in the software area. Both are hampered by extended patenting possibilities (H10). Bessen (2001) speaks in reference to the inclusion of later users in the development of the superior effectiveness of 'self-selection' in the course of open source development, as opposed to the central selection by software firms. In contrast to the classical products of manufacturing industry, the complexity of software and the possible variety of the applications leads to the situation that a greatly differentiated demand and utilization arises by single adaptations and in principle can also be satisfied. A central argument is that the parallel, interactive and transparent development of software programs by a large number of developers and testers, even possibly including the later users of the program, leads to programs and applications which are already in the development process being better adapted to the needs of specific groups of users than is possible in the traditional mode (Bessen 2001; Gross 2001). At the same time, these products, as a welcome side-effect, are relatively free of errors, more reliable and more stable compared with products with closed code.[21] The synergies of parallel development and open communication lead finally to lower costs for 'customizing' and 'de-bugging' (see also Horns 2000 §57 ff; Lerner and Tirole 2000). Added to this individual satisfaction comes a faster diffusion through the acceleration of sequential development processes, a greater variety of development results and new application possibilities (see for example Smarr and Graham 2000), as well as an improved interoperability of single programs (Murillo 1998). Finally, the transparency of open source programs serves as a guarantee for the greatest possible security for software,[22] a postulation that was last year confirmed by a top-notch committee of experts

---

[21] Quoted from Bessen (2001), p. 5.

[22] According to a study of the University of Wisconsin, which compared the open source products with commercial products (http://www.ccic.gov/pubs/pitac/pres-oss-11sep00.pdf). The present study does not go into the security aspect of open source in any detail. This aspect was the core of the study by Lutterbeck et al. (2000).

convoked by the President of the USA (among others Smarr and Graham 2000). In principle, these functions of open source are now very seldom denied (see Endres 2000) (H15). In addition, the disclosure of code has a number of important strategic motives and thus the innovation dynamic is accelerated (H17).

The question is now what impacts the various forms of intellectual property rights, especially patents, have on open source development and thus on the development of these postulated positive effects. Moderate representatives of the open source movement themselves, as well as a number of scientific authors, consider the usual patenting practice as incompatible with the open source development (Bessen 2001; Gehring 2000; Lutterbeck et al. 2000; Smarr and Graham 2000; Smets-Solanes 2000). They fear that a stronger patenting in the area of software- and computer-related inventions could limit the open source model; many open source developers even speak of the threatened end of this model[23] (H26). The basic problem for the open source developers consists in the fact that, even if they do not pursue their activities commercially in the narrower sense – and therefore a patent infringement because of commercial dealings is not actually given – they still run the risk of infringing the patents of other parties (H11). The reasoning is that 'regular provision and the regular sales' can offer grounds for patent infringements (Horns 2000). Open source freeware or shareware are characterized by particular features which are especially conducive to the development of software (open, dynamic system, high compatibility and so on), which are not met by proprietary software to the same degree (H15). Furthermore, the development efforts in the area of open source will not be increased by patents in the area of software- and computer-related inventions, because other motivations dominate here. Patents in the area of software- and computer-related inventions can even hinder the open source movement, or reduce its efforts, because as a result of easier patenting the alternative incentives for software programmers increase (H35). The given complexity and sequentiality of innovations in software products make an unnoticed patent infringement more probable than, for example, in the manufacturing industry (Dam 1995).

These basic problems are worsened by further structural problems, for open source developers are for the most part not attached to large enterprises and so are structurally unprepared for the requirements of patenting, either by information on existing patents, or for their own patent applications (Académie des Technologies 2001; Gehring 2000; Horns 2000 §55–56). Unlike large enterprises, especially from the manufacturing sector, they lack resources, time and know-how. Established, especially large enterprises on the

---

[23] For the discussion of the open source community in Germany, see http://www.swpat.ffii.org.

contrary have appropriate resources and knowledge[24] (H21). Hardware manufacturers have an advantage in the patenting of software because of their size and due to established patent activities (experience, fixed costs) (H6).

The discussed alternatives for protection rights in the area of open source development range from an undifferentiated inclusion of all inventions with 'technical reference' in patenting, regardless of the original model, up to a radical refusal to patent software developments generally. Beyond these extreme positions, various differentiated demands are to be found in the literature, which attempt to reconcile the significance of open source on the one hand, and the existing framework of patenting on the other. They consist in for example under certain conditions removing the open source codes from patent protection (Smets-Solanes 2000), in other words, to introduce a kind of 'source text privilege'' (see also Horns 2000, §80; Lutterbeck et al. 2000, p. 9).[25] A further suggestion is to introduce a novelty grace period, in recognition of the short innovation cycles of the software sector and the significance of open source for speed of the developments; this would enable the initiator of new code to communicate the same without forfeiting his claim to a patent by this action (in particular see Gehring 2000) (H30).

Few authors also see a chance for the open source movement in the trend towards more patenting. Nichols (1999) for example assumes that stronger patenting will lead to intensive competition between a few, presumably lucrative applications, and the open source movement would concentrate on the multiplicity of specific niches. For Smets-Solanes (2000), who basically emphasizes the negative consequences of patents for open source developers, patents have on software at least the effect that the codification, publication and thus also the diffusion of technological knowledge, as in other sectors also, would be improved by patent applications and publications. However, this information function might not play an important role in the software sector, as the information about new developments runs through other channels here and is available via other mechanisms (H28). In this way open source developers can also be informed about algorithms, which are not available to them at present because of the usual secrecy practices of large

---

[24] See for example an internal information brochure published by the patent department of Siemens which calls on its software developers: 'Do you think that software is not patentable? Read this brochure!'

[25] Without going into a legal discussion at this stage, we point out the problems of this demand. The construction of a source text privilege does not remove the problem of patent infringements, but postpones it. As the framework of intellectual protection rights otherwise remains and thereby in particular industrial application would establish patent infringements, then a potential industrial user of software which was developed on an open source basis and contains a code which is part of a valid patent, would run the danger of infringing a patent. This would consequently limit the attractiveness of open source developments which would continue to be carried out without recourse to patent searches for industrial clients.

software companies. A report for the European Commission acknowledges that the balance of positive and negative effects of patents in the software area is somewhat less favorable than in many other sectors, but it considers patents to be fundamentally reconcilable with the conditions of the software sector and therefore also open source development (Hart et al. 2000, in particular pp. 31 ff). The authors stress the possibility, with reference to the USA, that independent developers can also realize economic advantages through patenting (similarly Murillo 1998, p. 198). However, the strategic significance of patents, which extends beyond the mere protection from imitation, is more important for large enterprises with activities abroad (H28). In addition, patents on the capital market count as significant measures of the value of an enterprise and thereby possess direct economic value. Therefore, patent protection facilitates market entry for young software enterprises, as it offers them easier access to the capital market and gives them time to expand their production capacities (H31). Hart et al. (2000) see no empirical evidence that the independent developers would already be hindered in the existing patenting practice in Europe by large enterprises. However, they too warn of the danger that, as in the USA, too many trivial patents are awarded and thereby too many algorithms could be blocked.

As a result of this short discussion of the broad literature on open source and intellectual property rights, it can be determined that the economic and technical significance of open source is mainly undisputed, even if empirical data are missing. As regards the consequences of increased patenting in the software sector for the development of open source activities, on the other hand, there is no conformity. The review however showed that the problems in this area tend to be seen more strongly than in the software sector generally or even in other sectors. This lies especially in the particularly open forms of communication, which many authors and developers regard as threatened by protection rights. But in the area of open source development, there is a dearth of empirical data on the role of open source software in the software sector and how the developers of open source software are disadvantaged by patenting.

2.3 SUMMING UP: SUMMARY OF POSITIVE AND NEGATIVE IMPACTS OF PATENTS IN GENERAL AND SOFTWARE PATENTS IN PARTICULAR

The entire literature overview and this selective compilation have made one aspect clear: not only are the active market participants divided on the question of patenting software, but the scientific literature also does not present a uniform picture. If the history of the discussion about patenting is regarded

(Boch 1999; Gerster 1980, Chapter 2), there have always been conflicts about the private ownership of ideas. The qualitative novelty in this discussion, as appears from the literature screening, derives from the particular character-istics of software and the market for software: sequentiality, incremental deve-lopment processes, interoperability, multiple network effects, extremely short innovation cycles, parallel and complementary developments, confusion about authorship of partial inventions (code), cheap, worldwide diffusion of pro-ducts via the Internet and finally, unique in industrial history, interactive, trans-parent developments of innovations without the protection of patents. More recent empirical studies by Bessen and Hunt (2004a; 2004b) and their critical assessment by Hahn and Wallsten (2003) underline the controversial discussion and the difficulty of achieving a final conclusion. In addition, these character-istics provoke different consequences in the different sub-markets of the soft-ware sector. Finally, market participants from widely differing sectors with widely varying traditions, routines and long-term interests with regard to intel-lectual property rights confront each other. Software-developing companies in the manufacturing industry have developed a culture of protecting their intellectual property, similar to enterprises that mainly produce hardware.[26] Independent developers and small software firms, which achieve a part of their added value via product-oriented services, at least according to a rea-sonable assumption, have neither sufficient knowledge of property rights nor do they see possible advantages of such protection rights for themselves.

Against this background, in various places in the literature (Holmes 2000; Murillo 1998; Nalley 2000; Smets-Solanes 2000; Stolpe 2000; Thurow 1997) – although always with different nuances and limitations – a technology- and market-specific differentiation of intellectual protection rights is repeatedly called for (*sui generis*). Oz (1998) ascertained in a survey that enterprises, and patent attorneys, would also be in favor of such a system of property rights. More moderate deviations from current patenting practice demand granting privileges to open source codes (Horns 2000; Lutterbeck et al. 2000), and specific grace periods for novelties in conjunction with compulsory licenses (Gehring 2000). Other authors reject a *sui generis* solution for soft-ware out of hand (Dam 1995) or refer to the legal problems of a comprehen-sive differentiation (Horns 2000 among others).

The empirical study was designed to be open ended (that is, without pre-conceived results) and attempted primarily to differentiate the surveyed basic population from the primary and secondary sectors[27] – as far as possible – into sub-groups, in order to question the diffuse ideas about specific practices

[26]   See Graham and Mowery (2003) for an overview of trends to protect intellectual property in the US software industry.
[27]   See Chapter 3, Section 3.1 on the methodology of the empirical survey.

and attitudes and to make the discussion objective. Thus the empirical investigation should show to what extent patenting practice and attitudes towards patenting of the various software types, enterprise forms and sub-markets differ, and which conclusions can be derived for a differentiated patent protection system, from an economic perspective.

The literature overview presented and discussed a number of potential advantages and disadvantages of intellectual property rights. In the following passage, the most significant of these advantages and disadvantages are briefly summarized.

2.3.1 Potential Advantages of Intellectual Property Rights (IPR)

General

- increase overall welfare by higher incentives for R&D and innovations,
    - ensuring innovation rents,
    - risk premium for R&D;
- protection from imitations;
- acceleration of growth through accelerated knowledge production;
- increase the attractiveness for direct investments and improve technology transfer;
- control efficient follow-up innovations and prevent unnecessary duplication of research outlay;
- ensure better and faster diffusion of new knowledge (by disclosure and licensing).

Software-specific

- broaden the knowledge flow through disclosures;
- encourage incremental and sequential development work by the disclosure of new knowledge and thus increase variety and interoperability;
- lengthen the often very short innovation lead times;
- guide innovation activities towards radical innovations, which are not tackled without patents;
- make possible penetration price strategies, which could contribute to overcoming critical user numbers
- increase the market transparency and reduce the transaction costs in the dynamic and confusing software market;
- insure the most important asset of the enterprises – knowledge – with which also SMEs and young enterprises can protect themselves against the market power of the large companies;
- facilitate access to the capital market, especially for young enterprises.

2.3.2   Potential Disadvantages of IPR

General

- lead to losses of welfare through creation of lasting monopolies;
- block the innovation activities of competitors;
- brake the diffusion of innovations (forbidding imitation, expensive license purchase);
- limit the variety of functionally equivalent products;
- lead to additional state and private administrative costs;
- reduce imports because of competition-distorting protection advantage for domestic producers;
- hinder the development of technical standards.

Software-specific

- are not suited to the idiosyncrasies of the sector (difficulty to determine the state of the art, complementary developments and so on);
- hinder freedom of information and communication about algorithms;
- hinder incremental and sequential development work (forbidding use of protected algorithms);
- thus reducing the variety and interoperability and restricting the open source movement in particular:
  - possibly blocking a great number of applications and further developments,
  - decreasing the innovation speed in the entire software sector;
- lead to misallocation of resources,
  - raise costs because of alternative designs for functionally equivalent, interoperable applications,
  - more resources for lawyers and lawsuits than for R&D;
- restrict, even if they protect only surfaces (copyright), the competition in supporting functionalities and thus prevent incremental innovations;
- cause rather long-lasting monopolies in combination with network effects;
- prevent imitations, whereby the probability of further innovations (sequentiality) and positive network effects decrease and thus the net effect (higher incentives for the first innovator) of IPR becomes negative;
- create artificial legal uncertainties;
- lead to very high additional administrative costs, relative to the R&D costs;
- lead to structural disadvantages for the more dynamic SMEs and young enterprises.

3. Empirical Investigation: A Representative Survey

Against the background of the political discussion in the years 2000 and 2001 and the hypotheses derived from the literature analysis on the pros and cons of patenting computer-implemented inventions, in spring 2001 a representative investigation was conducted of German companies that develop software. Chapter 3 contains the descriptive depiction and analysis of the answers of the sample of the representative survey, as well as the results of the statistical tests of hypotheses derived from the literature analysis, among others. The structure of the chapter is oriented on the questionnaire. The second case study based investigation, which refers not only to the sample of the representative survey but also to additional companies and cases, is presented in Chapter 4.

In Section 3.1 the composition of the total population and the realized sample are presented in detail first of all, because in the meantime software is not only produced by classical software firms, but also by companies in the manufacturing sector, that can as a rule look back on long experience with patents. Starting from the thought that the type of software produced influences the attitude to and utilization of protection strategies, the activities of the enterprises in connection with the type of self-developed software are firstly described in a differentiated manner (Section 3.2). Then a detailed depiction of the innovation activities of the companies follows (Section 3.3). This is necessary, to analyze the connection between innovation and the meaning respectively use of protective strategies in a later step. Section 3.4 is devoted to three specific characteristics of software often mentioned in connection with patenting, namely, the sequential development process, the practice of code disclosure and establishing interoperability. In Section 3.5 we show which experiences the enterprises have had with property rights and their attitudes towards them. Section 3.6 describes and analyses the estimation of possible alternatives to the status quo in property rights regulations for software and the assessment of the possible consequences of an extended patenting practice, from the perspective of companies and independent open source developers. Instead of a short summary at the end of each section, a final section (3.7) summarizes the essential results of the representative survey in an overview.

One basic hypothesis of the investigation assumes significant differences between enterprises whose main purpose is to develop and market software (primary sector), and companies of the so-called secondary sector, which besides a traditional main business also manufacture software for commercial use. For this reason the answers are basically differentiated according to these two groups in Chapter 3. In some cases, in which the group of independent open source developers differs strongly from the other firms within the primary sector, the answers of the primary sector are shown divided into independent developers and other companies. In the test of the working hypotheses, the differentiation between the primary and secondary sectors is retained if the significance test can prove an essential difference between the sectors. If this is not the case, then the hypotheses are tested on the basis of the whole sample, as there is no danger of a statistically subcritical number of answers. Finally, in selected questions, it was determined that the enterprise size has a fundamental influence on the answers, so this differentiation is additionally shown.

3.1 METHODS AND SAMPLE

The questionnaire and the hypotheses were drawn up in February and March 2001 by the whole project team, with the support of the Max Planck Institute for Intellectual Property, Competition and Tax Law and the Fraunhofer Patent Office, with the Fraunhofer Institute for Systems and Innovation Research ISI as project leader. In March 2001 the resulting drafts were discussed and co-ordinated with the BMWi (Federal Ministry for Economics, meanwhile the Federal Ministry for Economics and Labour) in several feedback loops. This co-ordination also covered checking and commenting on the questionnaire drafts by experts named by the BMWi, as well as experts contacted by Fraunhofer ISI. After two pre-tests in April the actual survey was carried out in April and May 2001 as an Internet-based survey, that is, the addressees received in an e-mail or fax the Internet address URL of the survey as well as the appropriate password for the respective group of the sample (see below), answered the questions directly on the Internet and sent the results by mouse click to Fraunhofer ISI, where they could then be fed directly into the electronic data processing system.

The first URL despatch to the relevant addressees (see below) took place in mid-April, the first reminder was sent at the beginning of May, the second in mid-May. At the end of May the response return was cut off, the data set prepared and the analysis begun.

The empirical investigations addressed firms that develop software in Germany (primary sector domestic), companies from selected sectors of the manufacturing industry, which also develop software within the scope of their activities (secondary sector domestic), as well as enterprises of the primary sector in selected European countries (primary sector abroad). The sectors selected from the secondary sector, and also the choice of countries, were agreed with the BMWi. As the enterprise databases in the primary sector do not as a rule contain the so-called independent open source developers, but they are significant for the subject of the study, at the suggestion of the BMWi a number of independent developers were contacted as a fourth group whose addresses were supplied by the BMWi (independent developers). This last group received the same questionnaire as the firms of the primary sector and is also grouped under the primary sector in the analysis. If necessary, the answering behavior of this group can be considered separately.

The investigation followed the principle of empirical social research, according to which a random sample of the relevant parent population must be taken as the basis, in order to gain generalizeable statements. Two software-developing sub-sectors as well as the independent developers group were identified as the relevant basic population. By use of the random sample in the defined parent population of the software-developing sector, this investigation differs from consultations running chronologically parallel in the European Commission and Great Britain, which cannot claim to be representative due to the openness of the consultations and the different mobilizations in this process via the Internet.[1]

3.1.1 Primary Sector Domestic

In this study, the companies belong in the primary sector whose corporate objective according to the generally accepted NACE classification[2] is the development of software (NACE 72.202), complemented by a number of independent software developers.

Enterprises of the primary sector
Target figure for the despatch of the questionnaire here was 300 enterprises. The basis for obtaining the addresses was the company database Hoppenstedt, the leading company database in Germany, which also classifies the firms according to the NACE code. From the total number of companies under NACE Code 72.202 (software development), for pragmatic reasons those were chosen whose e-mail address was recorded in the database. The second filter was a question about the willingness to participate in the study.

---

[1]   For results of the EU consultations, see PbT Consultants (2001), the results of the British consultations are found under http://www.patent.gov.uk/about/consultations/conclusions.htm.
[2]   Nomenclature générale des activités economiques dans les Communautés Européennes.

In a first mailing, all companies were requested to give us the e-mail address of the head of the software department, and inform us of their willingness to participate. The response to this first letter formed the basis of the parent population of the domestic primary sector.

Independent software developers
A number of independent developers complemented the group which was recovered from the Hoppenstedt database, as there – other than in tax statistics – the very small or one-man companies are not or are too poorly represented, but these micro-enterprises play a large role in the software sector (see Stahl et al. 2000). The addresses of the independent developers were mainly provided by the BMWi and are thus not based on a random selection. The independent developers did not receive a first contact letter.

3.1.2   Secondary Sector Domestic

The sectors which were agreed together with the BMWi were vehicle construction (NACE 34), electro-technology (NACE 30-32), telecommunication (NACE 64) and mechanical engineering (NACE 29). In order to adequately limit the parent population (targeted size: 300 firms), we tried firstly to determine, for all four sectors, those companies which also claimed activities in the area of data processing and databases (NACE 72) as a second string. It appeared that this led only in the field of electro-technology to a sufficient number of firms; the number of hits was subcritical in all other sectors. As the number of companies found by this method was small, it made sense that in the vehicle construction, telecommunications and electro-technology sectors[3] all enterprises whose e-mail or fax address was quoted in the Hoppenstedt database should be contacted in writing with an invitation to participate. In order to include the ten largest companies of each sector in the survey, their e-mail or fax address was retrieved, in the cases where no contact address was given in the Hoppenstedt database. The positive responses to a first contact letter analogous to the primary sector formed the basic population of the actual survey.

Mechanical engineering was a special case. Due to the extremely high total number of enterprises, we refrained from writing to all companies with an e-mail address. Instead, a complete survey was carried out of those mechanical engineering enterprises which are members of the VDMA Expert

---

[3]   In the field of electro-technology, all enterprises of NACE Code 30 were written to, supplemented by those of Code 31 (manufacture of appliances to produce and distribute electricity) and Code 32 (radio, television and telecommunications technology), which declared activities in the area of software.

Committee Software and which can therefore be regarded as relevant for the survey. A first written request to participate was not sent in this case.

3.1.3 Primary Sector Abroad

In order to obtain the addresses of relevant enterprises in the selected countries (see below), two commercial databases were utilized.[4] In all countries a random draw was conducted in the relevant NACE Code (or in the corresponding SIC Code). We attempted to maintain a relative distribution, not only between the countries, but also between the various sizes, which corresponds approximately to the ratios of the semi-official Eurostat statistics. A first contact letter was not sent to firms abroad.

According to these criteria, 1085 company addresses were finally ascertained – for an original target of 600 enterprises. As a result 822 enterprises were successfully written to. Unfortunately, the response, even after two reminders, was extremely low, a mere 23 enterprises from abroad completed the questionnaire and returned it on-line, so for this reason the foreign enterprises could no longer be taken into consideration in the following analysis.[5]

3.1.4 Statistics to Determine the Random Sample

Table 3.1 depicts the sample drawn, as well as the number of usable responses and the resulting response rates. The sample (column 2) is composed of the enterprises which declared their willingness to participate in the survey, and which passed on the address of their head of software development.

By comparison with other empirical surveys of this kind in Germany, the response rate of 16 per cent for the primary sector lies above the average. The low response rate in the secondary sector can be explained by the fact that only every third to fifth enterprise develops software for the market in this sector (Stahl et al. 2000, pp. 54 f). Against this background, the real response rate here also lies between 10 and 15 per cent. As far as the response rate is concerned, it should be mentioned that response rates under 10 per cent have been noted even for studies commissioned by the European Commission.

---

[4] The database of Dun & Bradstreet, the market leader in the field of enterprise addresses and data, was able to supply meaningful (that is, with fax or e-mail) address lists for Italy, Austria, the Netherlands, Spain and the United Kingdom. For the other countries (France, Finland, Sweden, Denmark and Norway), addresses were chosen from the Amadeus database of the Bureau van Dijk.

[5] As there was also no response worth mentioning for a non-response analysis, the reasons can only be speculated on. Obviously, there is no incentive for a foreign enterprise to participate in a study for a German federal ministry, even when the question addressed is of relevance Europe-wide.

Table 3.1   Statistics of the survey

	Advance contact	Number of questionnaires successfully sent	**Sample: usable responses**	Response rate 1 (columns 3/1)	Response rate 2 (columns 3/2)
Primary sector					
Enterprises	1202	304	**149**	12.4%	49.01%
Independent developers	–	113	**38**	–	33.63%
Not clearly classifiable	–	–	**9**	–	–
Sum	1202	417	196	16.31%	47.00%
Secondary sector					
Electrotechnology	521	79	**33**	6.33%	41.77%
Telecommunication	214	16	**6**	2.80%	37.50%
Vehicle construction	873	40	**6**	0.69%	15.00%
Total (without VDMA)	1608	135	**45**	2.80%	33.33%
Mechanical engineering (VDMA)	(170)	170	**17**	–	10.00%
Sum	1778	303	67	3.77%	22.11%
For information:					
Abroad		871	**23**		2.64%

Note: Primary sector: NACE 72.202; Secondary sector: NACE 29; 30-32; 34; 64.

3.1.5   Non-Response Analysis

In the invitation to participate or in the reminders, the companies were asked to quote one or more reasons for their non-participation. This non-response analysis makes it possible to attain insights into the relevancy of the subjects for the enterprises outside the group of participating companies. A total of 432 domestic firms gave reasons for non-participation: 293 from the secondary sector, 138 from the primary sector. For the primary sector, the most important reason is the time and effort involved in answering which might be due partly to the size structure of the firms questioned (see next section). At any rate, a quarter of all enterprises do not undertake software development themselves, despite the corresponding classification in the database, and a fifth do not perceive the subject of property rights as influencing their business activities. The most significant reason by far for non-participation for the secondary sector was that the subject was not relevant for them: 73 per cent did not develop software, over 16 per cent developed only for their own use, and over 17 per cent did not see their business activities affected.[6]

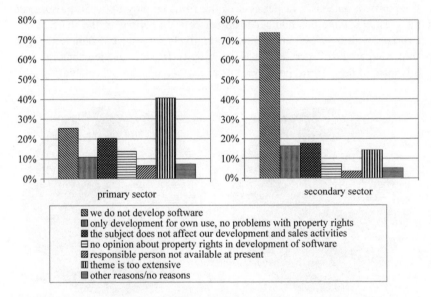

Figure 3.1   Non-response analysis: Reasons given for non-participation in the survey – primary sector and secondary sector (multiple choices possible)

3.1.6   On the Representativeness of the Sample

Regarding representativeness, two characteristics appear relevant to the subject of the study: the distribution of the kind of software developed and the size of the companies. While data are available on the size distribution from tax statistics and enterprise databases, no representative data are available for Germany on the distribution of companies according to the kind of software developed.

---

[6]   Multiple choices were possible.

As already mentioned above, the primary sector was very narrowly de-fined (NACE Code 72.02), in order to focus the survey on as many relevant companies as possible. A full survey was conducted for this narrowly defined basic population. The restriction thereby to the firms which had given an e-mail address in the database utilized for the survey was without consequences for the size distribution, as the relative size distribution is identical in both groups. If the response to the survey is compared to this size distribution (Figure 3.2), then it becomes clear that the survey shows a certain bias to-wards medium-sized enterprises. Whereas in the basic population of the Hoppenstedt database, 72 per cent of the firms employ up to 50 persons, in the present sample this number is 58 per cent. In particular, the share of en-terprises with over 500 employees is relatively large in the sample (12 per cent compared to 2 per cent in Hoppenstedt). In view of the economic sig-nificance of these firms, however, this evaluation appears acceptable.[7]

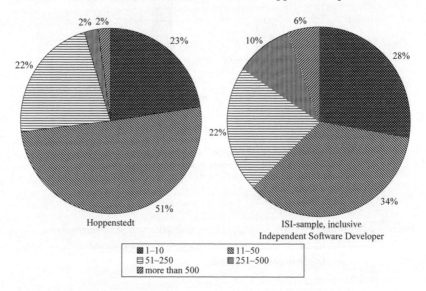

Figure 3.2   Size distribution of the primary sector: comparison Hoppenstedt, sample of the present study

With reference to the subject of this study, a further criterion for the repre-sentativeness is the nature of the software developed. No official statistics

---

[7]   In relation to data from sales tax statistics, this bias is even more evident. However, the official tax statistics encompass every company registered in the area of data processing and thus a confusing multiplicity of mini firms, which do not undertake development themselves (see Stahl et al. 2000, pp. 51 ff).

whatsoever are available on this subject. A recent study on the importance of the software sector in Germany can be taken as a reference (Stahl et al. 2000), in which based on a survey of 207 enterprises of the primary sector (defined as WZ 72: Data Processing and Databases)[8] the distribution according to type of software was extrapolated (ibid, p. 66). According to this estimation, in area WZ 72 approximately 17 per cent of the firms (also) produce systems-related software, whereas the share of user software is estimated at 55 per cent (business management software), 46 per cent (multi-media) respective 33 per cent technical software). If the critical figure for classification as systems-related producer is assumed to be a turnover share of systems-related software of at least 10 per cent, then 19.9 per cent of primary sector firms in the sample can be counted as producers of systems-related software.[9] 62 per cent of the firms claim to produce no systems-related software (see Figure 3.7). Measured against the existing data sets, the representativeness of the sample in the primary sector can thus be described as very good.

No data are available for the secondary sector, which refer to the distribution of kinds of software development. Figure 3.3 shows the distribution according to size classes.

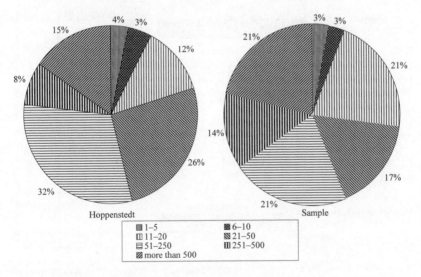

Figure 3.3   Size distribution of the secondary sector: comparison Hoppenstedt, sample of present study

---

8   The comparative study defined the entire area of the economic sector statistics WZ 72 'Data Processing and Databases' as primary sector.
9   A further 18 per cent claimed to produce systems-related software in a volume of up to 10 per cent of turnover.

3.2 TYPES OF SOFTWARE DEVELOPMENTS AND THEIR SIGNIFICANCE

In order to differentiate the importance of intellectual property rights for the software-developing enterprises in Germany, the firms were first of all asked how their turnover was distributed among various types of software. A first dimension is the independence of the developed product, which ranges from the so-called stand-alone solutions to complete integration in other software or hardware. Figure 3.4 depicts clear differences between the primary and secondary sectors. The average turnover share with independent software products amounts to somewhat over 58 per cent in the primary sector; in the secondary sector to somewhat more than 35 per cent. For the turnover share of so-called 'embedded software', that is, software which is an integral part of hardware and only functions in conjunction with it,[10] this ratio is reversed, as expected.

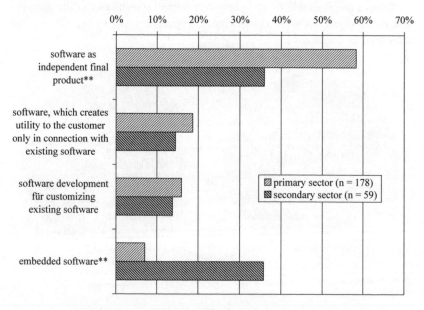

Note: The asterisks (*) at the individual criteria signalize significant differences between primary sector and secondary sector based on t-tests (** = 5 per cent significance level, * = 10 per cent significance level).

Figure 3.4   Turnover shares of various types of own (developed) software

[10] For instance, this is the case for automatic control software in mechanical engineering or vehicle construction.

In the primary sector, the average share of embedded software amounts to only 7 per cent, while it accounts for nearly 36 per cent in the secondary sector and thus corresponds mainly to the share of independent software. This distribution corresponds to the claims about own production of hardware: 85 per cent of the enterprises in the secondary sector and 44 per cent of the firms in the primary sector develop and also produce hardware (Figure 3.5). These differentiations according to primary and secondary sector are both statistically significant. These distributions mean that the particular problems of embedded software do not play an essential role for the primary sector, whereas for the secondary sector not only the specifics of independent software, but also the idiosyncrasies of embedded software are relevant. Furthermore, in both sectors hardware producers also increasingly produce embedded software (H2).

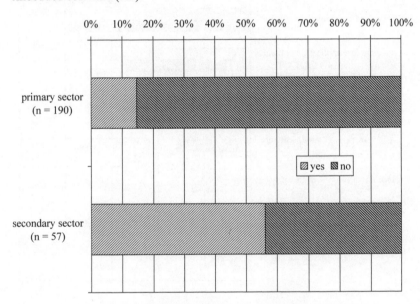

Figure 3.5　　Share of enterprises, which (also) produce hardware

As the consequences which software patenting will have for the company possibly differ regarding the functionality of their products (H3), the sample was asked about the various application areas of their software products (Figure 3.6).

It appears that the secondary sector has the largest share of turnover with systems-related software, followed by approximately equal shares of user software from the areas of business management, technical applications, automatic control engineering and multi-media. In the primary sector, on the other hand, user software plays a greater role (with business administration software in the lead), and systems-related software takes fourth place here with only 11 per cent.

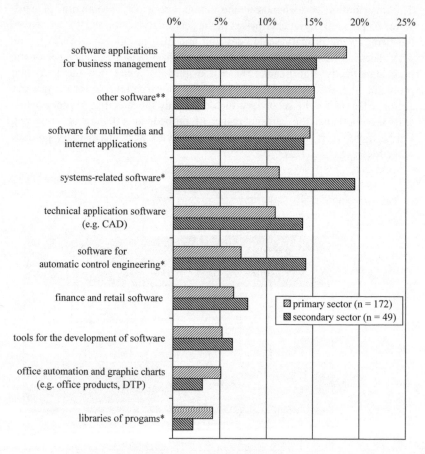

Note: The asterisks (*) at the individual criteria signalize significant differences between primary sector and secondary sector based on t-tests (** = 5 per cent significance level, * = 10 per cent significance level).

Figure 3.6   Turnover shares with software of different functionality

A closer look at the distribution of the turnover shares with reference to the generation of systems-related software (Figure 3.7) shows that over 19 per cent of the enterprises in the primary sector and over 28 per cent of the firms in the secondary sector achieve over 10 per cent of their turnover by means of systems-related software.

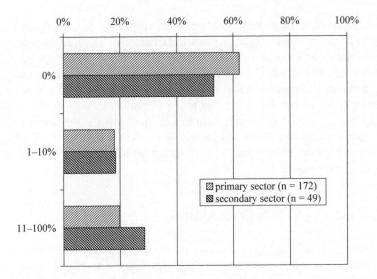

Figure 3.7   Turnover shares with systems-related software (shares of the enterprises with corresponding turnover shares)

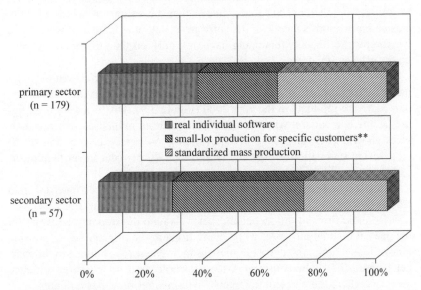

Note: The asterisks (*) at the individual criteria signalize significant differences between primary sector and secondary sector based on t-tests (** = 5 per cent significance level, * = 10 per cent significance level).

Figure 3.8   Turnover shares of software products according to customer classes

A final differentiation among the firms regarding their products distinguishes between them according to what extent they develop their products as individually tailored software solutions for single customers, or small groups of customers. The underlying assumption is that the patenting of products for the mass market is of greater significance than for custom-made articles (H4). Figure 3.8 shows that in the secondary sector most often small series are developed for certain customer groups, whereas the primary sector is more strongly polarized and clearly more than a third of their turnover stems either from client-specific, customized developments or from products for the mass market.

3.3   INNOVATION DYNAMICS

In order to gauge the significance of intellectual property rights in the software sector, it is necessary first of all to visualize the innovation behavior of the software enterprises. There are two reasons for this: firstly, only thus can the central assumption of the adherents of property rights, especially patents, be tested, according to which intellectual property rights stimulate companies to greater innovations. Secondly, it can then be estimated which idiosyncrasies innovation behavior in the software-developing industry displays and which specific impacts this could have, not only on the utilization, but also on the effects of patents.

Software development is characterized by very short cycles and high dynamics. Approximately 90 per cent in both sectors state that they developed new software products in the year 2000 (Figure 3.9). This is a very high figure, as the comparison with the share of innovators in business-oriented services shows. There the share of innovators is 64 per cent according to the most recent innovation survey and is thus over 20 per cent lower than in the software area.[11]

A difference between the primary and secondary sector becomes apparent when one considers to what extent the innovations represent market novelties. Here the firms of the secondary sector claim to develop new software for the market on a larger scale, while many firms in the primary sector develop innovations which are admittedly new to their enterprise, but not to the market (Figure 3.10). In comparison to the whole area of enterprise-oriented services, where the share of companies with market novelties amounts to 37 per cent, the software sector achieves average figures. These firms support and make more use of patents (question 5, sub-question 'yes', 24). Thus the

---

[11]   Cf. Janz et al. (2001), p. 2. The following reference figures also come from this source.

relatively high shares of innovators are put in the right context and can be so interpreted that the software sector produces many above-average incremental innovations, but only an average number of radical ones.

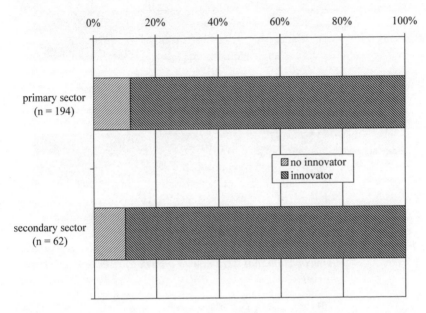

Figure 3.9 Share of enterprises which developed new software products in the year 2000

A further measurement for innovation dynamics customarily used in innovation research is the turnover share with products that were completely new to the company. For the year 2000 a left-skewed U distribution appeared. The majority of the firms attained between 0 per cent and 30 per cent of turnover with completely new products. In this area the firms of the secondary sector have somewhat higher shares, whilst the primary sector is more strongly represented in the area of highly innovative companies. Here 15 per cent of the companies claim to have made over 50 per cent of their turnover with completely new products; for a quarter of the firms the figure is over 30 per cent (Figure 3.11).[12] By comparison with the whole area of enterprise-oriented services, however, these figures are slightly under the average, as the turnover share with new products here amounts to 29 per cent.

---

[12] However, the differentiation between primary and secondary sector is not statistically significant in this case.

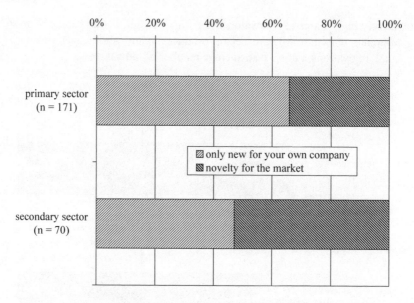

*Figure 3.10   Shares of enterprises which introduced innovative products in
the year 2000 that were new to the enterprises and new to the
market*

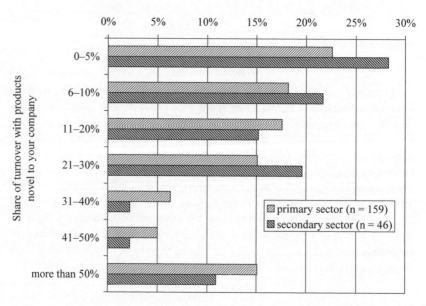

*Figure 3.11   Turnover shares with completely novel products in the year
2000 (share of enterprises)*

The high dynamism is also reflected in the development cycles. In both sectors, product development does not take longer than six months in over 40 per cent of the enterprises. On the other hand, less than a third of all products require a development time of over 12 months (Figure 3.12).

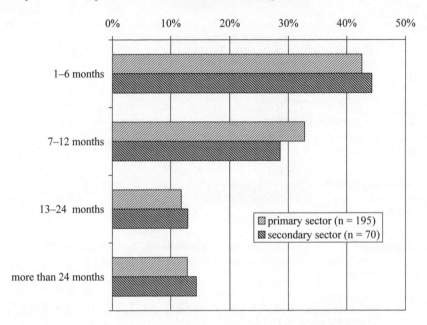

Figure 3.12   Average development duration of software products

The very short cycles correspond to the demand behavior in the software industry anticipated by the firms questioned. Over 75 per cent of the clients in the primary sector (secondary sector: approximately 66 per cent) replace their software by improved products in the period of one year (Figure 3.13). Forty per cent of the clients in the primary sector replace their software within two years on average with completely novel products. The demand behavior is less dynamic in the secondary sector, but here too almost 80 per cent of the clients want completely novel products within two years.

To sum up, it can be said that developments in the software area are characterized by a very high market dynamic, not only in the primary but also in the secondary sector. The average duration of development in both sectors is correspondingly short. This leads to a competitively crucial significance of fast innovations and effective development processes. Obstacles to conducting development work are therefore even more serious in the software industry than in other fields of industry.

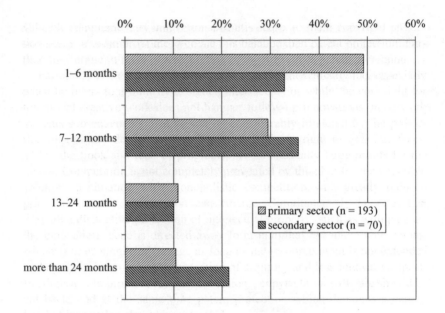

*Figure 3.13   Share of enterprises whose clients on average demand
                an improved product within certain time periods*

3.4 SPECIFICS OF DEVELOPMENT ACTIVITIES IN THE SOFTWARE AREA

A main argument of many opponents of the patenting of software is based on the fact that specific conditions predominate in the area of software- and computer-related developments, under which patenting would have counter-productive consequences. These specifics concern principally the sequentiality of software developments, the utilization and disclosure of open code (open source) and the resulting principles, such as the necessary interoperability of software products. These conditions were discussed in the literature analysis and included in the questionnaire. Whether the software development process is really characterized by these three idiosyncrasies will be covered in the following chapters.

3.4.1 Sequentiality

A first dimension for the idiosyncrasies of software development is the recycling of code and thus of sequentiality. One assumption by critics of patents is that patents limit the access to existing codes (H10). An indicator for sequentiality in the software development is the degree of reutilization of existing code for own developments. It states the percentage of the input for new developments attributed to code reutilization (Figure 3.14). The result is unambiguous: in almost a third of all enterprises, more than 50 per cent of the input for new developments consists of already existing code. Almost two-thirds of the enterprises quote a share of over 30 per cent for code re-utilization. The significance of sequentiality in software development is thus unanimously confirmed (H12).

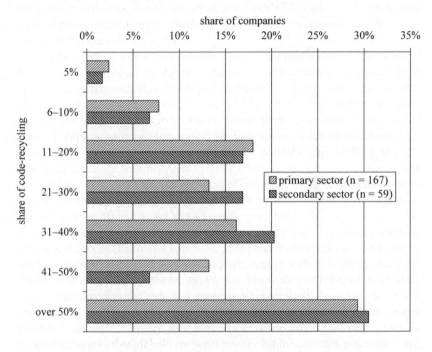

Figure 3.14   Share of code recycling in self-developed software

In order to estimate the significance of sequentiality for the question of in-tellectual property rights, not only the extent of code recycling is relevant, but also and above all the origin of the program components which flow into the developments of enterprises (H3). It appeared at first (see Figure 3.15) that the greater share of the code that was reused stemmed from own devel-opments and thus was not affected by intellectual property rights. This ap-plies to both sectors, but for the secondary sector with 70 per cent is however slightly higher than in the primary sector. In general, Figure 3.14 confirms that on average around one-third of software code is reused for further de-velopments, which indicates a certain degree of sequentiality in software development. Nevertheless, this sequentiality refers mostly to self-developed code and not to code from third parties.

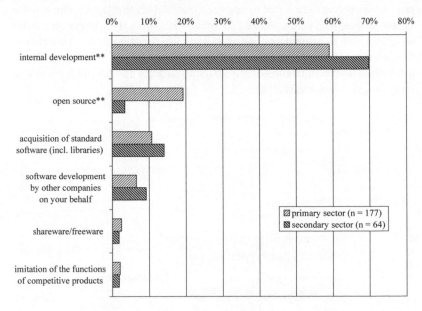

Note: The asterisks (*) at the individual criteria signalize significant differences between primary sector and secondary sector based on t-tests (** = 5 per cent significance level, * = 10 per cent significance level).

Figure 3.15   Origin of software in software products

3.4.2   The Significance of Open Source Software

The result significant for the importance of intellectual property rights is obtained from the analysis of the 'foreign' components in own developments (Figure 3.15). According to this analysis, open source software accounts for over 70 per cent of the input independent software developers use as a sub-group of the primary sector, and thus almost five times that of bought standard software, and ten times as much as specially commissioned software (H11). The imitation of foreign software plays a subordinate role, just like the use of free-of-charge software. Of all foreign components in the software developments in the primary and secondary sector, acquisition of standard software and specially commissioned software are the most significant. The great role which open source plays for the independent software developers cannot be observed for the primary and secondary sector, because these shares of open source barely reach 6 per cent.

In the secondary sector, the extent to which open source is used (3.5 per cent of the whole input for software developments) is significantly lower in comparison with the whole primary sector, while the shares of other 'foreign' components are at similar levels.

The estimation of future development is important to mention. More than 60 per cent of the enterprises in the primary sector claim that in future the importance of open source will increase. In the secondary sector, 70 per cent of the enterprises expect that the importance of open source will increase as an input for their own software development. And for the secondary sector it also applies that the dependence on external sources will increase, as well as the exchange of software components between enterprises. For this reason, influence on open source development through patenting policy in the future is also of increasing importance for the secondary sector.

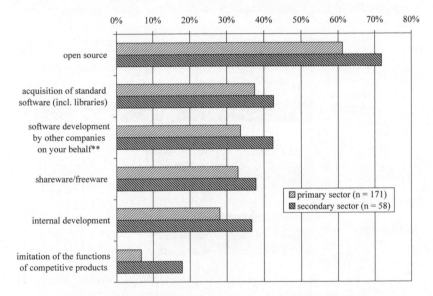

Note: The asterisks (*) at the individual criteria signalize significant differences between primary sector and secondary sector based on t-tests (** = 5 per cent significance level, * = 10 per cent significance level).

Figure 3.16   Estimate of the future change in importance of various sources for software development (share of the firms that count on a growing importance)

The estimate of future development is significant (Figure 3.16). Over 60 per cent of the primary sector companies claim that the importance of open source will continue to grow in future. Whilst this is the highest figure for all

sources of software development, own development – after imitation – has
the lowest rating. In the secondary sector, as many as 70 per cent of the firms
anticipate that the importance of open source as input for their own developments will increase. And for the secondary sector it also applies that the dependence on external sources and thus the exchange of software components
between enterprises will grow (Figure 3.16). Thus in the future an influence
on open source development through patent policy will be of increasing significance for the secondary sector also.

The significance of open source is manifold. Most important is obviously
its functional role as a development tool, that is, its use means increased
effectiveness of the development process in general (H14) (Figure 3.17). In
more than a quarter of the companies in the primary sector, further applications lie in their utilization as Internet software and as components for end
products. The shares in the secondary sector do not differ significantly from
this.

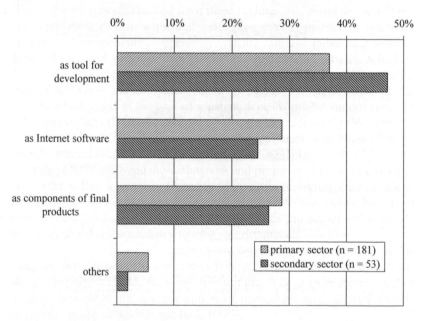

Figure 3.17   Use of open source

The last question about the use of open source for development work dealt
with motivation. Figure 3.18 makes clear that there are a number of motives
for utilizing open source software, all of which are given high marks for
importance. The most crucial motive is good adaptability, followed by high
topicality and low costs, which cannot be fulfilled by proprietary software to

the same degree (H15). All motives are judged slightly higher in the primary sector. The difference between the primary and secondary sectors is only statistically significant pertaining to security, which is graded much higher by the primary sector than by representatives of the secondary sector. It is interesting to note that security on the whole is accorded the least importance of all motives questioned.

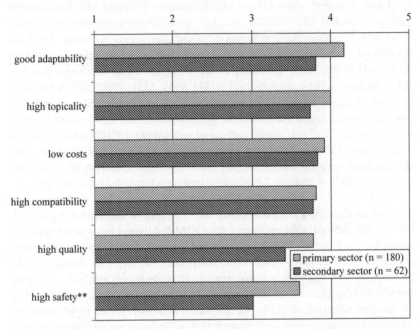

Note: The asterisks (*) at the individual criteria signalize significant differences between primary sector and secondary sector based on t-tests (** = 5 per cent significance level, * = 10 per cent significance level).

*Figure 3.18   Motives to utilize open source software
            (1 = unimportant; 5 = very important)*

Besides the utilization and application of open source, the practices and conditions for the own disclosure of open source software are interesting. Various modes must be differentiated here. Code is either made available free of charge and for general use, or for a fee for the general public, or only for specific clients. The only category of these three organisational forms in which significant differences are noted between the primary and secondary sector is the release to the general public for no fee (Figure 3.19). The majority of the enterprises questioned in both sectors admittedly is never prepared to commit to such an unconditional disclosure. This refusal is however unambiguous on the part of the secondary sector, and at 84.5 per cent, significantly higher than in the primary sector. In the latter, 13 per cent state that they generally release code (secondary sector 1.7 per cent) and approximately 10 per cent do this frequently (secondary sector 3.4 per cent).

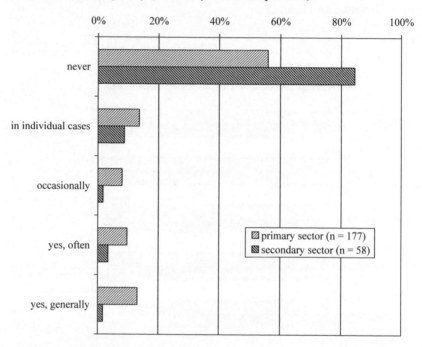

Figure 3.19   Diffusion of the practice of disclosing code free of charge to the public

If the independent developers (ISD) are separated from the primary sector (Figure 3.20), then the differences to the secondary sector are reduced to a marginal level, especially in the categories 'Yes, often' and 'Yes, generally'. Half of the independent developers however disclose code to the general public free of charge on principle. In other words, the majority of the independent developers, but also a number of enterprises of the primary sector, follow a business model in which code is disclosed for free and the economic incentives are obviously not based in the exclusive provision of software. Still less widespread is the practice of releasing code for a fee to the general public: over 84 per cent of the enterprises in the primary and over 87 per cent in the secondary sector do not do this generally, approximately 10 per cent only in individual cases.

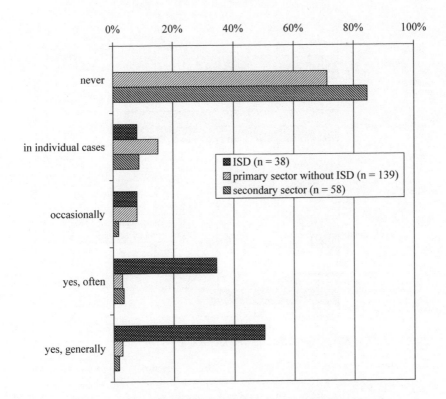

Figure 3.20 *Diffusion of the practice of disclosing code free of charge to the general public, differentiated according to independent developers*

The willingness to disclose is obviously linked to the direct client relationship. Only if the disclosure of code takes place within a client relationship do the practices alter, and to an equal extent in both sectors: only approximately 20 per cent still claim not to disclose in such cases, and somewhat more than a third disclose in individual cases in both sectors. Approximately 17 per cent of the enterprises of the secondary sector and slightly over 20 per cent of the firms in the primary sector generally disclose their code within the framework of client relations (Figure 3.21).

The disclosure of code is not limited to certain forms of software, but is customary across the whole range of software. It appears significant that for systems software the figures are pretty high, especially in the primary sector and here above all for the independent developers, which tends to raise the importance of disclosure for the functioning of whole systems. Otherwise there are no significant differences between the sectors (Figure 3.22).

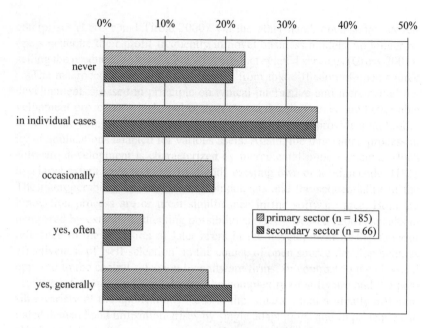

Figure 3.21   Disclosure of code to special clients for a fee

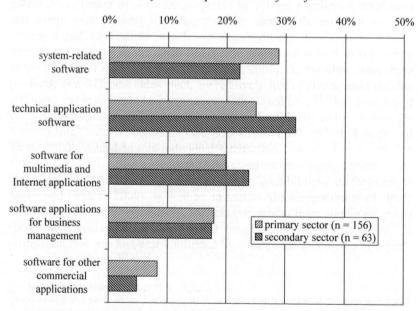

Figure 3.22   Share of enterprises which disclose code for various kinds of software

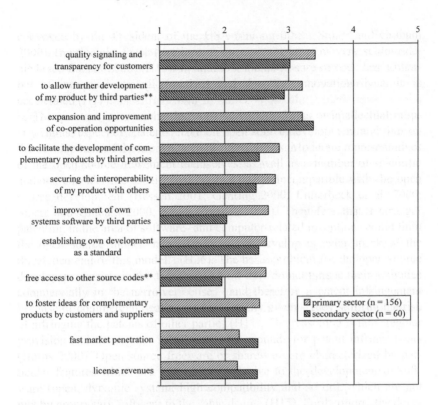

Notes:
The asterisks (*) at the individual criteria signalize significant differences between primary sector and secondary sector based on t-tests (** = 5 per cent significance level, * = 10 per cent significance level).

The distinguishing signs for the significance refer here again to the differentiation between primary sector (without independent developers) and secondary sector.

Figure 3.23   Motivation to disclose code (1 = very low, 5 = very high)

In order to understand the economic significance of disclosing code, the motivation must be exactly examined (H17) (Figure 3.23). Here is seen unequivocally that the majority of independent developers use open source according to the classical pattern: the four most important reasons correspond to the open source philosophy, whereby the disclosure leads to further development of their own product or to improvement of their own systems, the access to other code, as well as the quality of their own work demonstrated. Cashing in on license income plays no role whatsoever for the independent developers. The motives of the primary and secondary sector, which with few exceptions all give a rating under the medium significance 3, differ only slightly in their values, but show a somewhat different sequence. The most important reason for the firms in the primary sector is the proof of quality, whereas the secondary sector enterprises utilize disclosure most frequently to initiate and improve co-operations. Interestingly, the firms in both sectors quote as a relatively important reason (place 3) the possibility to develop their own product, while the potential of third parties gaining access to the code does not play an essential role. In other words, only the use of open source by the independent developers follows the comprehensive logic of 'quid pro quo' of this mode. Lastly, only a few enterprises attempt to establish their products and programs as standard software by employing the strategy of disclosing code (H18).

3.4.3   Interoperability

One last idiosyncrasy of software development in contrast with other products is the interoperability necessary between systems and applications or between various applications (H19). An argument of the opponents of patenting in the software area points out that patenting could prevent the rapid establishment of interoperability, especially by means of open code.

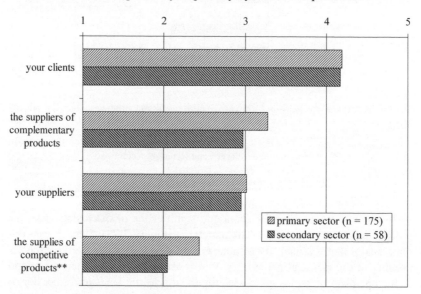

Note: The asterisks (*) at the individual criteria signalize significant differences between primary sector and secondary sector based on t-tests (** = 5 per cent significance level, * = 10 per cent significance level).

Figure 3.24   Importance of interoperability with software of various actor groups (1 = very low, 5 = very high)

Four dimensions must be differentiated regarding interoperability. Figure 3.24 shows that the interoperability with customer software is by far the most important criterion for both sectors. The interoperability with supplier products is of medium importance and is approximately as significant as the interoperability with products of complementary suppliers. The significantly higher figure of the primary sector regarding the interoperability with competitive products reveals the importance attributed to the functional compatibility of their own product with others on the market. This strategic motive on the other hand is not pronounced in the secondary sector.

In particular, software which is a partial component of other software is decisively dependent on interoperability. Therefore enterprises which produce software as partial components attribute a much higher significance to interoperability with the software of clients, suppliers and competitors than the other enterprises (H1).

In order to judge what importance patenting could have for establishing interoperability, we must first ask how interoperability can be established at all (H19). For all the relationships depicted in Figure 3.24, there are no significant differences between the two sectors. However, it makes sense to differentiate between the vertical level of clients and supplier relationships (Figures 3.25 and 3.26) and the horizontal level of competing and complementary products (Figures 3.27 and 3.28).

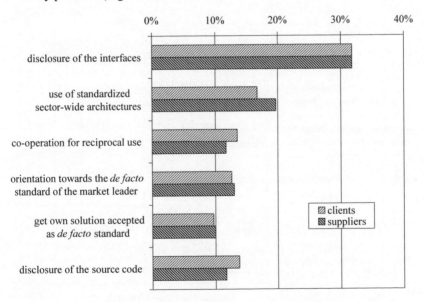

Figure 3.25   Securing interoperability to clients and suppliers –
primary sector

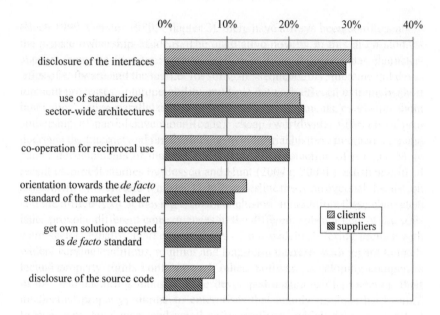

Figure 3.26   Securing interoperability to clients or suppliers –
secondary sector

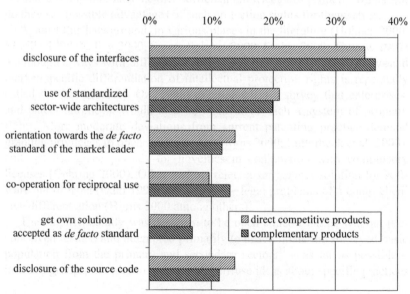

Figure 3.27   Securing interoperability with competitive and
complementary products – primary sector

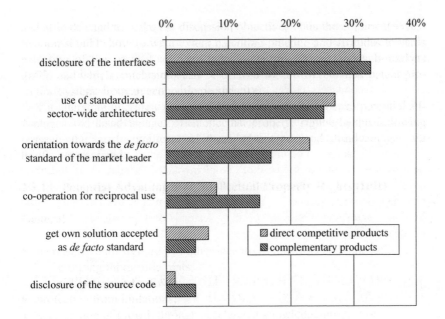

*Figure 3.28   Securing interoperability with competitive and
complementary products – secondary sector*

By far the most frequently mentioned instrument for all four dimensions is the disclosure of interfaces, followed by the use of standardized sector architectures, which is obviously somewhat more widespread within the secondary sector. The same relation applies to contractual co-operations, which is accorded slightly less importance. On the other hand, code disclosure plays rather a subordinate role, above all in the secondary sector. For the independent developers, however, code disclosure – or the disclosure of interfaces – is the most significant strategy to establish interoperability, not only to clients and suppliers but also to competitive and complementary products.[13] The assessment is surprising that, by comparison to the orientation to the *de facto* standard of the market leader, only slightly fewer firms attempt to have their own specifications accepted as a *de facto* standard.

If one leaves the vertical level of client and supplier relationships and turns to the direct competitive relations divided according to suppliers of complementary and competitive products, similar structures emerge. On the one hand, the disclosure of relevant interfaces is the preferred strategy of

---

[13]   We can dispense with a graphic depiction of the independent developers here, as they do not occupy a deviating position.

approximately one-third of all enterprises, not only for complementary, but also for competitive products. Further, a quarter of the firms in the secondary sector use standardized sector architectures. Only a fifth do so in the primary sector. It is remarkable that regarding the direct competitive products, above all in the secondary sector, an orientation to the sector standard takes place, while direct legally contracted co-operations are entered into especially with suppliers of complementary products. The enterprises obviously have greater difficulties co-operating with suppliers of direct competitive products on a contractual basis, as in certain circumstances conflicts can be caused in competition law by this. In the case of complementary products, these and other risks are less; on the other hand, the incentives for direct co-operations are obviously more pronounced. The disclosure of own code does not play a role in either sector and within the primary sector is only practiced by the independent developers.

3.5 PROPERTY RIGHTS IN THE SOFTWARE INDUSTRY: PRACTICES AND EXPERIENCES

After having presented the specific features of the products and the innovation behavior of the software sector as important background information, this chapter turns to the practical experiences with, and attitudes to, intellectual property rights. According to the questions in the study, patents are once again the centre of attention.

3.5.1 Organization of and Knowledge about Property Rights

An indicator of the way enterprises deal with intellectual property rights is to be seen in the organizational structures within the company (H21). It can be clearly seen that the secondary sector in practice has institutionalized its dealings with industrial property rights very much more strongly: 39 per cent of the companies of the secondary sector have a department or unit responsible for intellectual property rights.[14] In the primary sector this share is just under 12 per cent and is thus significantly lower. As despite the current discussion about software patents only 4 per cent of the enterprises in the software sector are planning to establish such a unit, there will be no principal changes in these shares in the foreseeable future (Figure 3.29).

In the comparison between those enterprises in the primary and secondary sectors which have established such a unit, in addition it appears that the

---

[14] In close conjunction with the better institutional equipment of the secondary sector is also the fact that it is more probable that hardware manufacturers have a patent office or unit.

departments in the secondary sector tend to employ more staff and the firms in the primary sector have also not set up large, costly organizations.[15]

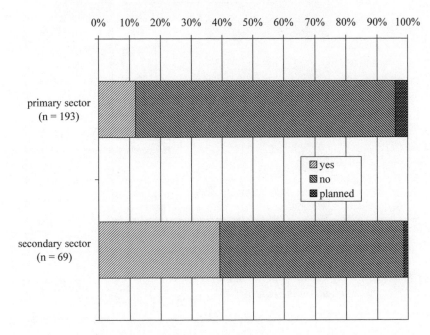

Figure 3.29 Share of enterprises which have a department or unit responsible for intellectual property rights

The age of the units or departments responsible for intellectual property rights differs again significantly between the sectors. Functional units of this caliber in the primary sector are a phenomenon of the last five to ten years; in the secondary sector they have been in place intermittently for over 20 years. This difference can be explained not only by the increasing relevance of patents, but rather because of the age structure of the companies themselves. For whereas in the secondary sector 50 per cent of the companies are older than 20 years, this is the case in only somewhat more than 10 per cent of the primary sector.

---

[15] Regarding the costs necessary to run such a unit, it was seen that the majority of the departments or units in the primary sector (67 per cent) do not cost more than €50 000 a year (primary sector 50 per cent). In the secondary sector the spread is greater. Here, two companies quoted costs in excess of €500 000. However, the differences between the primary and secondary sectors regarding size and costs of the departments – also due to the low number of cases – are not statistically significant.

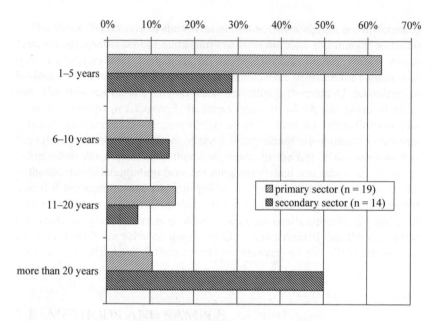

*Figure 3.30   Age of the functional unit responsible for intellectual property
                rights in the enterprises*

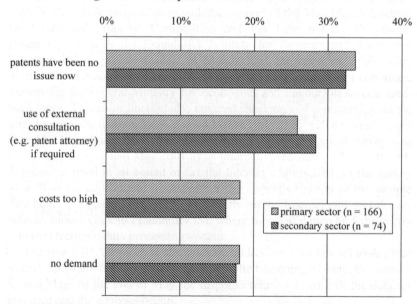

*Figure 3.31   Reasons to dispense with a functional unit to handle
                intellectual property rights in the enterprises*

With regard to the reasons not to establish such a unit, both sectors resemble each other very closely. In both sectors approximately one-third of the firms state that patents are not a matter for discussion for them and approximately 16 per cent see no need for such a unit (multiple answers were possible). For approximately 18 per cent of the firms in the primary sector and about 16 per cent of the secondary sector the costs are a main reason not to patent. Somewhat more than a quarter of all enterprises (primary sector 26 per cent, secondary sector 28.4 per cent) meet their manpower requirements to deal with IPR-relevant questions through external sources, for example through patent attorneys.

In the question as to how firms classify their own knowledge about the two most important intellectual property rights, patents and copyright (H22), there are also only very few differences between the sectors. It became clear that the firms are more familiar with copyright than with patent law. On a scale from 1 ('No knowledge') and 5 ('Very comprehensive knowledge'), the average value for patents in the primary sector is 2.17 and in the secondary sector 2.32; for copyright these values are much higher at 2.7 for both sectors.[16] At the same time, small and medium-sized enterprises not only have less patent units, but also clearly less knowledge about patent law than larger companies (H39). It is all the more surprising that the younger companies claim greater knowledge about patents, compared with the older ones (H41).[17] This high degree of ignorance must be taken into account when interpreting the answers to the following questions about patent law.

3.5.2 Utilization and Company-specific Significance of Patents

A crucial question of this study is the significance of various strategies to protect software- and computer-related developments. In order to determine the relative significance of the different strategies, the use on the part of the firm, together with the significance which it is accorded by the firm, must be individually observed.

Figure 3.32 shows firstly the number of companies which make use of the various strategies. It was shown unequivocally that intellectual property rights have a relatively low importance in both sectors and only complement the whole range of possible informal protective measures (H23). By far the most frequently used are various forms of internal confidentiality (secrecy

---

[16] The companies in the primary sector which also manufacture hardware have significantly better knowledge about patent law and consider patents to be more important than the other enterprises.

[17] Interestingly, the lawyers who answered the questionnaire did not claim greater knowledge for their companies than the non-lawyers.

agreements), followed by market leadership (time) advantage and customer relations management. One interesting, significant difference arises from the use of technical protection measures, which are much more widely spread in the secondary sector (41 per cent) than in the primary sector (22 per cent).

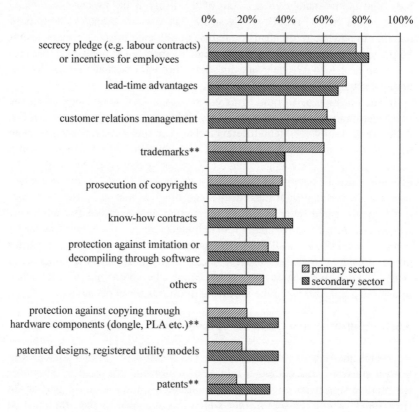

Note: The asterisks (*) at the individual criteria signalize significant differences between primary sector and secondary sector based on t-tests (** = 5 per cent significance level, * = 10 per cent significance level).

Figure 3.32   Use of various instruments to protect software- and computer-related developments

The intellectual property rights evince considerable differences between the primary sector and the secondary sector. Trade marks take first place in the primary sector and are utilized by 63.4 per cent of the companies; the upholding of copyright follows at some distance (43.3 per cent of the companies). Patents, on the other hand, are utilized by a mere 15.9 per cent of the companies in the primary sector. In the secondary sector, the divergences in the frequency of use are lower. Although trade marks (43.5 per cent) are also more important for the secondary sector than patents, patents are still utilized in this sector by more than a third of the enterprises (34.6 per cent). Thus the frequency of using patents is statistically significantly higher in the secondary sector than in the primary sector, whereas in the primary sector importance of trade marks is significantly higher than in the secondary sector. The independent developers take recourse to patents as a protective mechanism only in exceptional cases (7.9 per cent), whilst their utilization behavior of the other formal property rights is very similar to that of the other two sectors.

Furthermore, it was ascertained that producers of embedded software patent significantly more frequently than the other software firms. The former protect their software, which is integrated in hardware (H2) or other technical systems, that is, indirectly through the patent protection applicable to hardware. In the case of producers of individual software it could be supposed that they maintain the necessary protection through bilateral contracts with their customers and therefore are less dependent on patent protection. However, they do not differ from the companies which produce series or mass software regarding patenting the utilization of know-how contracts or in the significance which is attributed to both instruments. Basically, the utilization of know-how contracts and patents are positively correlated (H4).

Software is a good which can trigger off positive network externalities with increasing numbers of users. Theoretically, it applies that via high sales with low unit costs and the resulting *de facto* monopoly position, the development costs can be rapidly recouped, so that the enterprises do not need recourse to the temporary monopoly protection of patents. However, it appeared that companies which manufacture in large series utilize patent protection to the same extent and accord it the same significance as the other companies[18] (H5). A positive correlation could also be drawn between the age, the company size (according to the number of employees) and the export activities on the one hand, and propensity of a firm to patent on the other hand (H25; H31; H37; H38; H39).

An initial assumption was that the companies were given additional incentives through the award of patents to invest in the development of new products (H7). On the other hand, this positive incentive effect can change into the opposite, if due to a more effective utilization of these protective mechanisms a temporary monopoly can be maintained longer and thus innovation activities can be avoided (H7). It appears, however, that more R&D-intensive software firms with R&D expenditures of more than 10 per

---

[18]   Producers of large series, however, do not have significantly less competitors than the other firms. The motive, however, for them to make their own developments the standard by disclosing their source code, is more strongly marked than with other companies.

cent of turnover do not patent more frequently than the less R&D-intensive companies. Besides the R&D intensity, the product development and lifetimes also exist in a close context to the use of patents, for software is characterized by comparatively short product development and lifetimes, and short utilization times by customers. For these reasons, formal protective strategies such as patents are less important and should – theoretically – therefore be less utilized (H9). The analyses reveal, however, that the length of the development times or the utilization periods of customers do not correlate with the patent use. If the analysis is conducted separately for the secondary sector, then it emerges that companies with longer development times make greater use of patents as protective measures.

On the other hand, more innovative firms with a turnover share of more than 10 per cent in new products make greater use of patents than the less innovative enterprises. This result accords with the fact that pioneer firms, which introduce market novelties, use patents more and thereby guarantee the amortization of their high development costs and do not rely only on their first-mover advantage (H8). Further, the companies of the primary sector, which have fewer competitors, use patents as protective mechanisms to a greater extent. If one interprets these results in context, then it is true on the one hand that no positive incentive effect of patents for the R&D activities can be discerned, but enterprises which take advantage of patent protection are more successful in the market – and this possibly even at the expense of competitive intensity (see below).

In Section 3.4.2 we saw that under certain conditions some of the companies disclose the source codes of their different software products or make their software accessible free of charge, so that formal protective mechanisms are not necessary (H16). The analyses reveal that companies which patent disclose less code free of charge to the general public. Conversely, the firms in the primary sector which disclose their source code have a lower opinion of the effectiveness of patents.[19]

The firms which hold patents on software- and computer-related developments were also asked about the number of these patents. The great majority of the firms in both sectors hold less than five patents (90 per cent of the primary sector, 67 per cent in the secondary sector). Only three firms of the total samples are quoted as holding more than 50 software-related patents.

Besides the actual extent of use, the relative importance which the companies accord to the different protection rights is interesting (Figure 3.33). The result is unambiguous here: the significance of patents is regarded

---

[19] Anticipating the results of Section 3.6, it can already be seen that these firms and those which disclose their software free of charge have greater fears for the development of open source and innovation dynamics in the own company as well as for the whole sector.

as very low. They have the lowest value in the primary sector, and in the secondary sector also, only registered designs are considered to be of less importance. However, when comparing sectors it appears that the primary sector allots patents a significantly lower importance than the secondary sector. In combination with the low degree of utilization of patents this permits the conclusion that for the primary sector patents play a relatively small role by comparison with other protective strategies and by comparison with the secondary sector – at least in the year 2001.

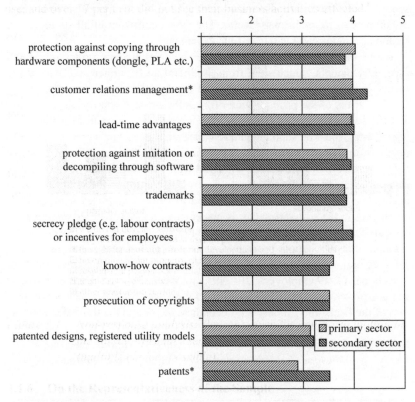

Note: The asterisks (*) at the individual criteria signalize significant differences between primary sector and secondary sector based on t-tests (** = 5 per cent significance level, * = 10 per cent significance level).

Figure 3.33 *Importance of various strategies to protect software- and computer-related developments (1 = very low, 5 = very high)*

However, in the primary sector generally intellectual property rights are allotted the lowest marks. The exception to this rule is trade marks alone, which are rated nearly 4 (great significance). It must be remembered though that the main motive in applying for trade marks lies not in the protection of innovations, but above all so that the visibility and the image of the company and its products are in the forefront (Bugdahl 1998, pp. 1–26). Interestingly, for the primary sector, the technical possibilities of protection represent the most important strategy, although compared with other strategies they are relatively less widespread, so that this average figure is based on relatively few responses (n = 40).

In the secondary sector the intellectual property rights also have the lowest scores. Trade marks are also the exception here, which have a similarly high importance as in the primary sector. The most significant of all strategies are customer commitment and lead-time advantage.

Based on the experiences or practice with intellectual protection rights, especially patents, which stem from the literature (Rammer 2003) on manufacturing industry, the differentiation of the sample from the enterprise survey into firms of the primary sector (the software sector in the narrow sense) and the secondary sector (software-developing companies from manufacturing industry) must be supplemented by the size aspect. For increasingly enterprises from manufacturing industry mutate into software firms, not only in the sense that their hardware is equipped with software components, but they also produce and market software independently. Further, the sample analysis made clear that the classical demarcation of small enterprises with up to 49 employees in the software sector is inadequate and even with 20 employees a critical size barrier has been crossed.[20] For this reason, the answers to the essential questions about protection strategies, preferences regarding various software regimes and possible evaluations are also calculated according to three size classes (1–19 employees; 20–249 employees; 250 and more employees) and are presented comparatively in the following. Table 3.2 shows the division of the firms into primary and secondary sector and the three size classes.

Table 3.2   Sample of the written enterprise survey (without independent developers) differentiated according to primary and secondary sector and sizes of enterprises

	Primary sector	Secondary sector	Total
1–19 employees	69	12	81
20–249 employees	86	29	115
more than 250 employees	37	23	60
Total	**192**	**64**	**256**

[20]   Calculations on the basis of the differentiation of companies up to 49 employees and between 50 and 249 employees show few significant differences, especially regarding attitudes, but also with reference to the various possible consequences of an extended patentability.

It emerges clearly that in the secondary sector the large enterprises are represented disproportionately often, whereas this is true for the small firms in the primary sector.[21] In Figure 3.34 the shares of the enterprises are depicted which utilize the various formal and informal instruments to protect software- and computer-related inventions. The differentiation into primary and secondary sector made clear that only in the applications for trade marks do the secondary sector firms display a significantly higher utilization intensity, while conversely the secondary sector companies make use of patent protection with significantly more frequency. The evaluation according to size classes illustrates that complementary to these differences between primary and secondary sector, the different size classes differ even more significantly in their behavior. The use of patents increases with increasing company size, which also applies for the utilization of trade marks, whereby in this case only the group of small enterprises stand out against the medium-sized and large ones.

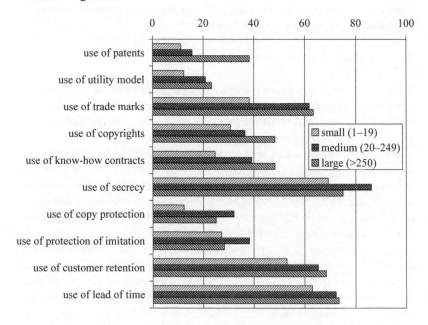

Figure 3.34   Use of various instruments to protect software- and computer-related developments differentiated by company size

---

[21]   The group of independent developers was intentionally not included in this analysis, because they only use protective instruments in exceptional cases and their opinions were explicitly rendered in the preceding study. See Blind et al. (2003b), pp. 95 ff.

For all formal protection rights, it is valid that active use increases with increasing company size. The same pattern emerges also for the very frequently used instruments of client commitment and the attempt to gain time leadership ahead of the competitors. The division into primary and secondary sector produced no clear-cut distinctions. With regard to the technical protection possibilities and confidentiality, we find an inverse U distribution, which signalizes that the medium-sized enterprises take advantage of these instruments more often than the small and large companies. The differentiation into primary and secondary sector shows, on the other hand, that the secondary sector firms make more intensive use of all these informal mechanisms.

If the findings of the analysis according to size classes are summarized, then it can be clearly observed that the differentiation into the selected size categories is even more meaningful than the division into primary and secondary sectors. Further, it became apparent that all protective mechanisms, with the exception of confidentiality and technical safety devices, are more often used with increasing company size. This is a crucial observation for the later derivation of policy recommendations.

3.5.3   Reasons for Patenting and Not Patenting

The decision as to whether a company should patent or not is determined by a variety of reasons, which extend beyond mere protection from imitation. Figure 3.35 gives the reasons for patenting and Figure 3.36 the ranking of the reasons which speak against patenting.

As to the reasons which lead to patent application, in the primary sector the defensive consideration to protect own developments from imitation has the highest priority,[22] whereas in the secondary sector the aggressive reason of establishing a market lead dominates. This reason is also frequently quoted by the large firms in the primary sector. At the same time, the secondary sector is more strongly oriented towards the importance of patent protection abroad, in particular in Europe, and less in the USA. The further reasons do not differ significantly in either of the sectors. It is interesting that not only the blockade of the software development by competitors which could prove detrimental to the innovation dynamics of the entire sector, but also the generation of licensing income or cross-licensing receive relatively low scores. Then again, the raising of the value of the firm through patents (signaling) is seen as clearly more important, in both sectors.[23] The argument that patents

---

[22] This motive is less important for export-intensive firms, as they are often confronted with cases of inadequate enforceability of their patent protection in the global context.

[23] Access to the patent pool is significantly more important for small firms in the primary sector than for large companies.

ease the entry of young software companies into the market due to easier access to the capital market could not be proved, because young companies do not accord to this motive any greater significance.

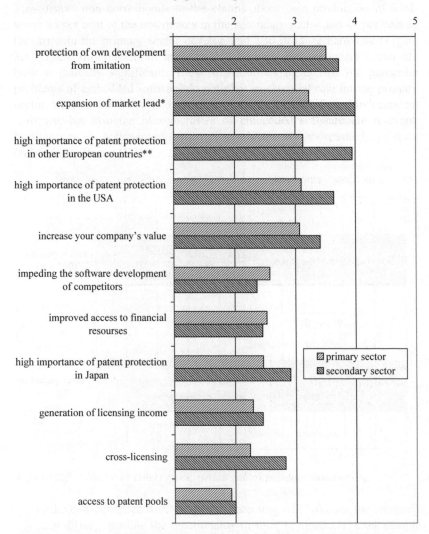

Note: The asterisks (*) at the individual criteria signalize significant differences between primary sector and secondary sector based on t-tests (** = 5 per cent significance level, * = 10 per cent significance level).

*Figure 3.35   Importance of various reasons for patenting
(1 = very low, 5 = very high)*

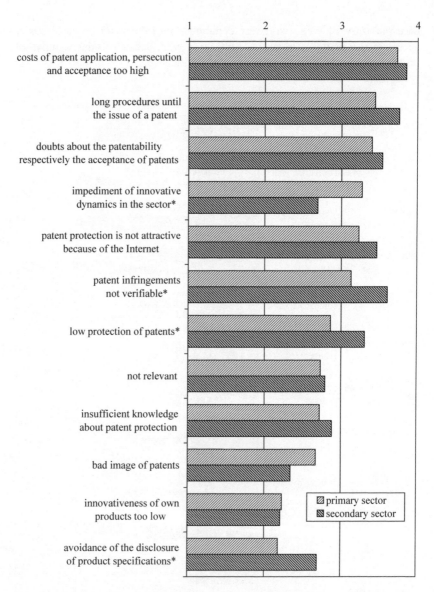

Note: The asterisks (*) at the individual criteria signalize significant differences between
           primary sector and secondary sector based on t-tests (** = 5 per cent significance level,
           * = 10 per cent significance level).

*Figure 3.36   Importance of the reasons not to patent in the area of
                software- and computer-related developments
                (1 = very low, 5 = very high)*

The reasons not to patent are also manifold. The sequence of the three most important reasons not to patent is the same for the primary and the secondary sectors. This means that the secondary sector judges the reasons which speak against patenting in the area of software- and computer-related inventions to be of the same significance as the primary sector. The most significant impediment is the high costs of applying for, following up and enforcing patents, whereby no differences exist between small and large companies. Whilst this reason is still independent of the specifics of computer- and software-related developments, the next two reasons are a particular problem in this area, namely the long duration of the process (with short innovation cycles, see Section 3.3) and the general uncertainty about the patentability of the inventions.

Of particular interest in the discussion about the consequences of stronger patents in the area of software- and computer-related inventions is the assessment in the primary sector that this impedes innovation dynamics (score: 3.27). This fear is significantly weaker in the firms of the secondary sector, which have worked with patents for decades in their areas of major activity. On the other side, these firms of the secondary sector see significantly greater barriers relating to the enforceability of a patent claim due to lack of verifiable proof or concerning the protection offered by patents. At the same time, the firms of the secondary sector have greater reservations about the obligatory disclosure demanded in patenting. On the other hand, the bad image of patents is much less of a problem for the companies of the secondary sector than those of the primary sector.[24] The lower scores in the primary sector in the pragmatic categories, such as costs and enforceability, were probably also caused by lack of familiarity with the whole issue of patents.

An initial assumption was that, in the area of software- and computer-related inventions, the significance of the reasons speaking against patenting depends on the different kinds of software products. Thus for producers of components, by comparison with producers of stand-alone final products, the more important reasons not to patent are the low protective effect of patents, too low a degree of innovativeness of their products and a bad image of patents. For the producers of embedded software, the low protective effect of patents plus the lack of verifiable proof of infringements, long process duration, high costs, limited national protected areas and the avoidance of disclosing product specifics are the more significant reasons against patenting. For the enterprises in the primary sector which produce software applications above all, almost all reasons not to patent are more important than for producers of system software.

---

[24]   However, this difference is not significant in the statistical sense.

3.5.4 Digression: Patent Applications and Awards in the Area of Software Patents

From the analysis of the use of the various formal and informal protection strategies, the low relevance of patent protection for the primary sector emerged clearly. In order to relate this data to the real application behavior, and to obtain indicators of the quantitative extent, the chronological development of the applications and awards in the narrower area of the software patents was determined, based on searches in patent databases. As no specific patent class exists for software patents, a very broad demarcation must be selected in order to encompass all software-relevant patents. However, the applications are also influenced by other factors which have no causal connection to the dynamics in software development and the use of patent protection. For this reason, the patent applications and awards were divided into two narrowly defined classes as an example. Patents for digital calculation or data-processing equipment or processes for computer-supported design systems (for example CAD) are contained in class G06F 17/50. Class G06F 17/60 comprises patents referring to digital calculation and data-processing equipment or processes for administrative, economic or business purposes. The applications to the European Patent Office mean all the direct applications without the transferred international or PCT applications. In the German Patent Office the direct applications of German inventors are recorded.[25]

Figure 3.37 makes clear that the development in both areas is clearly upwards, however, with different rates of growth. The total applications of processes for administrative, economic and business purposes at the European Patent Office have all doubled at the end of the 1990s, whilst the number of applications for the data-processing equipment and processes for design systems has only grown moderately. Between 6 per cent (G06F 17/50) and 8 per cent (G06F 17/60) of the applications originated in Germany. The applications of German applicants to the German Patent and Trademark Office are approximately four times more than the applications from Germany to the European Patent Office.

Whereas the application procedure presents an indicator for the demand of inventors for patent protection in software-relevant sectors, the patents awarded can give indications of the official award practices. Up to 1996, practically no patents were awarded by the European Patent Office *de facto* for the two sectors, although at that time a certain number of applications had already accumulated. In the meantime, the numbers of applications have

---

[25] The patents which were assigned to these categories in the second classification are not taken into consideration. These patents amount to approximately one-third of the number in the first classification.

drastically risen, but the willingness to award patents has also clearly risen, particularly since 1999. If one extrapolates not only the developments with the patent applications, but also the awards into the future, then within only a few years the stocks of European software patents will have grown considerably. The German Patent and Trademark Office has not yet awarded any patents in the area of computer-aided design systems, while since 1994 a total of 18 patents have been awarded in the areas of data-processing equipment and processes for administrative, economic or business purposes, although no trend is recognizable here.

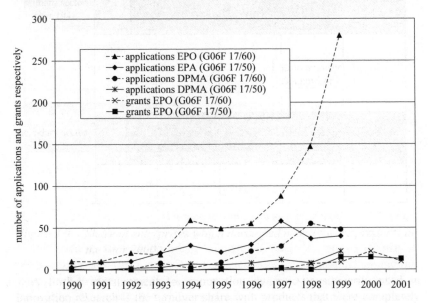

Source: EPAT and PATDPA.

Figure 3.37 Patent applications and awards in the area of software patents

These current tendencies must be seen as background information, if on the one hand the actual costs of patents are analyzed and on the other hand recommendations are to be formulated for the future structure of the patent system in the area of software patents, based on the results of the empirical and legal investigations.

3.5.5 The Information Function of Patents

Besides protecting inventions, an important classical argument in favor of patenting is its function of diffusing information about latest developments. If the companies are asked whether they conduct searches in patent databases, the clear-cut result is that this function is underdeveloped in the software sector (Figure 3.38).

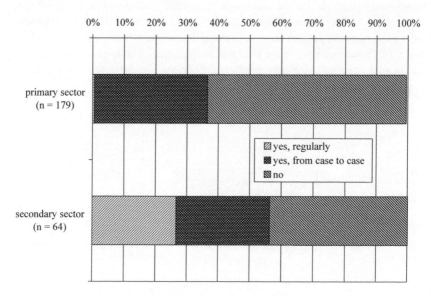

Figure 3.38   Frequency of searches in patent databases

Almost two-thirds of the companies in the primary sector never search through patent databases (secondary sector 43.8 per cent), one-third conduct searches from case to case, and only a very small percentage of the companies from the primary sector regularly conduct searches. In the secondary sector, however, more than a quarter of the firms do. This difference between primary and secondary sectors is significant. Basically, small and medium-sized firms conduct fewer searches in patent databases (H27). This finding agrees with observations on the part of the manufacturing industry, as the ability to utilize the information function correlates with the size of the enterprise and with its knowledge about the patenting system in general (ifo Institut 1998).

If one considers the ranking of reasons to search in patent databases (Figure 3.39), then the most important motivation to emerge is not gaining information as an input for own new developments. Rather, for both sectors, the most important reason is to avoid infringing the patents of a third party. This defensive reason is by far the most important in the primary sector, while the secondary sector also uses patent databases more strongly as an instrument to gain new input for own developments or for market analysis (H28).

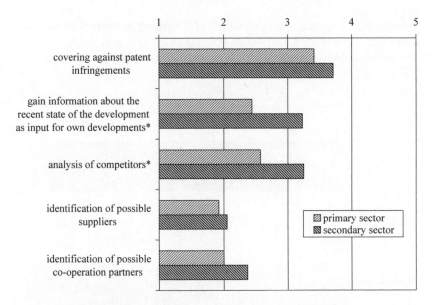

Note: The asterisks (*) at the individual criteria signalize significant differences between primary sector and secondary sector based on t-tests (** = 5 per cent significance level, * = 10 per cent significance level).

Figure 3.39   Importance of motives to search in patent databases
(1 = very low, 5 = very high)

3.5.6   Burdens of Patents: Extent of Litigation and Barriers to Development Activities

The significance of the patenting system for a sector is also reflected in the intensity and frequency of patent disputes, from which direct economic and administrative costs and burdens result due to patenting. It emerged that the firms in general had not been involved very frequently in legal disputes in the area of intellectual protection rights (H29), which was not surprising, given the slowly developing use of patents (see Section 3.5.4). Nevertheless, 38.8 per cent of the firms in the secondary sector and 20.7 per cent of those in the primary sector stated that they had been involved in a legal dispute (Figure 3.40).

Whilst the companies in the primary sector are charged not only in the area of patent law, but also under copyright law, rather than appearing themselves as plaintiffs, the firms in the secondary sector are more frequently plaintiffs than defendants in the patenting area, at least in Europe. This confirms the observation above that secondary sector firms tend to use patents rather as aggressive instruments, while in the primary sector a defensive attitude predominates. The probability of becoming embroiled in litigation correlates positively on the whole with company size and R&D activities, and in the secondary sector also with export activities (H29).

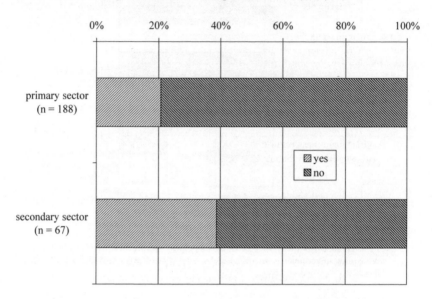

Figure 3.40   Involvement in litigation in the area of intellectual property rights

A further possible negative impact of protective rights could be seen in their deterrent effect on own innovation activities. Figures 3.41 to 3.43 point out several possibilities in which own projects are negatively influenced by (assumed) protective rights of other parties. The overwhelming majority of the firms do not quote any negative influences. In this context also the digression in Section 3.5.4 should be mentioned, which illustrates that the use of patents in the software industry is just getting under way. The enterprises whose own projects were negatively influenced belong to the primary sector to a much larger extent. In particular in the case of delays, price increases or slowing down, there are approximately 26 per cent of firms that are occasionally or frequently affected, a significantly higher share than in the secondary sector. At the same time, significantly more companies in the primary sector (17.6 per cent) have sometimes or frequently not started a project, by comparison with 10 per cent in the secondary sector. However, the higher rates for the primary sector are caused above all by the fact that over half of the independent developers see themselves threatened in their development activities (Figure 3.42).

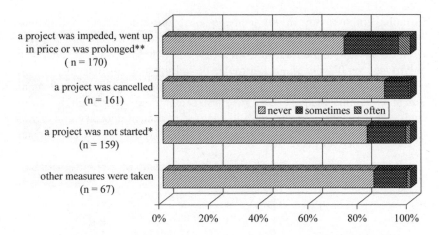

Note: The asterisks (*) at the individual criteria signalize significant differences between primary sector and secondary sector based on t-tests (** = 5 per cent significance level, * = 10 per cent significance level).

Figure 3.41   Share of enterprises and developers in the primary sector which were negatively influenced by a competitor's (assumed) property right

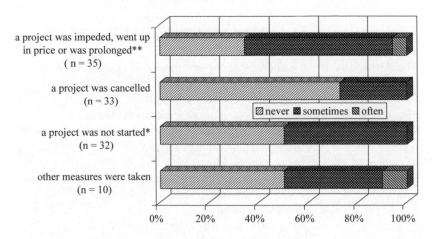

Note: The asterisks (*) at the individual criteria signalize significant differences between primary sector and secondary sector based on t-tests (** = 5 per cent significance level, * = 10 per cent significance level).

Figure 3.42   Share of independent developers who were negatively influenced in software development by a competitor's (assumed) property right

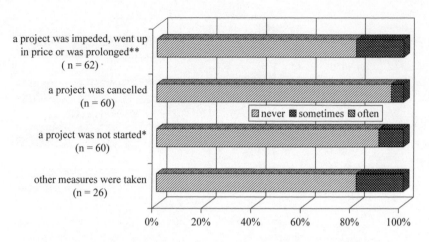

Note: The asterisks (*) at the individual criteria signalize significant differences between pri-
          mary sector and secondary sector based on t-tests (** = 5 per cent significance level, * =
          10 per cent significance level).

*Figure 3.43   Share of enterprises in the secondary sector which were
               negatively influenced by a competitor's (assumed) property
               right*

3.6   OPINIONS AND ESTIMATIONS OF THE ACTORS

The description of the responses of the enterprises surveyed ends with analyses of the attitudes and expectations of the actors regarding different possibilities of restructuring patent protection for software and concerning the
putative impacts of far-reaching patenting possible on the company, or on the
sector as a whole. These analyses provide a picture of the attitudes in the affected firms, but they are also an opportunity to learn about the possible consequences of alternatives to patents. Moreover, they form the basis for testing
numerous important hypotheses on the links between innovation behavior, utilization of intellectual protection rights and possible significance of patenting.

   As the opinions of the independent developers differ radically from those
of the other firms in the primary sector as regards patenting, the independent
developers are frequently considered separately in this section.

3.6.1   Opinions on Patenting of Software- and Computer-implemented
           Inventions

Firstly, the firms were asked to state whether they find a number of restructuring measures of a legal or administrative nature in the area of patenting

software- and computer-related inventions generally appropriate or inappropriate (Figure 3.44). These range from fundamental alternatives in the patenting of software in general, to administrative assistance and support measures.

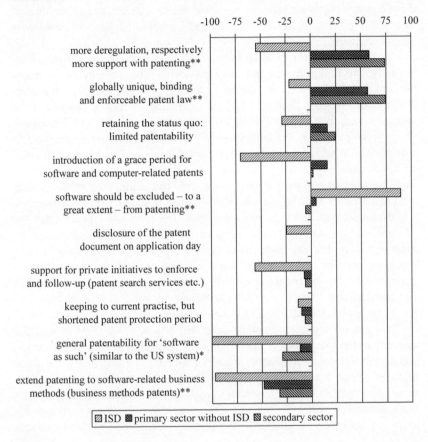

Notes:
Quoted are the difference of the shares of the enterprises (in percentage points), that consider the measure suitable and those enterprises that consider it inappropriate. The value for ambivalence is thus not demonstrated.

The asterisks (*) at the individual criteria signalize significant differences between primary sector without independent developers and secondary sector based on t-tests (** = 5 per cent significance level, * = 10 per cent significance level).

The figures for alternative answers 'immediate disclosure of patent specifications' amount in the primary sector without independent developers and in the secondary sector to zero.

Figure 3.44   *Attitudes towards possible different legal and administrative restructuring in the area of patenting software- and computer-aided inventions*

The figure shows clearly that the group of independent developers within the primary sector is characterized very strongly by a strict and very fundamental rejection of patenting in the software sector altogether, while the differences between the primary sector without independent developers and the secondary sector are more of a gradual nature. For this reason the discussion in the primary sector is differentiated between independent developers and other enterprises.

The fundamental rejection on the part of the independent developers does not only encompass the extension of patenting. The majority of the independent developers reject the current patenting practice, which is characterized meanwhile (see Section 3.5.4) by increasing awards of patents in the software area. In line with the majority demand to exclude software extensively from patenting, the independent developers are also not receptive to administrative assistance, to a grace period for novelties or state support within the patent system.

If the responses of the primary sector without the independent developers are compared to those of the secondary sector, it can be clearly recognized that the answers are much more moderate. At the same time, it seems that the opinions of both sectors tend in the same direction, with one exception. The main result is that the majority of firms of both sectors reject a broader patenting practice and of all the basic alternative answers speak out most strongly for retaining the status quo. The majority in both sectors are against the development towards patenting software 'as such' (US model) and in particular against the patenting of business processes.[26]

This general rejection must be adjusted, however, as there is a stable minority in the companies of the primary and secondary sectors which would welcome a development towards broader patenting.[27] Interestingly, the share of firms which would welcome patenting of software according to the US model is greater in the primary sector (without independent developers) than in the secondary sector,[28] whereas for the patenting of business processes the share of supporters is smaller in the primary sector than in the secondary sector.

The only alternative response, in which the direction of the agreement differs, is the general exclusion of software from patenting. In the primary sector, more than half the firms are in favor of excluding software generally

---

[26] This fundamental rejection is also confirmed in the British consultations (Webb 2001, as well as http://www.patent.gov.uk/about/consultations/conclusions.htm). For concrete examples which document the existing hindrances through the patenting of business processes and warn about the diffusion of this practice, see Sietmann (2001), among many others.

[27] In the primary sector for example 27 per cent of the companies welcome the patenting of 'software as such'.

[28] These differences are not statistically significant here.

from patent protection and thereby limiting common current practice. In the secondary sector, on the other hand, a narrow majority is against a general exclusion of software from patenting of any kind. This difference is statistically significant. The two alternatives assessed by the majority of the primary sector as appropriate – a globally uniform, binding and enforceable patent law, or administrative simplifications – should be rather based against this background on the fact that the firms promise themselves more neutral conditions for competition and cheaper collaboration in general patenting practice. In the secondary sector, however, the attitude towards patenting in the software area is more positive, and accordingly the approval rates for global uniformity and obligation or for administrative simplifications are also higher than in the primary sector.[29]

Both sectors are on the whole relatively ambivalent about individual regulative changes in the patenting system, such as the introduction of a grace period for novelties or an immediate publication of the patent documents. The latter measure is even rejected by the majority in the primary sector, although a central argument of the opponents of patenting – the reduction of the diffusion of new knowledge in the software area through patents – would be cancelled thereby. An initial hypothesis was that the introduction of a grace period for novelties would be supported by the enterprises which are engaged in the open source area, because they can thus apply for patents for their new developments despite the direct disclosure (H30). This assumption cannot be verified: only 13 per cent of the enterprises which themselves frequently disclose source code consider a grace period appropriate. On the other hand, 43 per cent of those companies which seldom or never disclose source code support a grace period for novelties. In total, the results suggest that the revelation of knowledge through disclosure is judged with skepticism.

A reduction of the duration of protection to accommodate shorter innovation cycles in the software area is also rejected by a narrow majority in both sectors. It is striking that both sectors (without the independent developers) reject the support of privately organized patent services, at the same time – as seen above – as they however support administrative simplifications. An obvious motive for this could be that triggering off an even more intensive private competition about patents by such services would set off developments which the majority do not want in the software area.

A series of statistical tests makes possible a further differentiation of the attitudes towards patenting in the software sector. It appeared that those enterprises which created organizational units for the utilization and

---

[29] These differences are not statistically significant here.

administration of patents, dispose of more knowledge about patents (see Section 3.5.1), and also the majority tend to view the patent system more positively.[30] The majority support the patenting of 'software as such' (according to the US model), administrative simplifications, introduction of a grace period for novelties, support measures by private organizations and finally, a globally standardized, binding and enforceable patent law (H21; H22).

There was a difference in attitude according to whether the firms are already patent-holders or not. Enterprises that already hold patents are ambivalent towards the extension of patents in the software sector, whereas the majority of those which do not hold patents reject general patenting. At the same time, a majority of patent-holders favor a grace period solution, while companies without experience of patents tend to reject this possibility. The size of the company, on the other hand, does not influence the attitude towards alternatives to patenting.

Whereas the prior differentiation into primary and secondary sector with reference to the option that software should be largely excepted from patent protection resulted for both sectors in a stalemate between supporters and opponents, a further analysis shows (Figure 3.45) that this undecided stance applies only for medium-sized firms, whilst the small firms clearly, and the large enterprises narrowly, declare themselves in favor of such a restriction (in a ratio 60:40). Correspondingly, a general patentability for 'software as such' is definitely rejected not only by the small but also by the large firms, while the medium-sized companies are rather undecided.[31] The division into primary and secondary sector resulted in a slightly more negative attitude of the secondary sector firms by comparison to those of the primary sector. Finally, maintaining the status quo, in the sense of a limited patentability with necessary technical reference, finds somewhat more supporters than opponents in the medium-sized companies, by comparison with the large enterprises and above all in the small firms, that are not at all united. Slight modifications, such as a curtailment of the protection duration, the introduction of a novelty grace period or the immediate publication of the patent specifications, find neither clear-cut majorities nor rejections. It can merely be noted that the last two options are somewhat more vehemently rejected by the small firms above all, whilst the large enterprises object somewhat more to a curtailment of the protection period. The division of the firms into primary and secondary sector result as a rule in even less differences between

---

[30] Interestingly, there are no statistical differences in attitudes to patent alternatives between the answers of lawyers and non-lawyers.

[31] The same pattern also applies for the introduction of patents for software-supported business processes (business patents).

the two groups. Finally, the reaction of the firms to three further complementary suggestions must be gone into.

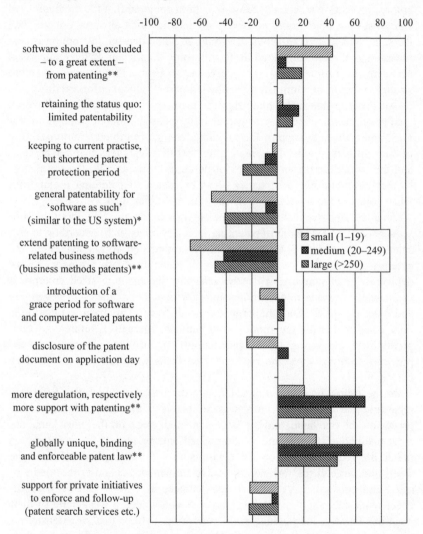

Note: The asterisks (*) at the individual criteria signalize significant differences between primary sector and secondary sector based on t-tests (** = 5 per cent significance level, * = 10 per cent significance level).

Figure 3.45   Attitudes towards different legal and administrative structural alternatives in the area of patenting software- and computer-related inventions differentiated by company size

With reference to easing the administrative burden, a globally standardized, binding and enforceable patent law and the support of initiatives to enforce protection rights, the constant pattern emerged that the medium-sized enterprises are much more positively inclined towards all three options than the small and large companies. It should be noted that the last option is also regarded by the medium-sized firms with some skepticism. In the comparison between the primary and secondary sector firms, the latter were more strongly in favor of administrative alleviations and global enforceability.

All these results make plain that the medium-sized enterprises above all tend to opt for the extension of patentability as an additional strategic instrument and a stronger support for patenting, or a more effective enforceability of their property rights. The small firms fear disadvantages than advantages, and the large enterprises have obviously come to terms with the status quo, so that the additional advantages of an extension of patenting possibilities when compared to the resulting insecurities are rather small.

As a last step, we differentiated the answers to the question about the consequences of an extension of patenting to 'software as such' according to size categories. In Figure 3.45, first of all the anticipated consequences for the enterprise as a result of the possibility of patenting 'software as such' are depicted. Fundamentally, it can be seen that the medium-sized enterprises estimate the various impact dimensions for their companies less negatively and more positively than the large and small firms. This basic estimation is thus consistent with the opinions on various alternative future structural possibilities pertaining to the patentability of software discussed in the previous section, where the medium-sized firms were rather in favor of an extension.

In the following, three dimensions are discussed in which the difference regarding the anticipated consequences between the medium-sized enterprises, on the one hand, and the large and small ones, on the other hand, are most distinctive. Firstly, the medium-sized enterprises expect on average a rather positive influence on the legal security for their firm, whereas the small and large firms foresee a negative influence. Secondly, the medium-sized enterprises believe their competitiveness in Europe will be strengthened, while the small and large enterprises anticipated a weakening of their position. Thirdly, the medium-sized enterprises believe that an extension of patentability positively influences the co-operation possibilities for their company, in that trade with more strongly coded property rights will reduce possible difficulties in the collaboration with other firms. The two other size groups see no effect, on average. By comparison to the differentiation into primary and secondary sectors, the division of the firms into these three size categories resulted in more distinct deviations among the groups. On the whole, the hypotheses established in the previous section are intensified, in that above all the medium-sized enterprises predict rather positive effects from an extension of patentability for their companies and the small and large firms are more likely to be skeptical in their attitudes.

A number of statistical tests facilitate the further differentiation of the attitudes towards patenting in the software area. It was seen thereby that enterprises that have created organizational units to exploit and manage patents possess more knowledge about patents (see Section 3.5.1), but also tend to have a more positive attitude towards the patenting system in general.[32] The majority favors patenting of 'software as such' (according to the model in the USA), administrative simplifications, introduction of a grace period for novelties, support from private organizations and finally, a globally standardized, binding and enforceable patent law.

A difference in attitudes is apparent, according to whether enterprises already hold patents or not. Enterprises which already hold patents are ambivalent about extending patents in the software area, whereas those that do not yet hold patents reject general patenting by a large majority. In addition, the majority of patent-holders are in favor of a grace period for novelties, whilst enterprises without patent experience tend to reject this possibility. The size of the company does not influence the opinion about alternatives to patenting in the least.

3.6.2 Anticipated Economic Consequences of Software-related Patenting

The attitudes towards various alternatives to software patenting do not say much about the possible consequences, that is, the economic and technological results for the company or the entire sector. A crucial indicator here is the assessment by the companies themselves. They were asked how the consequences of a broader patenting, oriented towards the practice in the USA of 'software as such' is regarded for their company and for the respective sector as a whole.

Figure 3.46 shows firstly the results for the evaluation of the consequences for the own firm, or own business activities. Directly understandable is the fear expressed by all groups to the same extent of rising costs for patenting in their company generally, be it for searches or for patent protection.

Analogous to the distribution of attitudes in the question of the desirability of various alternatives in the patenting system, the independent developers once again differ fundamentally from the two other groups. They fear negative consequences for their development or business activities, without

---

[32] Interestingly, there are no statistical differences in the attitudes towards patenting alternatives in the responses of lawyers and non-lawyers.

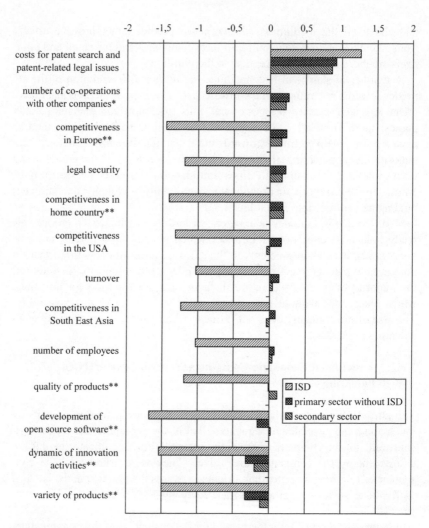

Notes:

On a scale from 1 (strong decrease) to 5 (strong increase) the firms should state which consequences would result for each dimension from a stronger patenting. From the arithmetical mean
of each answer category the mean value 3 was subtracted. A figure of +1 corresponds therefore
to an arithmetical mean of +4 and means that on average the enterprises assume that the respective dimension increases; a figure of –1 corresponds to an arithmetical mean of 2 and means that
the enterprises assume that the dimension decreases.

    The asterisks (*) at the individual criteria signalize significant differences between primary
sector without independent developers and secondary sector based on t-tests (** = 5 per cent
significance level, * = 10 per cent significance level).

*Figure 3.46   Anticipated consequences for the enterprise of the possibility
              to patent 'software as such' (– 1 = decreases, +1 = increases)*

exception. These fears are strongest for the development of open source. These fears correspond to the positive motivation for the utilization and provision of open source developments shown above. If negative impacts for the own open source development are anticipated due to patenting, then it is only consistent to anticipate a massive decrease in innovation dynamics and product quality. Own innovation dynamics plus the variety of end products would also be massively influenced, in the opinion of the free developers. The independent developers equate broader patenting directly with the loss of competitiveness. In short, the independent developers see their business model and their personal development opportunities greatly endangered by the patenting of software.

The enterprises of the primary and the secondary sectors have on the whole similar opinions with reference to the effects of broader patenting on their firms, which are however oddly divided into two groups. In competition with other companies, the firms associate the possibility to increase patenting with an increase in competitiveness, slight turnover increases and with better possibilities of co-operation with other firms. With regard to product quality and employment, the expectations are virtually neutral. On the other hand, both groups fear negative impacts on the development of open source, on their own innovation dynamics and on the variety of their end products. This last issue is more feared in the primary sector, which concentrates more on the production of software, than in the secondary sector, for which software represents only one part of the product palette or is frequently an input for other end products. Obviously, stronger patenting of software would not harm the product portfolio to the same extent.

Finally, Figure 3.47 illustrates the result with reference to the various impact dimensions, differentiated according to the size categories of the enterprises. The previous pattern is fundamentally confirmed, whereby the medium-sized enterprises assess the consequences for their own sector less negatively and more positively than the small or large enterprises.

This basic estimation is thus consistent with the attitudes discussed in the previous section towards various alternative future restructuring possibilities with reference to the patentability of software, where the medium-sized companies were most in favor of an extension.

In the following, three dimensions will be discussed in which the differences regarding the anticipated consequences between the medium-sized firms, on the one hand, and the large and small companies, on the other hand, are most clearly revealed. Firstly, the medium-sized companies on average expect a more positive influence on the legal security for their enterprise, while the small and large enterprises see a negative influence. Secondly, the medium-sized companies see their competitiveness in Europe strengthened, while the small and large enterprises assume a weakening

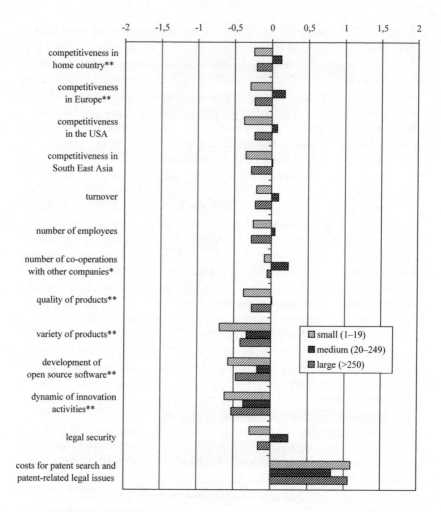

Note: The asterisks (*) at the individual criteria signalize significant differences between primary sector without independent developers and secondary sector based on t-tests (** = 5 per cent significance level, * = 10 per cent significance level).

Figure 3.47   Anticipated consequences for the enterprise of the possibility to patent 'software as such' (– 1 = decrease, +1 = increase) differentiated by company size

thereof. Thirdly, the medium-sized companies believe that an extension of patentability will positively influence the co-operation possibilities of their firm, in that the trade with more strongly coded property rights will reduce possible difficulties in collaborating with other firms. Both other size groups on average do not foresee any effect. Compared with the differentiation into primary and secondary sectors, the division of the enterprises into these three size classes produced more distinct deviations between the groups. On the whole, the hypotheses established in the previous section are reinforced that above all the medium-sized companies hope for positive effects from an extension of patentability for their enterprise and the small and large firms are rather skeptical in their attitudes.

In order to arrive at a more general picture of the feared or expected effects of a broader patenting, the companies were questioned about the impacts for their sector – in the sense of the relevant industrial sector. The resulting figure shows, to a great extent, analogous results (Figure 3.48). It is not surprising that the independent developers also fear exclusively negative consequences here, and most strongly for innovation dynamics, the variety of end products and interoperability, as well as the incentive structures for the development of open source.

The opinions of the companies of the primary and secondary sector are also largely similar in direction, whereby the secondary sector tends to be somewhat less critical or rather expects somewhat more positive effects. For both sectors, however, the division into positive and negative impacts can again be seen. On the one hand, most firms of both sectors assess the conse-quences on competitiveness, turnover, legal security, foreign direct invest-ment and employment as (slightly) positive (H32). On the other hand, they fear negative effects on the costs of formal standardization, the variety of products and components and innovation dynamics, as well as the number of firms. In particular, the anticipated negative effects on innovation dynamics are a key finding of the study and confirm a central, initial presumption of the study, according to which in sum the investments in innovations in the soft-ware area would decrease through patenting (H36). In addition, there is the remarkable influence on competition exercised by patents, from a regulatory perspective: the effects on the number of firms are evaluated as most nega-tive in both sectors, that is, the firms associate a concentration process with the patenting of software.

However, there are also interesting differences between the primary sector (without the independent developers) and the secondary sector. The primary sector enterprises expect decreasing product quality, decreased interoperabil-ity[33] and in particular less investment in the development of open source (H1; H19: H34; H35). Against the background of the significance of open source software shown in Section 3.4.2, which is bound to increase greatly in the

---

[33] There is, however, no difference about the assessment of the influence of software patenting on the interoperability between the companies which produce independent software and those which produce partial components.

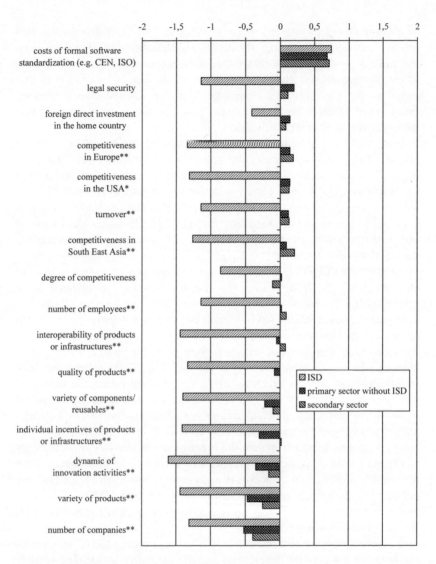

Notes:
See Figure 3.46 for the explanation of the scale.

The asterisks (*) at the individual criteria signalize significant differences between primary sector without independent developers and secondary sector based on t-tests (** = 5 per cent significance level, * = 10 per cent significance level).

'Sector' is to be understood as industry sector and not regarding the division into primary and secondary sector.

Figure 3.48   Anticipated consequences for the sector of the possibility to patent 'software as such' (–1 = decreases, +1 = increases)

future, stronger patenting would run counter to a central trend of software development.[34] As the users of open source see the advantages mainly in product quality, the negative expectations for product quality in the primary sector are merely consistent.

The secondary sector companies are less skeptical about the software-specific effects. They in fact assume – according to the patent logic of the secondary sector – improved interoperability of products and infrastructures (H1; H19; H34) and see no deterrent to the production of open source (H35). This demonstrates a crucial difference in the mentality of the two sectors: fears for closing a previously open system on the one side (primary sector) versus the prospect, by means of the patent publication, of being able to produce compatible products more easily (secondary sector). For all groups questioned, however, the fears of a decreasing innovation dynamic, loss of variety and products and fewer firms remain (H36).

The possible consequences of a broader patenting differ not only among the three groups of independent developers, and enterprises of the primary and secondary sectors, but in view of specific software products or development modes. Thus the widely differing utilization of external inputs for own development has (different) impacts on how important interoperability and sequentiality are. One initial assumption was that these two conditions were hampered by patenting (H10). Accordingly, the developers of system software, for whom interoperability and often also sequentiality are of great significance, anticipated greater problems for interoperability through software patents than the developers of application software. Further, the firms which depend strongly on their own developments see fewer problems for innovation dynamics and interoperability from the introduction of software patents. Into this picture fits also that enterprises which are characterized by a high degree of code recycling, are more uncritical towards the impact of software patents on competitiveness, variety of end products and innovation dynamics (H13). But firms with strong horizontal links, which accord great significance to interoperability with third parties, also see interoperability as more threatened by software patents.

A further differentiating characteristic of software-developing companies which is also related to the aspect of interoperability is the intensity of co-operation with other firms or independent developers. The effect of protection rights is ambivalent on co-operation behavior and protection rights can have the opposite impact, under certain circumstances (H40): on the one hand, they increase legal security and create clarity in co-operations, on the

---

[34] The assessments of the primary sector are here significantly different from those of the secondary sector, which only anticipates very minor effects on the development of open source.

other hand, however, they erect entry barriers, when firms without an IPR port-folio are not admitted. Further, they are then unnecessary when a controlled exchange of code and know-how takes place in existing co-operations.

The analysis shows two fundamental differentiations. Firstly, between those companies which already co-operate to a great extent and those which co-operate less, a difference can be observed regarding the significance for legal security accorded to patenting. The first group is better acquainted with the legal problems and even assumes a slight worsening of the legal security situation, whilst the companies whose co-operation behavior is more passive rather presume advantages for legal security.

The anticipated effect of stronger patenting on the co-operation behavior differs secondly with regard to the type of co-operation partner. The behavior in to co-operations with customers would not be greatly altered by broader patenting. Apparently, customer relations are adequately insured through contracts or the establishment of trust. Conversely, the firms which already co-operate to a great extent with competitors fear negative effects for the own firm and for legal security as a result of broader patenting more than the companies which co-operate less.

The descriptive statistics suggest that the primary sector has a high share of young enterprises by comparison with the secondary sector. This points to low market entry barriers and dynamic market development. An initial pre-sumption was that the extension of patent protection (patents for 'software as such') is particularly hampering for the development of new companies (H42). This assessment is supported by the survey, for within the primary sector there are significant differences concerning age: the companies which are less than ten years old view the impacts of patenting much more critically than those which are older than ten years. This assessment is not based on lack of knowledge, as the age of the companies could suggest; on the con-trary, the young enterprises in the primary sector claim to know more about patenting than the older companies (see Section 3.5.1).

One further initial premise was that the expected economic consequences differ with the degree of utilization of open source software, that is, that firms which use the open source code as input for their own developments are cor-respondingly more hampered by patents in the software area (H11). Conse-quently, among the companies of the primary sector, the open source users fear significantly more negative effects for their company and for the entire sector than the companies which do not utilize open source, with very few ex-ceptions. This becomes directly understandable if you remember that the inde-pendent developers in particular make use of and disclose open source (see Section 3.4.2 and Figure 3.20). These findings conform fully to the consulta-tions of the EU and Great Britain, as there too the supporters of open source, and thus most independent developers, are quite clearly opposed to patents.

Finally, Figure 3.49 illustrates the result of the various impact dimensions differentiated according to size classes of enterprises. Essentially, the previous pattern is confirmed, according to which the medium-sized enterprises reckon the consequences for the own sector to be less negative or more positive than the small or large firms. However, with a view to the sector as a whole, the medium-sized enterprises consider the consequences from the possibility to patent 'software as such' with skepticism. And there are some exceptions to the differences between small, medium-sized and large enterprises. For instance, it can be noted that the small companies estimate the negative implications for competitive intensity more strongly than the medium-sized and large enterprises. Obviously, the latter would be least negatively affected by such a regime change and would probably gain market shares at the expense of the small companies. A further aspect is that the medium-sized companies do not expect negative effects from the patenting of 'software as such' for the interoperability between different software programs, unlike the small and large enterprises. Finally, all firms foresee having to pay higher costs in formal standardization processes, as these groups will be confronted with increasing and wide-reaching property rights (H22).

If one sums up the results of the evaluation of the survey according to the enterprise sizes, it becomes very clear that the medium-sized firms adopt a special attitude. They argue most strongly for an extension of the possibility to patent 'software as such'. Parallels in attitude are to be found in the less negative or more positive expectations to various aspects relevant for their own enterprise or their own sector. However, it is apparent that the consequences for the own enterprise are seen more positively than those for the sector as a whole.

3.7 SUMMARY

The above detailed description and analysis revealed a number of characteristics, behavioral patterns and attitudes in software-developing firms of the primary and secondary sectors and the various size classes, which are of great relevance for the design of legal regulations for patenting software- and computer-related inventions. In the following the most important results are summarized once again, whereby a description of the composition of the investigated sectors (Section 3.1) was dispensed with. In order to present the key statements in concentrated form despite the complexity and variety of information received, this is done in the form of lists. The results summarized here, besides the results of the legal expertise not presented here, form the basis for the recommendations in the last chapter.

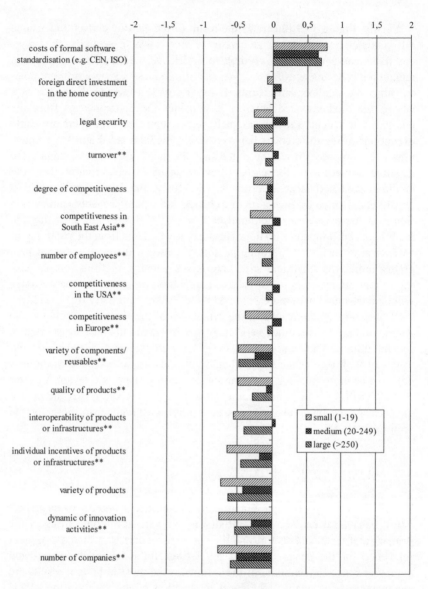

Notes:
The values in the scale and the asterisks (*) correspond to those in Figure 3.46, see there.
    'Sector' is to be understood as industrial sector and not referring to the classification primary and secondary sector.

Figure 3.49   Anticipated consequences for the sector of the possibility to patent 'software as such' differentiated by company size (–1 = decreases, +1 = increases)

3.7.1 Distinctive Features of Innovation Behavior in the Software Sector

In order to be able to assess the impact of patents in the area of software- and computer-implemented inventions, it was first of all investigated which idiosyncrasies characterize innovation behavior in the area of software development. The initial premise of particular dynamic and short-term developments of software development could be essentially confirmed:

1. Developments in the software area are characterized by very strong dynamics and short development times on the supply and on the demand side, both in the primary and the secondary sector.
2. The average development duration in both sectors is correspondingly short.
3. Compared with other areas of the service sector, market novelties are not more frequent in the software sector, but incremental further developments are clearly more frequent.
4. Rapid innovations and effective development processes are of even more decisive importance for competitiveness than in other service sectors.
5. Obstacles to conducting development work are thus even more serious in the software sector than in other sectors of the economy.

3.7.2 Distinctive Features of Software Development

Software development is characterized by three particularities which are important for the question of patenting and its consequences (see Chapter 2, Section 2.2): sequentiality, utilization and availability of open code and the necessity to ensure interoperability: The study basically confirmed the initial premise of the particular development conditions of software. These particularities must be taken into special consideration in the regulation of patenting.

Concerning these idiosyncrasies, the results from the survey are summarized in detail:

1. The rate of code recycling (sequentiality) is very high, approximately one-third of own developed software.
2. In both sectors own developments are increasingly dependent on the availability of compatible external inputs; the cross-company co-operation in software developments is steadily increasing according to these data.
3. Open source in the primary sector is already the most important external source of software components. This is the definite opinion of the

independent developers. If the primary sector is considered without the independent developers, then the application of open source in the primary sector is only negligibly greater than in the secondary sector.

4. The importance of open source will increase very greatly, in both sectors.
5. Open source has a generic character, that is, in many cases it is a functional input which makes the development of own software more effective.
6. There is not one main argument for utilizing open source, but a relatively well-balanced set of motives (among others: adaptability, state of the art, costs, quality).
7. Disclosure of code is mostly used as an information strategy to diffuse information about own performance: quality seal and transparency for the customers (primary sector), and signals for co-operation partners (secondary sector).
8. The classical open source mode, that is, making the code accessible for public use free of charge, thus contributing to a widespread diffusion of the new code, is still a clear domain of the independent developers, although approximately 13 per cent of the companies in the primary sector claim to use this custom.
9. Disclosure for special customers for a fee is practiced by roughly a quarter of the companies in the primary and secondary sectors.
10. Disclosure is especially customary for systems software in the primary sector, which tends to increase its importance.
11. For both sectors, interoperability is a crucial aspect, whereby the interoperability with customer software is by far the most important.
12. Interoperability with customer and supplier software and with competitive and complementary products is achieved above all by the disclosure of interfaces; the disclosure of code plays a very subordinate role here.

3.7.3   Practices and Experience with Intellectual Property Rights (Especially Patents)

A focal point of the analysis is the question of which experiences and practices with regard to intellectual property rights exist in the software area. Generally, it can be said that not only the use of, but also the enterprises' own organizational structures for dealing with intellectual property rights in this area are very underdeveloped. In detail, this means:

1. Of all protection possibilities, intellectual property rights have the least importance, especially for small and medium-sized enterprises.
2. Patents especially are the least widespread of all formal and informal protective strategies and have the least significance in the primary sector;

in the secondary sector only design patents are less important. The utilization of patents increases significantly, however, with the enterprise size. In very few cases have enterprises built up a whole portfolio of software patents; as a rule they hold only a small number of patents. The actual trends in patent applications and above all patent awards in the software-relevant area, however, show a clear upward trend.

3. The use of patents is more widespread in the secondary sector or in firms which also produce hardware.

4. There is also a positive correlation between age, enterprise size (according to number of employees) and the export activity, on the one hand, and the propensity to patent of a company, on the other hand.

5. The significance of patents for innovation activity and innovation success in the software sector is not clear-cut. Whereas the R&D intensity does not correlate positively with patent utilization, enterprises which are very innovative in the market make more frequent use of patents.

6. The reasons for patenting are manifold; the primary sector emphasizes the defensive nature (protection from imitation), while the secondary sector sets more store by strategy (exploiting the market advantages, reacting to the conditions abroad). Blocking competitors' developments is not an important reason for patenting.

7. Similar to the disclosure of code, signaling is a relatively important motive, whereas strategic cross-licensing is not yet very developed in the primary sector.

8. The theory that patents facilitate market access, above all for young companies, could not be confirmed.

9. Reasons for not patenting in the primary sector, besides costs and insecurities, are general reservations against the widespread effect of patents on the innovation dynamics of the whole sector.

10. Even for the secondary sector, more experienced in patenting matters, the lack of verifiable proof, enforceability and thus protection afforded by patents in the software sector is a great problem.

11. The function of patents to inform is only perceived to a small extent in the software sector, and if at all, for defensive reasons.

12. Dealing with property rights is still not much institutionalized in the primary sector, and where a need is seen, external consulting is mainly used.

13. There is a general dearth of knowledge about property rights, especially patents, in both sectors. Knowledge correlates with the existence of functional patent management units.

14. The negative aspects of patenting are based on:
    a. legal disputes: Almost 20 per cent of the primary sector and almost 40 per cent of the secondary sector were already involved in lawsuits

pertaining to the general area of intellectual property rights. The enterprises of the primary sector are mainly involved as defendants, the secondary sector companies on the other hand are also often plaintiffs.

  b. hindering own development activities: Approximately one-third of the companies in the primary sector and over two-thirds of the independent developers have already been hindered in the execution of their own projects by patents belonging to others; the number of those who were often impeded amounts to under 10 per cent.

3.7.4   Opinions and Estimations of the Companies on Possible Alternative Structures of the Legal Framework and Increased Patenting in the Software Sector

Alternative possibilities

1. The independent developers reject patenting on principle and are in favor of a general exclusion of software from patenting, which would mean a restriction of current award practice.
2. The independent developers also reject administrative simplifications and support measures out of hand.
3. The companies of the primary and secondary sectors are in favor of preserving the status quo and tend to have a skeptical attitude towards a spread of patenting practice in the software area. In principle, the medium-sized firms are rather in favor of an extension of patentability, the small and large enterprises rather less.
4. The companies in the primary sector, however, are polarized, for over 25 per cent of them are in favor of an expansion of patenting practice according to the US model. The supporters of such a broad patenting are more numerous in the primary sector companies than in the secondary sector companies.
5. In the primary sector the number of those who advocate the exclusion of software from patent protection is greater by several per cent than those in favor of such an exceptional ruling, whereas in the secondary sector the number of opponents of an exceptional ruling clearly predominates.
6. An extension of patenting to include business processes is rejected by a great majority in the primary sector. The majority in the secondary sector also reject this, but not to the same extent, as over a quarter of the companies signalize agreement for the patenting of business processes.
7. Administrative simplifications and support measures are greeted by both sectors (without the independent developers), with the exception of support of private initiatives on patent enforcement.

8. The existence of functional patent units, the possession of own patents, as well as knowledge about intellectual property rights, tend to produce a more positive attitude towards patenting in the software area.

Impacts of a broader patenting

1. Regarding the impacts of a broader patenting along US lines, the independent developers foresee negative consequences in all dimensions, not only for their own business model (open source), but also for the development of the sector and technology in general.
2. The expectations of companies in the primary and secondary sectors are ambivalent regarding their own enterprise and also the development of the sector as a whole. On the one hand, they expect a strengthening of national and international competitiveness; on the other hand, they fear a restriction of innovation dynamics, product variety and the development of open source.
3. After cost increases for patent searches and for achieving legal security, with respect to patent infringements, the anticipated consequence most often mentioned is the reduction in the number of enterprises and resulting concentration in the software market.
4. System software developers fear considerable problems due to broader patenting with regard to interoperability, more than do producers of application software.
5. Young companies have a more negative attitude towards patenting than established ones.
6. The more companies know about patenting, the more positive their estimation of the consequences thereof.
7. Fundamentally, the medium-sized enterprises anticipate most of all a positive influence from broader patenting.

3.7.5 Overall Results of the Representative Survey

1. Patents played a relatively small role in the software sector until the year 2001, that is, they hampered the development relatively little, but are neither a significant protective nor a strategic instrument.
2. The actors in the software sector have widely varying estimations of the impacts of patents. Independent developers are completely negative in their attitude, feel that they are already greatly hampered and consider administrative simplifications and adaptations in the existing system are not target-oriented.
3. The majority of companies in the primary sector and many enterprises in the secondary sector are ambivalent to many questions about patenting; as

a rule they have not developed an active patenting strategy and do not aspire to this. Knowledge and awareness are limited.

4. The number of companies which perceive the significance of patents as a strategic instrument is limited. These enterprises are as a rule internationally active and belong to the secondary sector.

5. The empirical survey basically confirmed that software development is characterized by the three distinctive features of sequentiality, utilization and availability of open code, and the most often necessary interoperability. The form of patenting possibilities regarding software has far-reaching implications for these three core elements of software development, in the opinion of the enterprises involved.

6. Basically, the majority of the enterprises, especially those of medium size, call for stronger support in patenting. In view of the fact that most enterprises claim that the state of their knowledge about patenting is low, or have not built up any in-house competence in this field, this is justified.

7. A further basic demand is aimed at realizing a globally uniform, binding and enforceable patent law. The question, in which direction harmonization should be pushed ahead, is not answered unambiguously. Adapting to US customs and making 'software as such' generally patentable is rejected out of hand by the independent developers and a majority of the companies in the primary and secondary sectors. As regards the size class, the medium-sized enterprises are the most open to an extension. Conversely, the option to maintain the status quo and to award a patent only on technical grounds achieved a very small majority. This means that as a whole the enterprises questioned (without the independent developers) – if they had the choice – would rather wish that their domestic system would assert itself worldwide.

8. The study confirms a recognizable trend that broader patenting does not find a large majority, even with those who do not utilize open source. This result agrees basically with the most recent results of the consultation with the British government (Webb 2001) and does not differ fundamentally from the results of the consultations with the EU Commission (PbT Consultants 2001). In the British case, a difference is drawn between organizations and individuals, whereby the organizations view patenting ambivalently and the individuals reject it. The results of the EU consultations also show that the vast majority of open source users speak out against the patenting of software, and those who do not utilize open source also signal slight approval for software patents.[35]

---

[35] The authors of the summary report of PbT Consultants interpret the results of the EU consultations in such a way that those who do not use open source are in favor of software patents (PbT Consultants 2001). A more exact statistical examination also shows, however, in the

9. A qualified majority – also from the companies – spoke in favor of not allowing patents for software-aided business processes. This result corresponds to the British consultations.[36]

10. The impacts of more widespread patenting are judged differently. The independent developers, who also supply the most open source, are very negatively minded in all dimensions. The enterprises of the primary and secondary sector, on the other hand, see the impacts in a more differentiated way, and this differentiation points to a division into short- and long-term effects. In the short term, the enterprises will achieve a greater scope for action regarding their patenting activities through the wider-reaching options of the US system, which increases their competitiveness. In the long term, however, they see dangers for competition and innovations dynamics in the increasing proprietizing of software. The further development of open source as a kind of public good, that on principle is available for use by all economic units and in the sense of the new growth theory thus promotes the general technical progress, and therefore innovation dynamics, is perceived to be in special danger. Once again it is the medium-sized enterprises which most expect positive impulses from an extension of patenting.

Small changes in the existing regulations are thus no solution to the above dilemma, for modifications of existing patent law, such as the immediate disclosure of the patent document, or a reduction of the protection period, are judged completely ambivalently. Only the introduction of a grace period for novelties could seem productive in view of the lukewarm approval of the enterprises and the fundamental rejection of the independent developers, as it makes possible the early publication of inventions and the prevention of sequentiality by patents.

EU consultations a rather ambivalent attitude in those who cannot be unequivocally reckoned as belonging to the open source movement. The interpretation of PbT Consultants of the results of the EU consultations cannot be endorsed here. The results show unambiguously that almost half (46 per cent) of those who do not count themselves as belonging to the group of open source developers reject software patents (n = 185, PbT Consultants 2001, p. 12, own calculations), In many countries (France, Italy, the United Kingdom) it is more than half. For Germany, the share of those who do not use open source themselves, and reject patents on software, lies at 35 per cent (ibid.)

[36] See Webb (2001) as well as http://www.patent.gov.uk/about/consultations/conclusions.htm, accessed 11 April 2001.

4. Context-specific In-depth Analysis: Case Studies

4.1 INTRODUCTION: MOTIVATION AND GOALS OF THE CASE STUDIES

In September 2001, the results of the representative survey were made available to the public. The results revealed an aggregated picture of the practices and attitudes of the software-developing industry. In the course of the analysis, and also during the broadly based discussion of the results, it became clear that the interpretation of the aggregated results was in part difficult because the context-dependent development and protection of software could not be depicted. By means of the survey alone, for example, it could not be adequately explained which mechanisms in each enterprise lead to positive or negative economic consequences of a certain regulation. At the same time, the written survey revealed that the majority of firms wish neither an extension of patenting nor for an exception for software-based inventions from patenting. Despite this, in this grey area of diffuse agreement, dissatisfaction and fears about the existing system were clearly expressed. This dissatisfaction of the majority of enterprises can only be understood with the aid of detailed case studies and an analysis of the firms' concrete experiences.

For these reasons, the contexts of the firms were also subjected to scrutiny in a follow-up study, based on 22 individual cases. The aim of the case studies was to present the concrete impacts of the existing property rights regulations in the software area on the innovation behavior and competition strategies, and to assess their possible advantages and disadvantages for the individual enterprise or for enterprise types. The definite emphasis thereby will be focused on the patenting possibilities. The in-depth and differentiated insights gained then permit a better and valid evaluation of the empirical data from the representative company survey. Further, they can contribute to a confirmation or even further differentiation of the conclusions and recommendations for action derived from the survey.

The sample of firms for the case studies was basically selected from the enterprises questioned in the preceding written survey. In order to guarantee a broad coverage of various types, the sample for the case studies was differentiated according to sector membership (classical software firms vs. enterprises from manufacturing industry), age, size and the spectrum of business models. In order to depict all essential enterprise types identified, in a later phase individual firms which had not participated in the first survey were also identified. The perspectives and problems of the developers, who work in open source mode and formed an independent group in the written survey, were also included in the investigation. This took place by identifying firms which base their business model on open source, whose members were either independent developers themselves or still place important findings of their development work at the disposal of the open source community as source code, and obtain the essential inputs for their own developments from the open source community. According to this categorization, three companies represent the attitudes, practices and problems of the open source community.

The advantages of a collection of case studies, that is, the reference to context and qualification of specific characteristics, also naturally contain its greatest limitations at the same time. The analyses are differentiated, but at the same time the findings and conclusions which result from this analytical step can only be understood with regard to the case studies discussed. The disaggregated picture which results can provide a better understanding of concrete facts and situations, but individual results cannot be generalized merely on this basis. For this reason, the analytical summary of the case study results is linked directly with the most meaningful statements of the written survey. The written survey is thus qualified and set in context. Such a procedure moreover ensures the consistency of the presentation throughout both partial studies.

Chapter 4 on the case studies consists of three sections. The methodological procedure is explained in Section 4.2. This contains the typology development and the selection process for the enterprises, as well as the introduction of the interview and the catalogue of main questions. Section 4.3 briefly summarizes all cases according to a standard pattern. These summaries are grouped according to the four enterprise types identified in Section 4.2. After presenting the enterprises, a summarizing discussion follows for each group which contains the first concrete conclusions.

4.2 METHODS

4.2.1 Selection and Classification of the Enterprises

The written survey had confirmed the theoretical premises of the investigation that patenting behavior and the attitude towards patenting depend on different characteristics of the firms. For the selection of cases it was intended to differentiate according to these essential distinguishing features and to cover different enterprise types.

The analysis had revealed that a crucial identifying criterion for the use of and attitude towards patents was whether an enterprise is to be classified as secondary sector or primary sector. Enterprises of the primary sector are those which exclusively produce and sell software for the market. For these firms the regulations governing the protection of software automatically concern their core business; simultaneously, these are the firms which traditionally possess relatively little experience with patents and which feel insecure about the preconditions for patenting, in particular the technical reference (H23). At the beginning, the firms of the primary sector were further differentiated according to producers of system software and manufacturers of mass-produced software. This last classification, however, turned out to be insufficiently selective in the identification of enterprises and also in the first case interviews. As the transitions were very fluid, many firms could not exactly define their main focus or gear their protective strategies to sub-areas of their products which do not always coincide with the main focus of their business activities. Additionally, it appeared that the enterprises do not differentiate their requirements of the patent system very strongly according to this criterion.[1]

Secondary sector firms are those which stem from manufacturing industry or produce their software basically in connection with their own hardware. In these companies it is argued, on the one hand, that their software developments are indirectly protected by the formal and informal protection mechanisms applicable to the hardware, so that patents in the area of software- and computer-related inventions are of less significance, compared with independent software (H2; H6). On the other hand, hardware producers have an advantage in patenting software because of their size and established patenting activities (experience, learning curve effects, fixed cost digression) (H21).

Besides the division into primary and secondary sectors, a further group of enterprises was specifically identified, the so-called start-up companies. The investigation of this group is based on the one hand on theoretical assumptions, especially in American literature, according to which patent protection facilitates the market entry of young software firms, as it affords them an easier access to the capital market and gives them time to build up larger production capacities (H31). Conversely, it is postulated that very young

---

[1]   Therefore we do not classify or systematize according to various software types in the following. The case studies do, however, cover the entire spectrum from system to mass-produced software, whereby cases are also covered in which firms modify their user software specially for clients.

enterprises or one-man businesses play a disproportionately large role in the development of software. This points to low market entry barriers and dynamic market developments. Suspected negative impacts of an extension of patent protection (patents for 'software as such') would be that they hamper the development of new companies (H42). The written survey produced only unclear results on this score and it appeared important to select this group of enterprises specifically.

The written survey also made clear that there are entirely contradictory patterns of patent utilization. Therefore we also differentiated, in addition to the sector dimension, according to patent utilization and attitude towards patents. The users of patents were subdivided in both groups into adherents and skeptics according to their views on the desirability of a broad patentability for software. The first group was identified because of their support for the 'US model', the second group according to whether they preferred the general exemption of 'software as such' from patenting. The non-users were divided, using the same criteria, into potential users and convinced opponents, whereby the potential users gave procedural problems above all as the reasons for their non-utilization of patents. In the group of convinced opponents were also the advocates of the open source mode.

Table 4.1 depicts the initial matrix of the case numbers, which resulted from applying these pre-considerations to the sample of the responding enterprises. The number gives enterprises which were to be clearly identified with addresses and which in view of their entire response behavior led us to conclude they would be meaningful cases.[2] In the table very few firms are duplicated, if they significantly produce not only embedded but also stand-alone software.

Table 4.1   Initial matrix for case selection: number of enterprises in survey

	Hardware	SW System	SW Mass	Start-up	**Total**
User, adherent	6	6	1	4	**17**
User, skeptic	4	1	3	1	**9**
Non-user, potential user	3	1	5	1	**19**
Non-user, convinced opponent	4	1	9	2	**16**
Total	**17**	**9**	**18**	**8**	**50**

---

[2]   In some cases the firms did answer the questions which were necessary for categorization; in many other questions which were interesting for the findings of the study, the answers were missing.

When setting up the interviews in the firms it soon transpired that size was a crucial influence variable for utilizing different protection strategies and for the attitude towards altering official patenting practice. For this reason, all efforts were made to include various size classes in the case study mix.

The objective of the study was to investigate between 20 and 25 cases. In an initial round of talks on the basis of the above illustrated matrix, 13 of the original 50 enterprises which came in question were willing to take part in a detailed interview. In order to reach the necessary number of cases, enterprises were searched for very specifically in a second round. As this search was conducted on the basis of the first interview results, it was possible to look specifically for those enterprise types which appeared particularly important, but which had not previously been covered in the sample of the representative survey. In this category belonged for example the search for companies that had claimed in the survey that they had already been massively hampered by patents or had already been involved in a legal dispute. In this way, two further cases could be identified from the sample and successfully approached. In addition, a patent search was undertaken, in order to gain further potential interview partners for the group of patent users. By this means young enterprises (start-up companies) in particular were identified.[3] Furthermore, two very large enterprises were contacted which are active particularly in the secondary but also in the primary sector, in order to better depict the positions of these very large enterprises in the exemplary cases. Finally, an additional company was sought out which bases its specific business model on open source. Thus a total of three enterprises are represented that mainly have recourse to open source.

The first interviews showed that the grouping of firms is more consistent if the enterprises are differentiated according to the criterion of attitude towards patenting software-related inventions. This makes more sense, especially for primary sector companies, which do not yet make use of patents, but are contemplating their use (potential users). It makes a great difference whether patents utilization is contemplated, because the instrument of patenting 'software as such' is welcomed and the firms would gladly use this in future proactively, or whether the enterprise is in favor of a general patenting of software only relatively restrictively and conditionally, but in recognition of the facts is considering a (limited) utilization. For this reason the investigated companies were classified into the three categories of adherents, skeptics and opponents.

This classification is, however, above all a heuristic means, for the borders between the groups are fluid. Adherents either support an extension of

---

[3]　Source for the firm foundation and thus the qualification as start-up company was the enterprise database Hoppenstedt; specifically the information in the company homepages.

patenting practice according to the US model, or absolutely do not want to return to the current practice of relatively restricted patenting. Skeptics are those firms which do not principally reject the legal protection of inventions based on software, but recognize great dangers in broadly based patenting and therefore – for different reasons – want to see the patents bound by restrictive criteria. The opponents, finally, are those firms which reject the patenting of software even according to the present practice in Germany and insist on an exception for software-based inventions. According to this classification, the sample contains nine adherents, seven skeptics and six opponents.

All in all, 22 enterprises were investigated. The selection of the case studies has a strong weighting in the direction of patent-active or especially patent-damaged enterprises. This distortion had emerged already in the responses to the questionnaire because the use of patents, or the actual experience as a party injured by patents, correlates with the willingness to participate in written surveys or even in single case studies. As the purpose of this study is not to produce a representative portrait of all software-developing enterprises in Germany, but the in-depth depiction of specific, patenting-related circumstances, this distortion is not only justifiable, but desirable.

Table 4.2 presents the distribution of the enterprises according to the categories mentioned. It also differentiates, unlike the starting matrix, according to size, but abstains from differentiating the primary sector into system and mass-produced software. Start-up companies are not depicted as an independent category, but are marked with an asterisk (*), enterprises which use open source code in essential parts and also champion this model, are marked with a cross (†). The firms which were not selected on the basis of the company survey, but were specifically searched for afterwards, are given in italics.

The firms are coded and not mentioned by name in the entire report. We thereby comply with the request of numerous companies which were only willing to be interviewed under this condition. In order to facilitate the recognition and classification of the cases in the report, the codes were so chosen that the position in the matrix was apparent from them. Each code contains firstly the consecutive case number from 1 to 22. Thereafter follows the size data (l, m, s) and the sector category (S, P). Last of all, the information about the attitude to or utilization of patenting is registered, which emerges clearly from the information in the left column of the matrix in brackets. For instance, the code 10_lPApU means that case 10 is a large enterprise of the primary sector (P) and an adherent (A) of broadly based patenting, does not have patents in the software area nor has yet applied for any, but is contemplating using patents (potential User).

The hatching in the matrix characterizes clusters of enterprises for which sufficient correspondences emerged, not only in the activity (sector), but also

Table 4.2 *Matrix of investigated cases*

		Secondary sector (S) Embedded software focus hardware		Primary sector (P) Pure software supplier or also IT service provider		
		large (over 250)	medium-sized/small (1–249)	large (over 250)	medium-sized (20–249)	small (1–19)
Adherents	Users	*1_lSAU* *2_lSAU* *3_lSAU*	4_mSAU	(1_lSAU)	7_mPANB*	8_sPAN* 9_sPAN*
	Potential users	–	–	10_lPApU	–	11_sPApU
Skeptics	Users	5_lSSU	–	12_lPSU	–	13_sPSU
	Potential users	–	6_mSSpU	14_lPSpU	15_mPSpU	16_sPSpU
Convinced opponents, non-user		–	–	–	[17_mPO 18_mPO 19_mPO† 20_mPO]	21_sPO 22_sPO

Notes:
italics = enterprises which did not participate in the survey

* = start-up companies (foundation from 1998)

† = enterprises which make great use of open source and partly develop in open source model

in the attitude towards software patenting. These groups of enterprises will be introduced and discussed together in Section 4.3. The columns on the left (above) in the matrix encompass all enterprises of the secondary sector (cases 1–6). For this group with focus on embedded software in the survey and also in the preliminary talks no 'convinced opponents and non-users' were found. Firstly, this is not surprising, given the tradition in manufacturing industry and secondly, it is not detrimental to the knowledge gains of the study.

The second group are companies from the primary sector, which support a broad patenting of software-based inventions. Three of these companies hold such patents themselves (cases 7 to 9); all three are start-up companies. Two further ones are considering using patents on their developments in the future (case 10) and also support an extension of patent protection to graphical user interfaces (GUIs) (case 11). The next group of enterprises (cases 12 to 16) includes those software-sector enterprises which are skeptical about the effects of patents on software to different extents and do not reject patenting, but want to see it handled restrictively. Two enterprises already hold a patent for a software development (cases 12 and 13); three do not exclude an application for the future (cases 14 to 16). The last group – bottom right in the matrix (cases 17 to 22) – consists of enterprises of the primary sector, which decidedly oppose an extension of the patenting of software and as a rule regard the present borders of patentability as already too wide.

4.2.2 Conduct of the Case Studies

Data sources
The central part of the case analysis was a 60- to 120-minute interview with from one to four company representatives. An identical guideline was used as framework for all interviews (see below). In the cases where the firms had participated in the survey, the staff member who had completed the questionnaire was always among the interview partners. Mostly this was a manager from software development or – in all small and many medium-sized enterprises – the top manager. Only in the very large firms of the secondary sector were the interview partners representatives of patent departments. In some cases, besides the R&D managers, other functionaries such as the standardization and quality control manager, competence manager or product manager participated in the interview.

Besides the interview evaluation, a further source of the analysis was the case-related assessment of the complete questionnaire of the written survey of all enterprises which had also taken part in the written survey. This eased the interview and supplied some important quantitative data on the enterprises. Further, the Internet pages and – if available – business reports were examined.

Box 4.1   Question catalogue for company interviews

---

1. Characteristics of the enterprise and its markets
Characteristics of the product and service range of your firm, markets (among others, competitors) in which your enterprise is active. Which factors decide your competitiveness?

2. Innovation activities
Software development process in the company based on dimensions input, sequentiality, interoperability. What role does open source play as a source of the software products? To what extent does the firm contribute itself to the development of open source and if yes, why?

3. Experiences with property rights
Relevance of protection strategies and rights for competitiveness. Knowledge level in the enterprise about the protection possibilities, including patentability of software.

a. Experiences with own property rights
Activities (resources, organization, range and kinds), changes; motives; experiences (enforceability, pursuit); reasons for non-use of some types of property rights.

b. Experiences with property rights of other parties
Role of property rights of others for software development. If no, why not; if yes; how do you handle this: searches (systematic, sporadic or not at all) and your motives; information function of property rights (state of the art, competition analysis, co-operation partners); licensing (cross-licenses); obstacles due to high license fees respectively blockade; reaction to accusations about infringements: settlement reached in or out of court?

c. Standardization activities and the role of property rights
A number of specific questions were posed here, which however were only answered by very few and above all large enterprises.[4]

4. Attitude to present system and possible future changes
How will your enterprise deal with the possible easier patentability of software?
Will you make more frequent use of this possibility? How will you react to the probably increasing patenting activities of your competitors? What support do you hope for from state institutions? Improvement of knowledge (among others by means of organized exchange of experience); improved search possibilities, administrative easing-up or support in applying for patents.

5. Special question for start-up companies
Which conditions or securities do venture capital investors demand to grant your company a loan? What role does the know-how of your company play, in particular registered intellectual property rights (patents, trade marks, design/petty patents, copyrights)?

Source: Fraunhofer ISI.

---

[4]   The questions on standardization were: To what extent is your enterprise involved in formal or informal (*de facto*) standardization activities? If yes, which general difficulties arise hereby? What role do property rights play here? What strategy do you pursue with reference to your own property rights? How do the standardization committees handle third party property rights? How are relevant property rights of third parties identified? Which licensing practices exist? Which possibilities are used to resolve conflicts?

This not only provided insights into the activities of the firms, but also enabled an analysis of supplier and sales markets, as well as characteristics of innovation approaches (interoperability with clients/suppliers, attitude to open source, innovation speed, range of offer and so on). In the enterprises specifically sought from outside the survey, in addition the results of a patent search and the information from the commercial database Hoppenstedt were also included in the analysis.

Catalogue of main questions
All enterprises were questioned according to a standardized catalogue. This catalogue was very comprehensive and also contained special questions on standardization and on start-up companies. From the differing contexts of the companies it naturally followed that the willingness and possibilities to impart information on the various thematic groups also varied. The interviews focused mainly on the enterprises' strategies to utilize patents for various goals (H21–H29) and on the attitude of the interviewees towards a desirable patent system and their assessment of the effects of different suggestions for a modified patenting regime for software (H30–H42) where the written survey showed no clear-cut results. The following overview gives a summary of the questions which the interview partners received prior to the interview.

4.3   SUMMARY AND ANALYSIS OF THE ENTERPRISE EXAMPLES

In the following chapter the essential characteristics of the individual company cases are shortly presented. These presentations follow a standardized pattern. For each single enterprise, the activities, size and experiences with property rights are stated and their attitudes and demands are sketched out. The portraits are divided into the four enterprise groups identified in Section 4.2:

1. Secondary sector
2. Primary sector – adherents
3. Primary sector – skeptics
4. Primary sector – opponents

The idea behind this division is that the firms in each group exhibit similarities, despite all the differences of their specific situations regarding the use, attitude and effects of patents. For this reason, the short portraits of all cases in a group are followed by a synoptical appreciation of the sketched facts and the conclusions directly resulting from them. In the discussion of the findings for each group, references are given to those hypotheses that are supported by the respective empirical material.

4.3.1   Secondary Sector

Three of the six enterprises of the secondary sector are very large, internationally active corporate groups (cases 1 to 3), which also each have a certain and continually increasing share in pure software development. They all utilize patents in the software area very intensively and want to maintain at least the status quo of the present award practice, and support an extension of patenting. One further large enterprise (case 5) is a mechanical engineering firm which holds a number of traditional patents, which have an essential software core. This firm feels insecure in the true software field and applies for patents here only hesitantly. Of the two medium-sized enterprises from the manufacturing industry, one has developed activities in the patenting of software (case 4); its patents, however, are (still) registered under the traditional classification of control engineering. Whereas this firm also sees chances in the patenting of software and supports this, the other medium-sized company has not yet used patents on software, but sees itself forced to patent in the future because of negative experiences in this area (case 6).

The cases
Case 1: 1_ISAU
The enterprise is the German subsidiary of a very large corporate group, active worldwide, which offers nearly the entire range of IT hardware, a broad spectrum of software – especially in the e-business field – and IT services. The German subsidiary has altogether approximately 26 000 employees, of whom 1700 alone are employed in an independent German development firm. The US mother company was awarded the most patents in the USA in each of the last years. The German subsidiary is also very active in patenting in Germany – in the year 2000 it contributed 80 patent applications to the company portfolio. Besides this strategy to protect intellectual property, the enterprise promotes open platforms and interfaces and also supports Linux, in order to exploit the advantages of open and proprietary systems synergetically.

   The patenting activities are centrally organized and in principle are not differentiated according to business fields, that is, software development is also systematically urged to patent via an integrated patent process, and is secured against existing patents. Patents serve primarily to secure the freedom of action for their own technological development in view of competitors' existing patent portfolios and technology exchange. The infringement of their own patents is strategically pursued, that is, in particular if the economic significance of the patents (important technology, important competitor) make this appear necessary.

The enterprise does not see the variety in software development endangered by patenting in the present mode, as the number of possible collisions is very much less than maintained, particularly by the open source movement. As patent protection assumes a technical and non-obvious invention, only a few programs are protected in this way. With the help of the mostly free search possibilities on the Internet, small enterprises or even individual persons can obtain sufficient information about such inventions. The company does not support an extension of patenting practice according to the US model, as this could lead to dangerous wild proliferation. The necessary technical content, as well as the possibility to revoke unjustifiably awarded patents via appeals and nullity suits in court, are crucial characteristics of the European system. The current tendency of some examiners in patent offices to reject patents on principle if they contain a software component was criticized. A careful examination of novelty and inventive quality of the application is supported, in order to prevent trivial patents.

Case 2: 2_ISAU

The enterprise is a corporate group operating worldwide that offers a wide range of products, systems and solutions for industry. Its main motive for utilizing property rights is to manage the portfolio of property rights in such a manner that it harmonizes with the goals of the business units. Important motives, especially for the patenting of software, are concretely protection from imitation, improvement of its own negotiation position vis-à-vis competitors, but also the improvement of its own corporate image. Property rights also fulfill an information function for the enterprise, and portfolio analyses are conducted in the business units on main technology areas. As the company is the technology leader, the information function of others' property rights is only of subordinate significance. The documentation of other parties' property rights is used less as an input for the firm's own developments, but serves to control its own technology and market leadership.

The company hopes for clear and unambiguous, legally codified regulations dealing with the patentability of software and business methods from state institutions. Legal clarity is the top priority for the enterprise. Of secondary importance for the company is to what extent software and business methods will be patentable. The company, however, has been dealing successfully for many years with the patent regime of the United States, so that the experiences gathered there with the patenting of software and business methods represent an immense lead in experience compared to competitive companies, which the enterprise would gladly utilize.

Case 3: 3_lSAU

The firm is a German subsidiary of a system provider which is active world-wide in the telecommunication field with a very large product range. It holds thousands of patents; in the last few years approximately 70 of the patents contain an important software component. The management of property rights, in particular patents, is highly developed and differentiated between the firm's locations. No difference is made between software patents and tra-ditional patents. Patents with a large software content played an important role in the dynamization of patent practice in the 1990s. Developers were sensi-tized to patenting, and the search system is well developed. The most impor-tant motives for patenting lie in ensuring technological freedom of action and in the possibility to exchange cross-licenses with competitors and suppliers.

The infringements of own patents by third parties is proving problematical as is the ban of the 'discovery procedure' usual in the USA, in which the docu-ments of the patent infringers can be extensively looked into. In addition, the proof of the infringement of embedded software through a tradable up-date version is very difficult. A more restrictive patenting in Germany or Europe would mean a competitive disadvantage compared with other international corporate groups; the enterprise prefers globally standardized regulations according to the US model for patents on software (not business models).

Case 4: 4_mSAU

The firm presently employs 40 staff and has an annual turnover of approxi-mately €5 million. It is active in the area of automation, measurement and control engineering and works in particular on innovative large projects for the international market and technology leaders. The company holds two patents; a further one is still in the application process. The patents of the enterprise belong in the area of measurement and control engineering, al-though the patented processes are always realized in the form of software.

In patenting practice, the enterprise is above all concerned with the crea-tion and guaranteeing of competitive advantages vis-à-vis its usually very much larger competitors. In cases of conflict the firm mostly cannot enforce its demands alone, because of limited resources, but can however frequently rely on the support of its big clients. The only case of conflict up to now was resolved in this way by the intervention of the client, who for its part threat-ened to withdraw orders from the competitor. With foreign clients the enter-prise patents are utilized as an effective instrument to underline clearly the technological leadership over the competitors.

For the enterprise the present ban on patenting software is insignificant, as it can formulate all claims in the language of automation technology, which is not critical from a patenting viewpoint. As software of sufficient innova-tiveness and with technical content is regarded equally as an engineering feat, the enterprise advocates an extension of the patentability of software for reasons of equality with other technology areas.

It criticizes above all the tendency observed in international large corporate groups towards wide-scale patenting, that is, to block whole business areas with trivial patents in the run-up to development. This not only hampers the innovation dynamic of software development, but also acts as the source of grave distortions of competitive positions between SMEs and large corporate groups.

Case 5: 5_lSSU

The company is a supplier to the automobile industry and sells software-supported controls for pneumatic systems. The medium-sized firm is meantime part of a foreign corporate group. It holds numerous patents, which increasingly contain software components, but which are applied for in the context of machines and machine parts as traditional patents. At present an unresolved conflict exists, because in the course of a routine search it was discovered that in a third party patent, software components are protected which are already contained in one of the firm's broader patents.

Although the firm is experienced in dealing with traditional patents, the patenting of software developments is regarded as especially difficult and full of preconditions. At the same time, the increase of pure software patents is observed in the market. Wide-scale patenting and the generic character of software holds the danger for the firm that their development activities will be obstructed by a multiplicity of software patents which are foreign to the market and technology, and that patent searches will become increasingly costly. The extension of patenting is vigorously rejected; the technical reference must be retained as a criterion. The European Patent Office is criticized above all for allowing ill-considered patenting in the software area.

Case 6: 6_mSApU

With its 30 employees, the firm develops and markets CAD systems and client-specific business management application programs. The former were developed in series and adapted and globally marketed; the latter are restricted to the German market. The annual turnover amounts to approximately €30 million.

The enterprise has three trade marks, but no own patents. This has reduced its market chances severely, as an important customer in the hardware field adopted the unprotected features of the firm in its own software program and integrated it into its whole system. First of all, the firm was not conscious of how susceptible the lack of patent protection made it, then it was unclear for a long time if its own development was protectable in the sense of being patentable.

The company does not reject the protection of software-based developments on principle, but calls for a better clarification of patentability and a shortening of the procedure.

Discussion and conclusions

The enterprises which produce both hardware and software often have a long tradition of patenting from manufacturing industry, mostly in the electro-technology area. The patenting practices developed as a rule because of the increasing software content of self-manufactured hardware, which was then continued in the software area. Thus the enterprises from the manufacturing industry, and the enterprises with large shares in hardware production, are drivers of patenting and transfer an active patenting mentality from the manufacturing industry context to the context of the software-developing enterprises (H21, H22).

However, in the discussion the companies of the secondary sector must be differentiated regarding their size, market and share of independent software. For the three very large corporate groups, which also very actively patent in the software area (cases 1 to 3), the protection of their own developments is daily practice for software and the advantages possessed by these large corporate groups are very obvious.

On the one hand, the large enterprises under observation here pursued expansive strategic patenting (H25). In a study conducted at the Fraunhofer Institute for Systems and Innovation Research it is shown that the annual applications of the large enterprises have nearly doubled (Blind et al. 2004). The reasons for this development are manifold, but basically patenting has become a strategic instrument to secure freedom of action in technological development. Patent portfolios are not only established for direct protection from imitation, but are being increasingly utilized, for instance, in the case of a possible collision with other enterprises in order to be in possession of sufficient critical mass to negotiate about cross-licenses or to present a potential threat. Additionally, patents also increasingly serve as evidence of technological leadership and therefore as an important marketing instrument, and when rendering accounts to the stockholders. Thus a kind of patent race with smaller, but more numerous patent claims and more widespread protection strategies has developed, above all among the large hardware producers. This is comprehensible and rational in the context of the large enterprises and their technologically based competition. It also has visible impacts, however, on patenting in the software area, because this area is naturally not excluded from strategic patenting.[5] Consequently, a dynamization occurred here which

---

[5]   This pattern was also unambiguously confirmed in a study of patenting in the service sector conducted on behalf of the European Commission. Here too the large concerns which have

could not be explained only by the interest in protection from imitation – also according to the statements of the enterprises themselves. Especially in the software area, according to the opinion of most interview partners, an imitation is frequently unavoidable despite patent protection, and many developers could copy functionalities in such a manner as not to infringe the patents. That means at the same time that the pure software developers have a structural competitive disadvantage in direct competition with the companies from manufacturing industry.

The subjectively perceived strategic necessity to patent is accompanied in the large corporate groups of the secondary sector by differentiated institutional abilities to patent. Sometimes very large patent departments are the driving forces within the enterprise behind more patenting and transfer patenting activities to new areas of the service spectrum and of software development (H21). They are thus essentially more effectively able to manage their own patents or fight off others' claims than are smaller firms or those without a tradition of patenting. These departments also form, as each functionally separate organizational unit does, their own institutional rationale, which leads to the permanent optimization of the patent portfolios being anchored in the company's strategies. A danger for the corporate group consists in this institutional logic becoming an end in itself, and that patenting will be disassociated from the technological and competitive rationalities.

Finally, the last aspect which contributes to the catalytic function of the large hardware producers in software patenting, is the keen, technology-oriented international competition against which these firms must hold their own earlier and more intensively than the many, mainly small and medium-sized, enterprises of the software sector. A legally secure stock of technologies is indispensable, and in all areas which are worth protecting abroad, especially in the USA. The clear majority of the companies investigated that do business in the USA and develop software themselves described the patenting activities there as a catalytic element for activities in Germany.

Summed up, this means that the large secondary sector corporate groups – for understandable reasons – have also become catalysts of patenting in the software area (H24). However, it does not follow that legislation and award practice should imitate the conditions in the USA. Based on experiences with US practice, some of the large enterprises of the secondary sector support an extension of patenting possibilities up to and including business patents. From an overall economic perspective, however, the preferences of these worldwide corporate groups need only be considered conditionally, because they possess sufficient competences to come to terms with most widely

their roots and main business fields in manufacturing industry emerged as the driving force for patenting, also in the service area, see Blind et al. (2003c).

differing patent regimes. Many of them will not suffer any competitive disadvantages as a result of more restrictive patenting in Europe, neither in the European nor in the US American market. Extending patentability brings these world corporate groups competitive advantages, compared to smaller enterprises and those only active in the European market, as they can call on their wealth of experience with US practices. More important than a copy of the US model for the firms questioned is, however, legal clarity and security, as these two factors could enormously reduce the costs for patent management.

The fact that large corporate groups utilize their patenting experiences from manufacturing industry also in the software sector, is not problematical for the overall economy, as long as this advantage does not become established permanently and damage competition intensity or lead to competitive disadvantages for 'inexperienced' firms. The enterprises which are more clearly anchored in the manufacturing industry find themselves in a transitional phase towards integrating software in their technology and property rights portfolio. In the case of two enterprises (cases 5, 6) a certain insecurity became apparent in this phase which led to manifest problems. Even in large firms it is still true today that the software developers must be more strongly encouraged to patent by the patent departments than the developers and engineers in the hardware area. In the enterprises participating in the study, which increasingly enter into the area of patentable software, for example in the field of mechanical engineering, this uncertainty is still tangible due to the increased software content in control systems. Own patents are perceived by the enterprises as patents in control or control and measurement engineering, but have a distinctly software core (H2). More and more firms, also from areas outside the manufacturing industry, apply for patents in areas traditional to the manufacturing industry, which are software patents at their core. As a result, the manufacturing industry enterprises find themselves increasingly confronted with a number of software patents which in the narrower sense do not stem from control engineering, but which restrict the technological freedom of action in control engineering technology, and simultaneously cause uncertainty with reference to their own developments and possible infringements of existing patents. This uncertainty will increase in breadth for firms in the manufacturing industry. In particular, the overview of possible competitors will be problematical, as the technology competitors possibly stem from areas of the software sector with which traditionally few points of contact existed, and it will be important in the future to point out more clearly the possibilities and dangers in patenting software for the core business. State support measures must take more strongly into consideration the generic character of software and thus the effects of patents on many areas of traditional business, that is, particularly in consulting activities pertaining to the novel problems caused by technology-unrelated software patents for many enterprises.

However, case 6 is simultaneously also an example for the dangers of a lack of protection. The case illustrates the vulnerability of SMEs that develop software in the manufacturing sector and cannot defend themselves without the protection of a patent against an imitation of their functionality by important clients. The problem is even graver within manufacturing industry because frequently here large enterprises as clients are at the same time systems sellers which can integrate the specific niche functionalities of their suppliers into their own systems. The case illustrated clearly that companies are often not able, even with the aid of their patent attorney, to identify the protectability of their developments (H39). The existing consulting institutions must be legally placed in the position to supplement or to compensate for the shortcomings often encountered in traditional patent attorneys in the area of software patenting. SMEs should be made more aware of these possibilities.

The large enterprises are very conscious of their structural advantage resulting from these practices. In order to retain the legitimacy and functionality of the patent system, the discussion partners from the large companies argued unanimously in favor of state support for SMEs in patenting software. The analyses have moreover revealed an implicit arrangement between the large corporate groups with a wide patent portfolio and the many small firms which deal with their niche markets. The large enterprises understand patenting as a strategic instrument, the most crucial point being guaranteeing their own technological freedom of action. This is usually not endangered by the multiplicity of developments which latch on to protected technologies and possibly also infringe patents thereby. It is true that no legal security has been created for the smaller enterprises, and they are also not freed from the costs involved in the obligatory search and validation, but the number of actual collisions is considerably less than the number of overlappings and infringements.

Case 4 is an example that it is also possible for a medium-sized firm in the context of the manufacturing industry to protect innovative software functionalities by patents and simultaneously use these patents in connection with client contacts, so that competitive advantages could be gained vis-à-vis very much larger competitors. However, even this enterprise, which is in favor of software patents, is frequently confronted with the problem of 'extensive patenting', with which usually large competitors try to seal off whole business areas by taking out a multiplicity of patents. The dangers of 'trivial patents' appear even more distinctly in the manufacturing industry than in the primary sector. One enterprise (case 5) complained that patents originating from the software sector and without technical and often without economic connections to its sector (mechanical engineering, automobile supplier) will represent a great danger in future, which makes the search for and awareness of these patents more difficult and will necessitate a change in the company's search practice. A further company in the secondary sector (case 6) expressed similar fears. The more widely patents are awarded in the software area and the less an actual proved reference to the technical application is given, the more difficult the protection situation will become for enterprises in the manufacturing industry. From this analysis stems the demand of practically all enterprises in this investigation, that only actually realized inventions should be patented and that the degree of invention and the technical reference should be very much more strictly inspected thereby. Even the enterprises which are very active in patenting meanwhile perceive the danger of blocking the system through over-patenting trivial developments.

The problem of widespread patenting also confronts some enterprises with the obstacle of internationalization (H38). Enterprise 4 explicitly named the danger of property right infringements as the most significant obstacle to activity in the USA. For some medium-sized firms from the manufacturing industry, as well as for numerous cases from the primary sector, the problem is reversed with reference to the deviation of the US model from the European model: the broader patenting in the USA presents a grave hindrance for export or activities abroad, especially for those enterprises which do not possess sufficient capacities in-house and are forced to rely on external experts in the US market. Here it is less the political actors and rather the chambers of commerce and associations which have the important function of diffusing information and raising awareness; they must point out to their member enterprises most strongly the possible dangers of patenting software, also for enterprises from the manufacturing sector.

On the whole the analysis of the secondary software sector provides evidence that these enterprises are indeed a driving force in favor of an expansion of patenting practice for software, mainly because their knowledge and awareness is highly developed and because they often have departments or partners that are able to deal professionally with the protection of intellectual property. Consequently their patenting strategies in the field of software are not much different from those in other fields, resulting in a dominance of strategic motives. This becomes more apparent with the degree of international activity and with the size of the enterprise.

4.3.2   Primary Sector: Adherent

The attitude patenting varies greatly within the primary sector companies. The spectrum ranges from the utilization of patents and support for widespread patenting according to the US model – partly including the patenting of business models – up to the rejection of software patenting on principle.

The five companies of the first group of enterprises from the primary sector are all adherents of the possibility of broadly based patenting. Three of these

16 firms (cases 7 to 9) already hold patents themselves on their software developments. These are all young enterprises (start-up companies).[6] Two further companies (cases 10 and 11) do not hold any patents yet in the software area, but are principally in favor of extending the patenting possibilities.

The cases
Case 7: 7_mPAU (Start-up company)
The firm employs about 50 staff. It is active in the area of IT security and develops software for secure communication as well as for smartcards. The enterprise holds one patent, and further patents are in the application process. The patents deal with cryptographic processes.

In its patenting practice the firm is above all concerned with the creation of a basis for communication with clients, in particular the PR-effective proof of its own qualifications and innovativeness, as well as a basis for the business model based on licenses. The essential competition-relevant knowledge of the enterprise is protected, however, by hardware and processes, not by patents. The enterprise searches patent applications in its core business activity area with the goal of preventing or avoiding possible patent infringements. Additionally, an internal database was established based on the comprehensive searches, which is utilized to increase the employees' know-how. In order not to obstruct development in the technology field, the enterprise does not enforce its patents against competitors. This is not possible for medium-sized enterprises anyway. Although the strongest competitor of the company holds a great number of patents, there has never been a legal conflict. This is attributed to the fact that because of the existence of 'prior art', many of the patents applied for are contestable. Far-reaching changes of patenting practice for software in Germany are regarded as not absolutely necessary, as innovative processes realized in software can today already be adequately protected under patent law. Therefore the interview partners from this company are not in favor of a clear extension.

Case 8: 8_sPAU (Start-up company)
The company was founded in May 2000 and employs four staff members. It developed a virtual reloading station for prepaid credit accounts on the Internet and already collaborates with notable partners in mobile telephony.

Protection strategies are essential for the enterprise. Assisted by patent attorneys, the firm has meanwhile been awarded a patent at the European

---

[6] All three did not participate in the original survey. In the response sample of the first investigation no pure software firms were found, which not only held patents in the software area but also were in favor of an extension of patenting, and were willing to take part in interviews for the case studies. In a few cases the enterprises no longer existed.

Patent Office. The protection afforded by copyright was regarded as inadequate, for an imitation of the program is possible – even without having recourse to the program code – without great effort or expense. The company can report numerous infringements of trade marks and patent protection. By observing the market and competitors, the enterprise noticed that attempts were being made to imitate the above-mentioned process. Property rights of others were not infringed up to now.

An extension of patent protection to software is welcomed. Innovative ideas in the software sector should be more strictly protected. This is justified, even if it emerges *ex post* that the protected idea is relatively banal.

Case 9: 9_sPAU (Start-up company)
The enterprise is a specialist for business-to-business transactions in the field of electronic procurement and sourcing, was founded in 1998 and since then has been on a growth path. The firm develops technologically demanding, flexible and secure software and platform architectures.

Awarded patents are decisive for the competitiveness of the enterprises because the imitation of its products by competitors can thus be prevented. Whereas trade mark applications do not play a role at the moment, as they cannot provide protection for innovations, patents are seen as a significant protection from imitation which is not sufficiently guaranteed by copyright.[7]

Until the year 2003, no experience has been made with the property rights of other companies. However, spot searches are increasingly being made for relevant patents of other companies, in order to avoid possible infringements and to analyze competitors on the basis of the information thus gained.

The enterprise emphatically supports the extension of patent protection to software, although till now it has had neither positive nor negative experiences. But it is planned to utilize property rights more than in the past, in order to obtain better investment protection for its own software developments.

Case 10: 10_lPApU
The enterprise, with its 35 000 installed licenses and more than 3000 clients, is the worldwide market leader in the area of software tools to model, assess and optimize business processes. These are extremely standardized products with interfaces to all leading business management software systems. The company employs 1400 staff and has an annual turnover of approximately €160 million.

The firm does not hold any own patents. The danger of infringing competitors' patents but also of infringement by third parties were regarded as

---

[7] With the term 'copyright' – if not expressly otherwise mentioned – German copyright law is meant. We thus adopt the general linguistic usage in the enterprises.

low because of the enterprise's lead in development and experience, particularly as important system elements are generally known. In the course of further internationalization and first (bad) experiences with other parties' patents, the enterprise is aspiring to extend its patenting activities.

In principle, the firm is in favor of the possibility of protecting innovative software elements under patent law. The practice of trivial patenting, however, is denounced as it leads to hindering innovation dynamics and is responsible for the bad image of software patents. Patents on inventions realized in software with a sufficient degree of novelty, on the other hand, are seen as beneficial for technical and economic development. Called for in particular is the prevention of trivial or petty patents and standardized guidelines for private, civil law licensing.

Case 11: 11_sPApU

The enterprise is a small software house with four employees, whose core products are a content management system and a software program for invoicing. It holds no patents and at the moment has no plans to change this, above all due to the high costs and the long application procedure. Apart from this, it is feared that through disclosure, the company's know-how would be available to competitors and that the firm could not defend itself because of its small size. The enterprise further regards user interface elements of software ('look and feel') as essential factors of its competitiveness, which are not protected under patent law.

On principle, the firm regards the protection of intellectual property in the software area as sensible, but not under the present regulations of patent law. The firm would welcome in particular a kind of 'mini property right', which is acquired automatically, like copyright. This would serve the interests of small enterprises better.

Discussion and conclusions

The examples show clearly that innovative software enterprises which seek legal protection for their developments are already in a position to patent inventions realized in software. The patents which were applied for by three of the companies discussed here were all described by the enterprises as 'software patents' which were awarded without big problems.

Patents also have different functions for pure software firms. For two of the three investigated enterprises, patents in a very traditional sense are important to retain competitiveness by protecting their most crucial asset, namely the exclusive right to exploit a self-developed application which can be successfully commercialized in the market (H31). These two young enterprises (cases 8 and 9) constructed their business models on the basis of protected technological developments, and their example shows that for start-up firms, patent protection can be of great significance and exercise a stabilizing influence in the market introduction process. Thus the patents are not held to be indispensable for acquiring venture capital, but have served as securities for third party and venture capital investors. In the case of enterprise 9, the enterprise founders had a sense of legal and planning security due to the patent protection. This was assessed as psychologically very significant to survive the risky start-up phase. In the case of enterprise 8, on the other hand, it is clear that small firms can also secure their stock by protecting software developments. With the help of a patent, which the firm itself characterizes as a patent on a 'banal idea', the crucial technological idea of the enterprise could be defended against various, mostly larger, mobile telephony enterprises. This is an example of the fact that the existence of a patent in the software area can secure the establishment in the market even against very large, financially strong and well-established competitors.

In the software area, however, a dilemma becomes apparent. The protection is regarded as essential, because it is very easy to imitate many applications and because the protection through copyrights can frequently be circumvented by minor changes in the program code. At the same time, however, imitation is still easy even if patents are held. The identification and proof of a patent infringement are extremely difficult for the enterprises, even if possible with legal assistance, as in the case of enterprise 8. Based on this perceived need for protection, the enterprises call for the extension of patent protection in respect of patentability, as this would facilitate the application and enlarge the mass of intellectual property to be protected.

Case 7, however, illustrates that patents in the software area can also be utilized strategically and independently of a need for protection. For the firm it was not the protection of the invention from imitation, but proof of quality and the corporate image vis-à-vis clients and competitors, as well as the establishment of a licensing practice, which were the decisive motives for patenting (H25). The enterprise applies for patents, although the protection of own developments can be sufficiently guaranteed through hardware elements. This use of patents involves the danger that far more patents are applied for than would be necessary to protect one's own technological freedom of action. Even if the enterprises concerned do not pursue infringements of image patents, in order not to put a brake on the innovation dynamic, the uncertainty in the field is raised and the degree of technological freedom of the competitor's decreases. If strategic patenting should become generally accepted in the primary sector also, then in view of the very large number of potential inventions this could lead to an increased patenting dynamic, which exceeds even the developments in the hardware area (H23). For this reason it must be ensured that the checking criteria for patenting are strictly adhered to and in particular the degree of innovation is closely examined.

The largest pure software company which was investigated within the study framework (case 10) is a vivid example for two common theses. Firstly, it had not applied for a patent up till then and had not yet paid systematic attention to the infringement of existing patents. This shows that large software firms are frequently indifferent to the patenting situation and can attain their market position in Europe even without the extended patenting possibility. Secondly, despite this, the firm calls vehemently for an extension of patenting according to the US model, in order to 'overcome the asymmetries of international business' (H38). This is proof of the theory that the patent conditions in important markets abroad form the norms and internationally active enterprises are keen to transfer the broader patenting regime of the USA to the domestic market. As in the large enterprises of the secondary sector, this behavior is quite rational from the firms' perspective, as it creates an advantage in the domestic market, if capacities and practices geared to the foreign market can be utilized at home. The large software enterprises that are active abroad often do not harbor fears regarding more intensive patenting of domestic competitors, because they have own patents and adequate capacities to manage them at their disposal. The logic of this argumentation for the overall economy is not plausible, for it is already possible for the firm examined to conform to the US model. Case 10 showed that large enterprises are capable of adjusting to changed conditions and can also be active under the US regime. The transfer of the US practices to the home market leads thereby – besides the additional competitive advantage for the large enterprises active abroad – potentially to an intensification of patent activities throughout the whole breadth of the software industry, without obvious efficiency gains for the economy as a whole.

In the investigation of the primary sector companies, which unanimously favor patents and would partly also welcome an extension, a number of problems in utilizing patents clearly emerged. As with some secondary sector firms, the software sector enterprises, especially the SMEs, see themselves hindered above all by (mostly contestable) trivial patents, as contesting them exceeds the company's economic possibilities, even with a sound knowledge of the patent situation. However, the practice of some firms to utilize patents not for reasons of protection from imitation, but to advance their technological image ('image patents'), promotes just this tendency. Even if trivial patents are not always concerned here, the 'image patents' do increase the insecurity in the sector.

In addition, the investigated firms in the software sector all see great difficulties with a possibly necessary enforcement of their own patents against infringements by large enterprises. The necessary resources are frequently beyond the financial means of the often very small software enterprises.[8]

---

[8]   The complaints that small software companies do not have possibilities to apply for patents due to lack of resources (case 11) are to be modified based on the example of the start-up

Secondly, these firms as a rule do not possess a patent portfolio, which in the case of collision could serve as bargaining material.

A further idiosyncrasy appears to be the search in patent databases, which as a rule has another more limited meaning for software companies than for secondary sector firms. Searches into the technological state of the art as input for own developments are the great exception (H28). Only the company in case 7 conducted patent searches in this sense and thus at the beginning of its business activity acquired a rapid overview of the key technology in the business field. However, this is an exception in the whole sample; a search is usually carried out in databases to secure an own development against infringements. But even this search overtaxes the enterprises. A considerable outlay is necessary to research the patent situation, even in narrowly limited areas, which start-up companies above all cannot cope with alone. As for the great majority of the firms in the software sector a search in patent databases is something completely new, but at the same time must be conducted to protect existing patents from infringements, it is necessary to inform especially SMEs and start-up firms better about the use of search possibilities. The deficit in experience compared to the established enterprises in the secondary sector is obvious and leads in daily business to a subjective feeling of over-taxation and being at a disadvantage. If even 'successful' patent users complain about this dilemma, then here is a significant lever for state support.

Generally speaking the supporters of broader patenting possibilities in the primary software sector show clear similarities with the secondary sector enterprises in their aim to use patents as a new means to increase their (international) competitiveness. On the other hand, virtually all enterprises have been successful without patent protection and have become aware of the issue only recently often through the public discourse in the media. There is some evidence that patents on software inventions may facilitate the market entry for young software enterprises as it offers them easier access to the capital market.

4.3.3   Primary Sector: Skeptics

The five companies in this second group are very heterogeneous. They stand for the large number of widely differing enterprises which have hesitantly begun patenting, or at least are considering activities in this direction. They are not opposed in principle to the possibility of protecting intellectual property also in the software area, but clearly reject a broad patenting and see a number of practical reservations too in the implementation of the current rulings.

companies. The problem consists rather in that a patent protection on a 'look and feel' application was wanted which cannot be awarded according to current law.

Two of these enterprises already hold a patent in the software area (cases 12 and 13). Case 12 is the only company in this group originating in the secondary sector with numerous traditional patents, whose competitors however meantime define themselves in terms of software development. The firm in case 13 on the other hand is a relatively young enterprise of the telecommunications sector that offers its services exclusively via the Internet. The company in case 14, however, sees no necessity to patent for its business area. Two further firms are beginning to systematically consider patenting. While the firm in case 16 is doing this because of insights into the conditions in the competitive environment, the firm in case 15 is being forced to do so by the new mother company.

The cases
Case 12: 12_lPSU
The enterprise employs over 550 staff, and its annual turnover is approximately €75 million. It sells systems for document management, and also develops and markets embedded software. The firm has a great number of patents, mainly for hardware solutions in the area of data systems technology; one patent at the European Patent Office is described as a software patent.[9]

The significance of patents has increased greatly in the firm's market in recent years, nationally and internationally. In the USA above all the market and technological environment of the firm is aggressive, also with reference to software patents. Not only patenting, but also searches to avoid patent infringements are perceived as much more difficult and costly in the software area; even for this large SME this cannot be systematically performed to the necessary extent (comprehensibility, classification). In particular, activities to avoid patent infringements had to be massively extended because of increased software patents. At the same time, tendencies towards patenting trivial inventions were observed by the enterprise, which increasingly encroach on its own competition-relevant area. The main cause is seen in the patenting practice of the European Patent Office, which is regarded as not sufficiently restrictive. Despite this, a more restrictive patenting practice for software in Germany is not desired, due to the given necessities of international competition.

Case 13: 13_sPSU
A service provider in the telecommunication sector with seven staff members offers not only on-line services, but also software products to optimize the utilization of telephony and the Internet. The firm holds several trade marks

---

[9] The company was classified as primary sector, because software development is increasingly the main pillar. Despite this, the hardware share still dominates quantitatively.

itself and also a patent for a specific application. The main objective of the patents is to prevent the imitation of a developed solution by a direct competitor. Conflicts were experienced previously only in the trade mark area, which were all settled out of court.

The greatest problem is the patent protection of interfaces (interoperability), which reduces the variety of additional and follow-on applications. An existing patent forced the firm to increase the price of a product in the low-price segment by the cost of the license fee, which led to reduced sales. A now available alternative solution is of lesser quality and compatibility. Thus the demand grew to create special regulations to ensure interoperability and generally to enforce the criterion of non-triviality more strictly.

Case 14: 14_lPSpU

The enterprise is a large medium-sized software firm with international subsidiary enterprises and activities. It employs a good 350 staff and in 2001 achieved an annual turnover of €35 million. The enterprise's core product is a system to manage documents and archives, especially tailored to medium-sized enterprises.

The firm does not hold any patents and considers this a rather inappropriate means to secure its competitiveness. The main reason for this is above all a general uncertainty about the patentability of the processes and algorithms used in the products, which are mostly estimated to be publicly known. Besides, the enterprise regards its selected user interface metaphor as the decisive competitive advantage. The design of user interfaces, however, has been assessed as non-patentable in Germany and also in the USA for some years now. The firm is always ahead of the competition in its particular niche market with this structure, and patent protection is thus not regarded as important.

The firm up to now has not perceived the danger of property right infringements by third parties and sees no great danger in this for the future. It takes a negative view of the possibility of broader patenting, in particular of algorithms and business processes. It fears above all that obstructions in development activities could occur in the market for business software, which is characterized by numerous providers and only incremental innovations.

Case 15: 15_mPSpU

The enterprise is the market leader in Germany in the area of the software-controlled planning and production of newspapers; it employs 130 staff members and has an annual turnover of €12 million. The most important functionality is the linking of the newspaper data with the printing presses. In 2002 the firm was bought by an internationally active printing press manufacturer.

The firm holds no own patents. The danger of infringement of patents by competitors and also by third parties is relatively small, because of its technical leading position, good market position and relaxed relationship with clients (no mass production). A new situation in dealing with patents arose through the integration with a mechanical engineering corporate group, as now the resources for patent applications and searches are available and the corporate group headquarters insist on property rights.

In principle, software-related patents on central functionalities are welcomed for reasons of legal security, but a number of practical problems are perceived (costs and the long patent application process). The danger is also recognized that by a further extension of patenting in the software area, its own developments could be hindered by trivial patents despite its technological leadership. Prevention of such trivial patents is called for, simpler and faster rulings and reduction of the protection period, in order to increase the pressure to market rapidly.

Case 16: 16_sPSpU
The company is a medium-sized software house with 25 employees, which conducts general software development on clients' behalf, with however a special focus on the telecommunication and automobile sectors. Since the beginning of the year 2000 a new business area is being established which offers control engineering on the basis of GSM mobile telephony standards.

The firm's own developments were not protected by patent law up to the year 2003, as the degree of novelty of its own developments was not considered high enough. On the other hand, frequently software developed on behalf of clients is concerned, which becomes the client's property. What is more, in connection with the new business area, the company wants to use the possibilities of patenting software which only functions in interplay with a special hardware. Patents on software are only supported in the case that an extremely high level of invention – for instance a new, complex algorithm – is involved.

Patents of third parties have so far not been infringed, and the firm does not conduct searches – above all because of lack of resources – to discover if its own developments infringe patents.

Discussion and conclusions
In this group of companies, it also emerged that enterprises which are acquainted with patenting practices from activities in the traditional manufacturing industry are more rapidly able to react to the increasing significance of software-related patents than are pure software developers (H22). However, enterprises with patent experience, even if they agree in principle with the status quo of the patent award practices in the software

area, have an immense need for learning and support with regard to software patents. The software developers in the firms are in even less of a position to interpret patent information than inventors in rather traditional areas, yet at the same time they consider the need for searches as higher, because of the generic character of many software applications and the necessary compatibility. Patents should be much more easily investigated and more easily explained to the developers. In addition, the patenting practice in the patent offices should be checked: the willingness to award patents too fast (trivial patents) causes not only uncertainty, but due to the increased need for searches also higher direct costs for the firms. The fact alone that objections can be raised or an action can be brought does not alleviate this problem, in particular in the case of limited resources and in dynamically developing areas.

For many small niche firms with products in the low-price sector, patents and the license fees involved with them lead to a considerable restriction of the range offered. As a result, the variety of applications which are complementary to existing, protected applications or need such protected functions as input (compatibility), is reduced (H34). The enterprise interviews have shown admittedly that in reality in the very great majority of cases an infringement of patents to achieve compatibility is not pursued. This happens mostly in the interests of the producer of an application which increases further in value due to complementary applications (network effects, variety of applications). However, this does not apply to all producers; and legal certainty is not given for many small enterprises in niche markets. The company in case 13 correspondingly calls for a ruling according to which existing patents may be infringed to establish interoperability. This demand is echoed by many enterprises in this survey. To make a specific criterion like interoperability a precondition for an exceptional case appears difficult, however, to realize in practice. It would be worth considering, however, that in patent offices during the time limit for entering objections the possibility would be granted to claim that interoperability is being hindered, and after successful proof of the same to enter into negotiations to concede a license acceptable to both sides. This procedure could be modeled on the licensing regulations in the standardization of patented functions; however, for cost reasons a binding conciliation board must be created within the patent offices to settle cases.

The examples of enterprises 14 and 16 show that enterprise success in the software sector (in particular in the area of business software) is frequently not based on extraordinary innovativeness, but on other factors not protectable by patents (H12). In company 14 this is the user interface, while company 15 is the supplier of not particularly innovative software components for other firms to realize functions in accordance with the client's specifications. Such enterprises have hardly any benefit from broader patenting, but are constantly in danger of patent infringements. As long as these enterprises have no concrete experiences with patenting themselves, many regard it naively. They mainly regard time leadership or a typical individual characteristic as sufficient. Precautions against imitation by third parties are thus not taken, and their own developments are also not checked for infringements of existing property rights (H9). As a rule, they express the typical SME complaints about the patent system (costs, complexity and so on). Only if a grave problem becomes virulent do they react, usually in the form of taking external legal advice. Preventive information is very frequently inadequate. The share of firms which display such inexperience can be estimated only with difficulty. On the basis of the written survey which preceded this investigation, it can be rated as very high, for even out of the sample of enterprises which were interested enough to participate, more than 60 per cent possessed little knowledge and more than 75 per cent had no department that was in charge of performing these tasks.

The conclusion already reached above, that the secondary sector is an important driver of patenting in the software area, becomes vivid in the case of enterprise 15. The firm became the clear technology and market leader entirely without patents and because of this lead never considered patenting, even in their new US business. The new mother from the secondary sector transferred the patenting mentality of the mechanical engineer into the software line of business. It confronts the enterprise regularly with printed patent specifications and demands a check of the technological abilities of the software house with the target of patent protection. Although this protection would not be necessary to protect from imitation and secure innovation rents, such protection is being seriously considered for the future, not only because the mother company insists on patenting, but also because it possesses the necessary know-how and capacities. This development corresponds to the rationality of the mechanical engineering corporate group, but leads to a situation where patents emerge in a field in which there is no economic reason for patents. At the same time, the software enterprise itself sees dangers in this extension of patenting, namely, when patents from other sectors on single software components limit the own freedom of action. Through pressure foreign to the sector – such as exerted by the mother company – this becomes more probable. Such a constellation and strategic behavior of enterprises, especially in the secondary sector, is not to be objected to by the state, but it again points to an important driver of patenting in the software area.

All skeptical enterprises in this group are not basically opposed to the possibility of protecting competition-relevant knowledge. The enterprise examples, however, show unambiguously that this basic support for patenting software, that is, of the real status quo, is accompanied as a rule by demands to improve the process. In particular, the examination of the degree of novelty must be a central criterion. The fear of trivial patents runs like a red thread through the whole investigation, but is greatest in this group. Just as frequently did the firms in this group call for better investigation methods, for instance by means of a horizontal category for software and by requiring the technicians to formulate the patent documents in understandable terms. A further recurring subject in this group is the difficulty of enforcing patents in the software area, especially for SMEs. The high costs of the application, on the other hand, are mentioned by small firms, but they play a subordinate role compared with the problem of trivial patents or the difficulties of enforcing patents.

The skeptical companies in the primary sector provide evidence that the software sector – in contrast to public opinion – is not exceptionally innovative in comparison to other high-technology sectors, but is characterized by a large number of incremental improvements and relatively few radical inventions (Rammer et al. 2004). Many of the less innovative but nevertheless successful software (service) companies see a realistic threat of losing their competitiveness when broader software patenting is used by strategically patenting (large) competitors. In the medium and long term this can result in a smaller product variety and a decreasing intensity of competition. At the same time, this group of companies has only little knowledge and awareness of software patenting issues.

4.3.4   Primary Sector: Opponents

The enterprises of this last group are all opposed to the patenting of software, albeit for various reasons and to different degrees. Some of the firms base their business model and their developments on open source (19, 20 and 22) and therefore regard the disadvantages of patenting as especially grave. The company in case 18 secured its technological freedom to act via bilateral contracts and was damaged by a patent which was later declared invalid. Case 17 rejects patents on software, but due to the general increase of patenting is toying with the idea of commencing to patent actively. Case 21 considers the protection of software as unnecessary for its business. Interestingly, enterprise 21 (as also 20) argues in favor of protecting only complex algorithms with patents, whilst enterprise 17 wants to exclude exactly this possibility.

The cases
Case 17: 17_mPO
This enterprise employs about 25 staff and has an annual turnover of approximately €2 million. It develops an ERP/PPS system[10] for medium-sized

---

[10]   Enterprise Resource Planning/Product Planning System.

manufacturing firms and is specialized in some sector segments. Besides this, product-related services are offered, especially client-specific adaptation and software introduction courses for clients.

The firm does not hold any patents, and indeed considers them unimportant or even damaging in relation to securing its competitiveness. The main reason for this is the comparatively low degree of innovation of many (also successful) ERP/PPS systems. In competitive terms, the non-technical factors such as flexibility, knowledge of clients and the sector are very much more important. However, patenting practice in other countries, especially the USA, present a major hurdle for a possible international expansion.

Case 18: 18_mPO
The enterprise sells services, software and systems in the telecommunication sector. The medium-sized company bases its developments on Microsoft products and has few competitors in its niche market.

The firm does not possess any patents of its own, and the need for protection and also the establishment of interoperability are maintained by bilateral contracts. The firm was accused, like a number of other companies, of infringing a patent on a technical arrangement, which for many years has been a standard for all suppliers in the market. By bundling resources and with the support of a large German enterprise, as well as of the patent attorney of a hardware manufacturer from the USA, the patent was revoked (on grounds of nullity) at the European Court of Justice. Despite the accusations being dropped, the firms were confronted with high direct costs and the entire niche market lost some of its dynamic.

The firm calls for the limitation of patenting to innovative processes. The greatest criticism is aimed at the Patent Office, which should employ many more software developers as patent examiners.

Case 19: 19_mPO (Start-up company)
The enterprise with headquarters in Sweden was founded in 1995 and in the meantime employs 60 staff in 14 countries. It markets a relational database management system, which is utilized by millions of users worldwide. The company offers support services and training courses complementarily.

Among the protection rights, copyright, trade mark protection and the protection of domain names have the greatest significance, while patents play no role whatsoever. The enterprise holds the sole copyright of the database software as the core of its business model. On the one hand, a licensing model is based thereon which is essentially free of cost for private users and only commercial users are charged license fees. This provides approximately two-thirds of the turnover. By means of this model, the further diffusion and improvement of the program is pushed ahead by the users. On the other hand, the enterprise offers support services and training courses. Foreign property rights, in particular patents, were not infringed up to the year 2003. Patent searches are carried out sporadically, in order to avoid infringements.

The enterprise argues in favor of overhauling the current patenting practice, in the sense that software should be widely excluded from patent protection. An adoption of US practice is rejected, because the protection via copyright is seen as sufficient and the patent offices are obviously not in a position to guarantee adequate quality in examining the degree of innovation.

Case 20: 20_mPO

The enterprise is an association of three firms which offers a wide spectrum of IT consultancy, services and developments for large industrial clients. An annual turnover of about €7 million is achieved with 60 staff members.

Own developments are not protected by patents, for patents on software are supported basically only in the cases where the degree of invention is very high – such as a new, complex mathematical algorithm. The firm makes intensive use of the possibilities of open source development. Up till now there has been only one problem with property rights, and that was in connection with one of the firm's trade marks; the dispute was settled with payment of a small compensation.

Third-party patents have not been infringed so far; even in the course of its international activities (with the USA) no accusations of infringement have been leveled. The company does not check whether infringements occur, for instance by means of patent searches, not least because of lack of capacity. However, in order to reduce the probability of an unnoticed patent infringement in the future, the firm records new developments on a CD and deposits it with a notary public. Thus it can be proved in case of doubt when the company had a certain solution at their disposal.

Case 21: 21_sPO

This enterprise develops and sells document management systems to libraries and archive systems to firms and research institutions and offers a number of related services.

The firm does not hold a patent itself and does not consider this meaningful, due to the disclosure of ideas and functionalities; copyright is adequate protection. Problems with third-party patents were few and far between till the year 2003. However, the patenting practice in other countries, the USA in particular, presents a crucial hurdle to possible internationalization.

Case 22: 22_sPO

The IT firm was founded in the year 2002, has five staff members and advises its clients about the utilization and the integration of open source supported applications. It develops software, but does not enter the market with it, instead defining this as part of the advisory service.

Due to the past experiences of the staff, the firm is generally opposed to patenting in the software area and holds no own patent. It is impossible for the staff not to infringe patents in their own developments. Patent searches cannot adequately safeguard against this danger. In addition, it would not be possible for the enterprise to defend its own patent in the case of collision, because a whole patent portfolio such as only large enterprises possess is necessary for that as a negotiating basis. These structural dangers of patent infringement were an important reason for the selected advisory model. Even if many of the existing patents owned by large firms are not pursued, as they benefit from the resulting variety and need not fear critical market losses, the permanent danger of infringing is a very great burden. This restricts the variety of possible applications in the market.

They demand renouncing patenting of 'software as such', to avoid a wild proliferation of trivial patents as well as to enforce the legal right to infringe on patent protection in order to establish interoperability, even in contravention of the private law regulations in the licensing documents of large firms.

Discussion and conclusions
The range of reasons to reject patents in the software area is as large as the variety of enterprise types, technologies and business models. Characteristic of all these enterprises, however, is that they have fought for their market position entirely without patents and entirely without concerning themselves with patenting, but are becoming increasingly unsure due to dynamic patenting in the software area, or have already made negative experiences, and now in part are beginning to take safety precautions, which are seen as one-sided burden to their business activities.

First of all, there are enterprises which base their competitiveness on factors which do not affect patent law. The enterprise in case 17, for instance, is a service provider which provides tailor-made ERP/PPS systems for clients and offers services in this area. Due to the low innovation level of the systems offered, the utilization of open interfaces and open source tools, as well as internal confidentiality and staff loyalty which functioned well up to the year 2003, this firm regards the development of patent activities as unnecessary and unhelpful. In addition, the special knowledge of the sector through the specialization in a niche market is a guarantee for competitiveness. Due to the intensification of patenting, the enterprise sees itself confronted with the danger that other market participants, in particular the market leaders, massively hinder its own competitiveness through large-scale patenting and trivial patents in its area, and thus harm the company's specific, established competitive advantages. This is exemplary for established enterprises, which have built up their markets not via technological leadership, but by working in niche markets and offering services; they now see their special competitive advantages endangered by patenting on the part of larger firms, and patents are therefore understood as competitive instruments, above all of the large enterprises (H10; H23; H25). Such a 'threat analysis' causes many of the software sector enterprises to reject patents on software, and if possible they would welcome an even more restricted patenting practice.

A second problem area, especially for SMEs, is presented by patent activities in other countries, mainly in the USA. This applies for some of the cases investigated here (in particular cases 17 and 21). The patenting possibilities and practices in the USA must be accepted as given. The statements of this firm show that especially small companies which had no problems in Germany with the existing practice, can only commercially market their software in the USA completely unprotected and only by taking certain risks (H24; H38). This leads to insecurity, which in view of the current discussions and increasing patenting in the software sector, also has repercussions on domestic business. The patent regime in the United States thus presents an obstacle to export or expansion which conversely does not exist for US suppliers. Measures to raise consciousness and to support the medium-sized software companies should be intensified on the part of public or semi-public institutions (foreign trade chambers, trade associations). Thus an enterprise that wants to export could be supported by patent consulting more suited to one of the functionalities of its applications, or even by a patent search.

Whereas the great majority of skeptics and opponents of a broad software patenting identify trivial patents merely as a possible or observed danger, case 19 demonstrates the negative effects of such trivial patents in a concrete example. This case also made clear that SMEs especially, even if they are active technology leaders in a small niche market, are exposed to great structural uncertainties and disadvantages. In the case of firm 19, the disputed patent, an arrangement patent, was so obviously trivial that despite thorough searches, the enterprise would not have searched in this area of the patent classification. In addition, it had been applied for by a one-man business which had not yet appeared as a market participant and was not recognizably active in the market with his own patent. In order to defend oneself adequately in view of such an aggressive patenting practice, software-developing firms must cover and evaluate all possible patent classifications. This is beyond the possibilities of many SMEs, for whereas the large enterprises have a much greater overview over bordering markets and new market participants and can structure their patent searches very thoroughly and broadly, this is not possible for SMEs (H27). Case 19 showed that small enterprises can only survive such a long-drawn-out and expensive procedure in association with one another and in co-operation with large enterprises with the same interests. Typical in this case is also that success at the patent court was essentially thanks to the activity of a US attorney, who on the grounds of many years' experience with such cases proceeded very aggressively. The threshold which spurs the large US corporate groups to activity is €1 million, a sum which is life-threatening for a single SME. State support in the form of a simplified presentation tailored to software developers and search possibilities could provide systematic remedial action. As patents can lead to large burdens even if they are declared invalid, the examination in the patent offices should additionally be much more thorough and properly conducted. Finally, it was shown that bundling resources to fight claims or trivial patents makes sense.

The above-mentioned case is also an example for a peripheral phenomenon which can, however, cause great damage and is based on the mechanisms of the patent system. The applicant for the now invalid patent had approximately 25 further arrangement patents in completely different fields, which were based for the most part on software. That means his business model consisted in driving developments so far that a patent could be applied for and this patent could then be used against market participants. This pattern was confirmed by examples cited by further discussion partners in this study; in the USA in particular there are a number of enterprises which achieve their turnovers not through actual market participation, but by asserting their patent claims. Such activities naturally hinder the regular patent process, make searches for patents more difficult, and shatter the trust in a well-functioning and legitimate property rights system. Enterprises, particularly SMEs, demand – besides the thorough examination of the level of invention – also a mechanism which guarantees that patent applicants should really try to exploit the patents commercially in the market.

The business model of the company in case 20 is based on the functioning and rigid pursuit of copyright protection with simultaneously high user numbers of database software. A highly innovative, software-based business model was successfully established, completely without patents and utilizing open source. The speed of the market and the functioning of the basic idea led to a client commitment which is far more important for the company than the legal protection of software functionality (patent) or the program code (copyright). This mechanism is moreover widespread in business models which are based on the Internet. Patents present a delay and uncertainty, without contributing to the actual market success (clients' commitment); therefore they are an obstacle for such business models. Although the enterprise can successfully survive in the USA despite the patents of the competitive companies, the – unproved – fear exists that adopting the US regimes could damage the innovation-friendly climate in Europe. As the enterprise takes over the copyright for improvements suggested by its users, if it comes to an agreement or respectively continually further develops the product it-self, it is feared that through the extension of the copyright to the patent protection, certain new functionalities cannot be integrated, if these are pro-tected by corresponding patents and no agreement is reached with the patent-holders. Because of the already wide diffusion of the program and due to the strong loyalty of the numerous private users, the enterprise was able to defy patent claims. Smaller enterprises with less widely diffused software pro-grams, that pursue a similar business model, could on the other hand be seri-ously hampered by software patents.

The company in case 21 developed on the basis of open source and open standards into a very successful service provider and application developer for the manufacturing industry. The clients have no problem with the util-ization of open source and the integration of these technologies into their own software systems. This enterprise sees its own activities endangered by a multiplicity of patents on functionalities, which are important as generic input for many applications (compatibility, sequentiality). In view of the growing uncertainty, the firm has started to develop a minimal protection of own developments, in that it deposits its own code with a secure date of mak-ing with a notary public. Thus in the case of conflict the exact moment of its own use of certain codes and functionalities can be proved. Other companies in the study also considered adopting this practice; it appears to be becoming a popular means to avert danger without much cost, especially for opponents of patenting who regard search practices as inadequate or too expensive (H42). Policy-makers should propagate this practice, but at the same time point out that naturally an infringement which occurred on the day of deposit is not to be prevented.

Case 22 is a further example of strategies by patent opponents to escape the consequences of patenting, without developing their own patenting and search activities. The company founders chose a business model that shifted the legal problems (besides property rights, also product liability) to the cli-ents, who have the full rights to the utilization of the software developed on their behalf. The enterprises paid for this protection in that their possible profit margins from a relatively cheap mass production are lost in a commercial distribution of their products. The example shows clearly which avoidance strategies are employed in the open source movement to avoid legal problems. The fundamental problem of this enterprise, like many oth-ers, is that for almost every commercially used application the interoperabil-ity to proprietary systems must be established, as open source applications are not closed systems. The open source companies complain that existing licens-ing duties are thus automatically infringed. Even if, in the overwhelming number of cases, the patent-holder does not even perceive a collision, or does not pursue it for economic reasons (further applications, diffusion), still many companies in the open source movement see themselves in permanent danger (H10). In particular, those enterprises which appear in the market as open-source developers with their own developments find themselves in the perception of the open source community permanently in a dangerous grey area, and are dependent on the non-pursuit of infringement by large manufacturers.

The interviews with different actors brought a distinct difference in perception to light, which is also a reason for the heated discussion about patents. The large manufacturers regard the number of cases of possible collisions between their claims and the activities of small enterprises as low. In addition, they prove that very rarely do they actually make open source developers take responsibility for infringements; in most cases the activities of the many small market participants are more positive than detrimental for the large manufacturers. From the perspective of the many small suppliers, in particular in the open source area, the danger analysis looks completely different. For them it appears virtually impossible to develop anything that does not infringe the rights of third parties. In the context of the collision between proprietary and open systems in the problems of interfaces, and the infringement of licenses to establish interoperability, finding an appropriate solution appears to be an urgent task.

The findings from the group of opponents in the primary software sector support the hypothesis that SMEs and freelance developers, that is, the majority of software enterprises at least in Germany, are facing less favorable conditions to benefit from broader patents on software inventions than larger companies or companies with a long patenting tradition. Moreover, the cases also indicate the problem that less innovation and more service-oriented companies fear the loss of their competitiveness to enterprises with a larger portfolio of (potentially trivial) patents. On the other hand, highly innovative companies (often start-ups) fear that they cannot exploit their inventions due to the high risks of infringing foreign patents and the disclosure requirement that gives more powerful competitors the chance to adopt and modify the protected invention. Finally, SMEs especially are often dependent on foreign input (often open source software) and interoperationality. Both are hampered by extended patenting possibilities.

5. Qualifying the Survey Results by Means of the Case Studies

5.1 INTRODUCTION

The central motivation for the case studies was to qualify and bring into context the results of the written survey presented in Chapter 3. The case studies should supply qualitative data on the experiences and practices with intellectual property rights and help to take a look 'behind the numbers'. Chapter 4 presented the individual cases and discussed essential characteristics and practices as well as first conclusions, which follow on directly from the cases. In Chapter 5 central results of the statistical analysis will be supplemented by the analysis of the case studies. In order to establish the complementarity to the representative survey, this discussion follows the presentation in Chapter 3. Thereby a certain – intended – redundancy results in the depiction of the results of the case studies, which make it possible to come to abstract conclusions from single cases and set general conclusions in the entrepreneurial context.

5.2 PRACTICES AND EXPERIENCES WITH INTELLECTUAL PROPERTY RIGHTS, ESPECIALLY PATENTS

The focus of the case studies was the experiences and practices regarding intellectual property rights in the software area. Generally, not only the utilization but also the enterprise's own organizational structure to deal with intellectual property rights are very diverse and in parts not very pronounced.

From the answers to the survey, it emerged that intellectual property rights possess the least significance of all protection possibilities for the enterprises. Naturally, the selection of the case studies has a certain bias in the direction of actively patenting enterprises, so that not only the use of patents, but also of other protective rights, such as copyright and trade marks, appear more strongly than in the survey. This stems also from the fact that the start-up companies which did not participate in the survey were identified for the case studies by means of a patent search. For this reason the companies in the case studies make greater use of patents in relation to other property rights than was the case in the survey. The survey revealed that in the primary sector patents had the least significance of all protective mechanisms; in the secondary sector only design patents were less significant. In very few cases had enterprises built up a complete portfolio of software patents; as a rule they hold only a small number of patents. In the case studies, however, it became clear that for the enterprises which utilize patents, this protective instrument assumes an important position in the quantitative and qualitative sense besides the other forms of property protection.

The use of patents emerged as low in the survey. In the case studies, however, a trend towards increased patenting became clear, even in those firms which have previously not patented. This dynamization of patent activities across the range of enterprises does not, however, express that the patent instrument is now widely accepted and considered a proactive instrument by the majority of enterprises. There are cases, admittedly (in particular cases 7 to 9), in which patents play an important role for the business model, or should play such a role in the future (case 10). The majority of the firms which will also use patents in the software area do so as a reaction to the current discussion or to concrete (negative) experiences, and in particular to patenting activities in foreign markets. With few exceptions (for example case 20) for all enterprises investigated that are contemplating or have begun to do business internationally, the property rights practice in the USA above all proved to be a catalyst for patent considerations.

The result of the survey, according to which the utilization of patents in the secondary sector and in companies that also produce hardware is more widespread, is indubitably confirmed (H6). All enterprises of the study whose portfolio contained not only hardware but also software, are either already very active in patenting software or are on the verge of supplementing their traditional patent portfolio with patents which they interpret as software patents. This development appears understandable and rational from the perspective of the secondary sector companies; software as a generic technology is increasingly a core component in many technical solutions.

However, two important qualifications must be made. On the one hand, the secondary sector enterprises are without a doubt the motors of patenting development and transmit their patenting mentality, tradition and organization to the primary sector. A vivid example of this is the firm in case 15, which is urged to patent by the new mother company from the secondary sector.

Some enterprises of the secondary sector, however, at the same time see great dangers in the dynamization of software patenting. For despite the tradition of patenting, experience in this area is frequently lacking, and simultaneously they are confronted with patents from technological fields which are new to the technology management of the companies. In addition, many companies from the secondary sector fear that software patents are more easily applied for and awarded than classical patents, and thus their own core business could be hindered by trivial patents foreign to the technology.

Irrespective of whether or not one welcomes this catalyst function of the secondary sector regarding software patents for the entire software sector, the tendency is that the structural problems of the SMEs will become more acute (resources, overview), if only due to the different size structure of the secondary and primary sectors.

The written survey demonstrated a positive correlation between age, enterprise size (according to number of employees, see Chapter 4) and export activity, on the one hand, and the propensity to patent of a firm on the other hand. This must be seen as unambiguously confirmed in the results of the case studies. Restrictions can be noted only with reference to the age as there are – albeit only a few – firms that applied for own patents already in the start-up process (see below).

Both the survey and the case studies showed ambiguous correlation between the significance of patents in the software sector and the innovation activities and the innovation success of firms (H7; H13). Only from the analysis of the start-up firms does one concrete correlation emerge between patenting and innovative activity and competitiveness, as its market success is directly based on its central patent (H31).

On the other hand, the non-users and opponents of software patents can also refer to successful business models and products. Some enterprises claim to be successful in the market not because of advanced software developments, but for a number of other factors, like comprehensive services, adaptation developments and so on. They also produce some process innovations hereby, for which they neither can nor want to claim protection. For these enterprises, firstly competitiveness despite low R&D intensity is important and secondly, the connection between low R&D intensity and low patent tendency.

From this it follows, firstly, that direct causality between the utilization of patents and the expenditure of resources in research and development or market success is not generally confirmed on the basis of the case studies, although in individual cases a direct connection cannot be denied. Secondly, however, a problem crops up which the statistical analysis could not grasp: enterprises not using software related patents feel more and more threatened by the increased patenting in the software sector, as they possess no patents to oppose them and simultaneously they find their freedom of action in developments restricted.

The survey demonstrated further that there are many and varied reasons to patent. The primary sector emphasized the defensive nature of patenting (protection from imitation), while the secondary sector referred more to market advantages and cross-licensing (thus also strategic patenting) and the conditions abroad. For both sectors blocking competitors' developments was not a significant reason for patenting, in contrast to signaling own competence, which was rated of increasing importance by both sectors (H25).

The case studies confirmed these fundamental tendencies, but also provided some extended perspectives. There are several cases in the primary sector, in which the main motive to patent or for the planning to apply for patents is the protection from imitation by competitors. However, in the primary sector – to a limited extent – strategic patenting is already to be observed. Thus patents are applied for in certain areas even when protection is sufficiently guaranteed by other precautions (hardware, contracts with employees). The patenting motive in these cases is rather the image as technology leader (signaling) and a precaution against the accusation of infringing the patents of other parties. Furthermore, not only the enterprises of the secondary sector, but increasingly also the firms in the primary sector are adapting to the respective customs dominant in the foreign countries they export to. On the other hand, enterprises which are actively involved only in the domestic or European markets, are only slightly influenced in their patenting behavior by the foreign circumstances which are given a high rating in the survey. This influence is rather indirect, for the heightened patenting activities in the course of international business strategies are also re-imported, so to speak, into the primary sector (see the intentions in case 10). However, it is also the case that for some, especially small primary sector firms, the necessary adaption to broader patenting (USA) represents an obstacle to internationalization as before. The enterprises of the secondary sector did not report such an obstacle.

Survey and case studies have shown without a doubt that strategic patenting is dominant for the large enterprises of the secondary sector in the software sector too. The motive to create a patent portfolio, in order to maintain the technological freedom to act in view of other parties' strategies ('leveling the playing field') and to go in for cross-licensing are absolutely central for these companies. One enterprise extremely active in patenting (case 1) explicitly described the protection from imitations as very difficult and almost not feasible. Accordingly, it does not play a role in the company's motivation. In the primary sector, patents possess little meaning as yet for strategic cross-licensing, although the exchange of technology is already widespread. A random patent analysis produced the result that even the very large, pure software companies do not have large patent portfolios at their disposal; technology exchange takes place above all on the basis of contracts or copyrights.

The technology-strategic motives for patenting are thus difficult for the primary sector, due to lack of negotiating mass. This asymmetry between the large firms that also produce hardware and the pure software enterprises has great impacts on the relations in software patenting. The software enterprises see themselves at a structural disadvantage, especially in the enforcement of their own patents. Large hardware enterprises are as a rule at a decisive advantage in negotiations because of their own numerous patents. Extensive patent portfolios always represent a certain potential threat, explicitly or implicitly, because the probability is great that other firms can infringe one of the patents, even completely unconsciously.

The theory that patents facilitate market access above all for young firms could not be confirmed on the basis of the survey. The case studies showed, however, that patents are becoming increasingly important for raising the firm's value, particularly of start-up enterprises, which can thereby achieve better access to the capital market. Patent claims can only support convincing business ideas. Without them, patents have no intrinsic value. And it must be remarked that patents of start-up companies are used only selectively, and only single cases from this small group of enterprises apply this asset actively in procuring capital.[1]

Reasons hindering patenting according to the survey were, for the enterprises of the primary sector, besides costs and uncertainties, general reservations about the long term, broadly based effects of patents (innovation dynamics). The first two reasons hindering patenting – costs and uncertainties – were absolutely confirmed in the case studies. Whereas the large enterprises (can) pursue a functionally differentiated patent management, which is increasingly mobilized for IPR in the software-related technologies, small firms are overtaxed for many reasons (H21; H37). This cannot be explained by lack of knowledge alone. As the case studies were biased towards enterprises which tended to have more than average knowledge about patent problems, lack of knowledge is not the most crucial reason here. Rather, due to limited resources, the small enterprises are not in a position to undertake sufficient patent searches to prevent all possible own infringements. Scale effects due to multiple and varied development lines, as achieved in the large enterprises, are not realizable for the SMEs (H39). The enforcement of their own patents appears to be simply impossible for many of them, as firstly, infringements are frequently not recognized, and secondly, the direct and indirect costs are beyond the means of small firms. The example of case 18 made crystal clear that only as a group of equally threatened enterprises, and

---

[1]   The basis for the identification of two of the three start-up companies was a patent analysis in selected technology fields, as none of the few start-up companies in the survey would agree to an interview.

together with two large companies from the hardware sector, was a successful patent challenge possible. Even if some enterprises can be considered inactive, naïve and unconcerned, the majority would be more than willing to take precautions if these did not exceed their financial means. In addition, patenting for these enterprises is not always a component of strategic reflections and is thus an incidental aspect of business activity, to which only limited resources can be allocated.

With reference to the survey result that innovation dynamics would be hampered in the sector if the usage of patents increased, the results are ambivalent. It was only seldom mentioned as a concrete reason not to patent. Only the enterprises which co-ordinate their business models closely with the open source movement explained their non-patenting by not wanting to hinder the dynamics of the software sector and to avoid contradictions with their enterprise philosophy. In the justification of the general rejection of patenting, however, this was a crucial point for all opponents of patenting (H33).

For the secondary sector companies experienced in the patenting system, the difficulties in furnishing proof, in enforceability and protection by patents in the software area were the main problems in the survey. This is not confirmed in the present enterprise sample which, however, may lie in the choice of the enterprises in the secondary sector. Only two enterprises (cases 5 and 6) of the secondary sector and one company that was attributed to the primary sector, but has an own tradition in the secondary sector (case 13), are examples of enterprises from the secondary sector that are slowly beginning to patent in the software area. The lack of enforceability is admittedly a problem for these firms, but the question of patentability as such is often more difficult. Neither the developers nor the legal departments have experience with software patenting; mostly they dare to take the step towards patenting software only after experiences of competitors or from the software sector become known (H23).

As already mentioned, the problem of lack of enforceability is more virulent for the small enterprises of the primary sector, and not because of the burden of proof, but because of the subjective feeling that – at least with large patent-holders – their own resources are insufficient for a conflict, or an open flank exists in view of the possible, unknown infringement of the patents of a third party which could be revealed by such a conflict.

The information function of patents was perceived very little in the software sector according to the survey, and if at all, then for defensive reasons. This was not altered in the findings of the case studies (H28). With one exception (case 7), in which the enterprise also accumulated important know-how by means of patent searches, the information function of patents in the software sector is fundamentally doubted, for they document already outdated know-how or describe the patented inventions in such a roundabout way that no worthwhile information can be derived from the documents for development activities. The case studies thus confirm impressively that the information diffusion function cannot be cited as a further economic justification for patent protection for the software area. It must be noted here, however, that the use of patent documents as a knowledge source for innovations has only low significance in other sectors also.

The self-estimation of the enterprises participating in the survey showed that knowledge about property rights, especially patents, was low in both sectors. In accordance with the procedure described in Chapter 4, Section 4.2, enterprises were contacted especially which made very active use of property rights, or had experienced concrete difficulties with the property rights of others, or were resolute opponents. That means that the discussion partners in this study were as a rule well informed. However, it could also be noted that experiences with the infringement of their own or others' property rights led to creating competence in-house or through close collaboration with patent attorneys, and that the level of knowledge within the entire sector is continually being improved.

Nevertheless, dealing with property rights in the primary sector is in general still hardly institutionalized and in case of need is usually met via external consulting (H21). To a certain extent this is also naturally an effect of size, as large enterprises have other organizational possibilities. Their patent departments were either strengthened by additional personnel or restructured, in order to possess the necessary competences in the software sector, and software patenting was made more effective by internal training courses or guidelines. The smaller companies in the secondary sector have an internal management problem (see above), while the SMEs in the primary sector almost all depend on external consulting with reference to legal implementation. Consulting with external lawyers, as is found in the primary sector in the great majority of enterprises, raises grave problems, however, which increase the structural disadvantages of the SMEs in the primary sector. The external lawyers advising the companies are not as a rule specialists in the patent system. The patent attorneys, on the other hand, usually have no experience in the area of software patents and have great problems assessing patentability and infringement claims. The communication between external legal advisers and enterprises is made even more difficult by the style of the patent documents. Some enterprises report that they frequently cannot fathom the meaning of the patent search results because of the 'legally roundabout' language.

The high percentages in the survey of almost 20 per cent of enterprises in the primary sector and almost 40 per cent of the secondary sector, which were already involved in litigation in the general area of intellectual property rights, is confirmed in the case studies only to a limited extent (H29). In the case selection we tried among others to include firms which had been involved in litigation. For the very large enterprises, lawsuits are on the daily agenda; however, in the large majority of cases a collision is settled by licensing agreements, technology exchange or other regulations. Disputes concerning infringements of software patents are still extremely rare in Germany.[2] The role distribution in plaintiff and defendant cannot be exactly determined on the basis of the case studies. However, the statement from the survey, that enterprises from the secondary sector are more often plaintiffs, can be explained above all by their size and the power asymmetry. The latter rather prevents small enterprises from taking large world corporate groups to court because of patent infringements. The hampering of development activities by patents or other third party property rights is a real problem which, however, has the character of an isolated case. Often licensing agreements can be found as a quick solution to prevent the infringement of other parties' property rights.

5.3   ATTITUDES AND ESTIMATES OF THE ACTORS TO ALTERNATIVE POSSIBILITIES AND EFFECTS OF SOFTWARE PATENTING

5.3.1   Alternative Patenting Regimes

The group of independent developers considered in the written survey is opposed to patenting on principle, and is in favor of excluding software from patent protection generally, which would mean a restriction in the present award practices. The enterprises examined in the case studies – which were founded by independent developers and developers close to the open source movement, or which are based on business models that utilize the input of independent developers, essentially support this position. Accordingly, lightening the administrative burden and assistance are regarded as not very effective.

However, there are some interesting qualifications with reference to such business models. The problems of these firms founded on open-source software are concentrated, as seen, in particular on the interfaces. These enterprises demand a weakening of patent protection, at least in order to establish interoperability and compatibility. It is a legal question to what extent such alternatives would be possible in view of existing civil law licensing agreements. In any case, it appears to be an urgent task in the context of collision between proprietary and open systems to find a reasonable solution for the

---

[2]   As mentioned above, statements differ as to how frequent infringements are.

problems of interfaces and the infringement of licenses in establishing inter-operability.

In the survey the firms of the primary and secondary sector mostly prefer the status quo to all alternatives and tended towards a skeptical attitude to a further extension of patenting in the software area. In general, the findings from the case studies support maintaining the status quo. However, an exact definition of patentability is fundamentally called for, so that legal security and clarity can be established once and for all. The most important qualification is that all firms questioned, even the large primary sector enterprises, also see a great danger from trivial patents already at present. The *de jure* status quo will continue to be accepted, because the principle of protecting non-trivial and commercially exploitable ideas is approved. In addition, the search possibilities existing at present must be immensely improved. Whereas some firms demand new classifications for software patents, others demand extending the patent documents by a text comprehensible to software developers, and thus reducing the usage of legal terms.

The polarization observed in the survey within the enterprises of the primary sector, according to which over 25 per cent support extending patenting practice according to the US model, can only be confirmed by the case studies to a limited extent. Obviously the voices in the USA criticizing their own system have led to a more differentiated attitude in Germany, too. Three groups of enterprises crystallize, which support an extension of patenting to a certain degree. Firstly, the large enterprises of the secondary sector for the reasons named in Chapter 4, Section 4.2.1 – in different stages – are in favor of extending patenting. Secondly, some hints emerged that large software houses construct similar argumentation to the large secondary sector enterprises. The company in case 10 supports an extension in view of its involvement in the USA, although it attained its own stable market position entirely without using patents. The case of the firm SAP is a matter of public knowledge, which in 1999 held only four patents, but in consideration of the tougher international competition and the intensification of strategic patenting[3] supports a broader patenting. A third group, whose size could amount to under 25 per cent, according to the survey results, are small software firms which have patents as an integral component in their business models and utilize them strategically, in particular for signaling purposes. The case examples documented that there are small enterprises which can also enforce the patents in the market (case 8).

While in the survey a majority of the companies from the primary sector still supported the exclusion of software from patent protection, in this

[3]   http://swpat.ffii.org/termine/2002/Europerl11/index.en.html.

collection of case studies only a small minority spoke up on behalf of such a restrictive model. Significant here is less the share of opponents or adherents: more important is the fact that many critics of the system and many persons having second thoughts in view of the consequences of an extension consider a form of protection legitimate in principle. The basic problem consists in the defective present form (see below). The result referring to the secondary sector, where the opponents of exclusion clearly dominated, could be confirmed by comparison. Although some skeptical enterprises feared wild proliferation and patents foreign to the sector as obstacles, in the software-developing enterprises of the secondary sector the demand for excluding software from patent protection can only be determined in exceptional cases.

Similar to the survey, the existence of patent departments and own patents, as well as knowledge about intellectual property rights, tend to lead to a more positive attitude towards software patenting in the enterprises investigated in the case studies. Once again, two qualifications became visible. On the one hand, there are enterprises which have already applied for patents or intend to do so, not because they welcome patenting, but because they see no other alternative under the given circumstances. On the other hand, enterprises without relevant competences, resources or even patents also have a positive opinion towards patenting, if they themselves have had the negative experience that other firms exploit their unprotected know-how in the market 115 (for example case 6).

The survey-based finding that enterprise size does not correlate with the attitude towards alternative patenting regimes must be differentiated. First of all, whereas the survey showed that young enterprises have more negative attitudes towards patenting than established ones, the case studies, in particular those dealing with start-up companies, made clear that in individual cases the existence of a single patent supports the foundation of enterprises and can secure the survival of the company, at least in the medium term. The case studies produced no additional correlations, however, between age of the enterprise and attitude towards patenting. Secondly, based on the case study findings, a new classification of the enterprises emerged which also contains an enterprise size dimension. If this size classification is applied, then it can still be seen that no linear correlation exists between company size and attitude towards alternative legal and administrative organizational forms (see Chapter 3, Section 3.6), but it also becomes clear that enterprises with 20 to 249 employees adopt a different attitude to small firms with up to 19 employees and large companies with 250 and more staff. These medium-sized enterprises are more in favor of extending patenting possibilities and simultaneously demand stronger state support.

Even if the subject of patenting business processes was not the main focus of the case studies, the skepticism expressed by the primary sector enterprises in the survey can essentially be confirmed. The outlook that business models can be patented is an important argument for many enterprises to reject an extension of software patenting. The same attitude applies for the secondary sector enterprises whereby here, similarly to the survey, isolated approval for patenting process methods was also signalized.

Lightening the administrative burden and support were welcomed in the survey and now also by the company representatives from both sectors interviewed in the case studies. The demands of the enterprises can be summarized as follows in a few key words:

- Guarantee that the patent offices conduct the patent examination according to the valid criteria. In particular, the level of invention (avoiding trivial patents) was named by nearly all enterprises as the most important criterion. For instance, it was proposed that the patent offices should employ more software specialists.
- Clarification of patentability and standardization of the interpretation of patentability in the patent offices. Many enterprises are very uncertain as to whether their developments are patentable; at the same time experiences were reported of different examiners in the offices deciding very differently.
- Simplification of searches and simplification of the language in the patent documents to facilitate communication between developers, management and lawyers.
- Guidelines and consulting with a view to export and internationalization efforts of SMEs.
- Acceleration of the application and award processes.
- Support for patent forums, to which interested or endangered SMEs can turn, in order to communicate or litigate with like-minded or similarly interested enterprises.

5.3.2   Impacts of Extended Patenting

From the perspective of the patent opponents, all disadvantages already perceived in the present system would be worsened and further entrenched. In concurrence with the survey, the companies founded by independent developers fear that an extension of patenting according to the US model will have uniformly negative consequences, not only for their business model (open source), but for the development of the sector and technology in general. Beyond the postulated 'ethical' resistance, the basic problem is that a further dynamism of strategic patenting activities is feared as a result of the extension. This would be accompanied by an increasing and more aggressive pursuit of infringements by the large software houses. For the companies investigated in the case studies which are decidedly opposed to the extension, the consequences of broader patenting would, however, not be foreseeable. Many enterprises have arranged their business models so that their own activity appears reasonably protected (for example consulting model in cases 20, 22; code deposition in case 20, technological leadership in case 13). However, the experiences reported by the interview partners also point out that a large number of enterprises, that intentionally act in a grey area and trust in the non-pursuit of patent infringements, could be threatened in their continued existence by an extension of patenting and increasingly more aggressive enforcement of patents.

Based on the survey, the expectations of the secondary and primary sector enterprises (without the firms based on open source software) with regard to possible consequences of broader patenting were ambivalent, not only concerning their own firm, but also concerning the development of the sector. On the one hand, they anticipate a strengthening of national and international competitiveness; on the other hand they fear a restriction of the innovation dynamic, of product variety and the development of open source. By contrast, the companies in the case studies as a rule do not anticipate strengthening their competitiveness, but also do not expect any significant disadvantages for the innovation dynamic or product variety. It must be explicitly mentioned that the examined start-up companies in part anticipate considerable advantages for their own enterprise and make their further growth expectations dependent on the fact that patenting possibilities will be extended.

Besides raising the costs for patent searches and patent-related safety measures, the majority of the enterprises in the survey expected a reduction in the number of enterprises and therefore a concentration in the software market. While the discussions in the case studies made clear that an increase in the search costs and other legal costs are expected, a wave of concentration throughout the software sector unleashed by the extension of patentability is difficult for the enterprises to assess. It is generally expected that the structural advantage of large enterprises through an extension of patenting could hinder the product variety in the software sector.

Detrimental effect of wider patenting regarding interoperability was encountered in the case studies only in isolated cases. Generally, the firm opponents of patenting see the biggest problems to be in the prevention of free production of interoperability, and accordingly fear an intensification of this problem. Up to now, the manufacturers of operating systems frequently tolerate a property right infringement in the interest of interoperability. This practice could become more restrictive if property right infringements were be pursued more aggressively on the whole because of the extended possibilities to patent. On the other hand, all the firms which produce interoperability within the framework of concrete contractual relations, that is, within bilateral contracts or close supplier–client relationships, do not see larger problems arising. For these cases an extension of patenting would be basically less problematical.

The survey made clear that with increasing knowledge about the patent system, the firms' estimate of the consequences of patenting became more positive. The interviews with the firms in the case studies passed on a more differentiated picture, for together with increasing knowledge about the patent system, the knowledge of the dangers of an extended patent system increase too.

6. Summary and Conclusions

Our two empirical studies furnished facts on innovation and patenting behavior as well as – against the background of real enterprise situations – preferences for various variations in the patenting system of software-developing firms. The empirical findings, as well as the literature analysis and a legal expertise by the Max Planck Institute for Intellectual Property, Competition and Tax Law,[1] show how complex and differentiated the question of the legal protection of intellectual property in the area of software development is.

In Chapter 5 above, the results of the written survey were specified and supplemented on the basis of the case studies. This summary need not repeat this detailed comparison yet again. Instead, the total result of the written survey will be further differentiated with the results of the case studies. Before this is done in Section 6.2, a short summary of the results of the case studies themselves follows. In Section 6.3 the advantages and disadvantages of patenting in the software area found in the literature will be briefly discussed in light of the empirical findings. In Section 6.4, recommendations for policy action are delivered. The book closes with some considerations on further research needed.

6.1 MOST IMPORTANT RESULTS OF THE CASE STUDIES ACCORDING TO ENTERPRISE TYPES

Because of the immense heterogeneity of the contexts, experiences and attitudes towards software patents which emerged in the course of the written survey, a conscious attempt was made to cover a wide spectrum of enterprises. Based on the survey results and the first interviews, four types of enterprises were finally identified. The classification and demarcation are not always straightforward, and also within the single enterprise groups a large degree of heterogeneity still rules. Despite this, the most significant results from the 22 case analyses which were presented in Chapter 4 can be summarized according to these groups, typifying the diversity of attitudes towards patenting in the software area.

---

[1] See Part C of Blind et al. (2003c).

6.1.1   Secondary Sector

The enterprises are characterized as secondary sector, which traditionally and still today make a large portion of their valued added in the hardware sector, but intensively construct and market embedded software, and increasingly also independent software. In the group of six secondary sector firms in the sample, only one is represented that does not utilize patents, and all are in favor of – some vehemently – software patenting. This corresponds in principle to the results of the written survey. The secondary sector enterprises frequently have a long tradition of patenting from the manufacturing industry, mainly from the electrical engineering sector. The practice of patenting in general developed through the increasing software content in self-produced hardware, but then continued in the software sector. Thus the enterprises from the manufacturing industry, or those with large shares in hardware production – reinforced by their international activities – are drivers of patenting. They transfer their active patenting strategies from the context of the manufacturing industry to that of software-developing companies, because they also possess the institutional infrastructures needed. Consequently, many of these firms have a preference for the more far-reaching US model, but the most important issue for them is a regulation of patentability, which creates legal security and clarity.

The medium-sized enterprises in the secondary sector have had not only positive experiences with their patent-protected software, but also negative experiences due to lack of protection. There are difficulties in exporting software, particularly to the USA, if no patent protection exists. For this reason export-oriented firms have a clear preference for comprehensive protection possibilities, whereby they want to see mechanisms implemented that prevent trivial patents.

6.1.2   Primary Sector

Sixteen companies in the sample could be assigned to the primary sector. They produce software exclusively or as a main focus, either directly for the market or within the framework of services for their clients. As emerged clearly from the survey, the attitudes and practices regarding patenting are very varied in this group. The classification of the enterprises follows the criterion of attitude towards and (potential) utilization of patents in the software sector. The most significant results of the three groups 'adherent of broad patenting', 'skeptics' of patenting in general and 'opponents on principle' of patenting are briefly summarized in the following.

6.1.3 Primary Sector – Adherents

In the group of the five enterprises in favor of a broader patenting of software, three start-up companies were identified by means of an active search outside the survey address pool. In addition, one enterprise is included which as a large software house is considering strategic patenting itself, although it achieved its market position without patents. One further enterprise is admittedly scared off by the administrative obstacles of patenting, but at the same time sees the necessity for a comprehensive protection of own-developed features.

Most of the enterprises in this group have experience that patents provide an effective possibility of protection. Simultaneously, patents are not generally necessary for the success of their enterprise. The protective function of software patents plays an important role for start-up companies – less in the acquisition of venture capital than in the consolidation phase, when they have to assert themselves against large competitive enterprises. Besides the protective function, patents are important for the enterprise image and the quality of its products. Further, patents impart a certain legal security to these firms about the basis of their own entrepreneurial activity. Finally, the companies demand an extension of the patenting opportunities as compensation for the present handicap against the US competition.

The critical aspects of extending patentability are also perceived. Thus the enforcement of claims is seen as difficult. Conversely, these enterprises are also conscious of the possible restrictions to their freedom of action. Therefore they urge that trivial patents must not be allowed under any circumstances, and that adequate search opportunities be available.

6.1.4 Primary Sector – Skeptics

The five enterprises of this second group in the primary sector are very heterogeneous. They represent the large number of widely differing firms which have cautiously begun patenting or have at least begun to contemplate it. They are not fundamentally opposed to the possibility of protecting intellectual property in the software sector, but clearly reject a wider patenting and see a number of practical objections in the implementation of the presently valid ruling.

Among the primary sector skeptics the conviction dominates that software patents are not necessary for their own enterprise's success. These firms see themselves rather in increased danger of infringing the patents of others. They fear trivial patents above all, which in spite of the possibility to lodge objections lead to high costs. Further, they see themselves increasingly restricted in their freedom of action by patenting activities on the part of the manufacturing industry. Finally, they feel hampered and unsure because interfaces are frequently protected and thus the interoperability of new developments is hindered. An infringement of such patents to establish interoperability usually remains without consequences at present. Whether this would remain the case after a further extension of patenting is still open to question. The restraint in the utilization of patents is partly explained by the high costs involved in an application. Lastly, the current search possibilities with regard to software patents and their effectiveness were complained about.

These firms are not fundamentally against patents, but in their view strong barriers should be erected in order to prevent a flood of trivial patents. Simultaneously, they call for better search possibilities. The possibilities to enforce patent claims are also regarded critically. Lastly, besides some skepticism as regards patents on software in general, in the context of interoperability they are judged very critically.

6.1.5   Primary Sector – Opponents

The companies in this last group are opposed to the patenting of software. However, the analysis showed that the convinced opponents have very different reasons for their opinion and in part also argue for contradictory limitations to patentability. Some of the firms base their business model and their developments on open source software and therefore consider the disadvantages of patenting as particularly grave. A further enterprise has already been concretely harmed and is therefore put off by the loopholes in the system and the costs of defense against unjustified claims, rather than being opposed to patents in principle. Two further enterprises have – up to now – considered the protection unnecessary. They do not doubt the essential point of protection, but want either only complex algorithms to be protected or argue – diametrically opposite – against software patents because algorithms are not worth protecting.

For this group of enterprises patents are not important for their economic success. Close contact with clients and excellent knowledge of the sector are the decisive success factors for them. But these enterprises are being increasingly confronted with the patenting activities of other firms. They also report concrete negative experiences and they see themselves as hampered particularly by trivial patents. As a consequence, safety precautions are taken which present a cost factor, but do not impact positively on the enterprise's development. Furthermore, they feel restricted in their freedom of action in their development activities. The increase of patent activities in potential export markets is perceived as a negative for their export activities. Lastly, the operators of open source-based business models, who are dependent on the input of independent developers, see the dynamic development of their products endangered by the increase in software patenting, whereas for their business model the important copyright on source code allows a higher flexibility to develop alternative solutions too.

6.2 QUALIFYING THE TOTAL RESULTS OF THE WRITTEN SURVEY BY THE CASE STUDIES

The written survey arrived at the result that the utilization of patents has played a relatively small role until now.[2] Even if the sample of this investigation for obvious reasons (willingness, relevance) displays a bias in favor of the enterprises which patent or intend to do so, or which feel upset by patents, it became clear that the question of patenting assumes a role of increasing importance. This happens in those enterprises which until now have undertaken few activities, mainly as reaction to the perception that the software-developing companies generally tend more strongly towards protection. In addition, increasing internationalization leaves most enterprises with no alternative but to concern themselves with property rights.

The heterogeneity and ambivalence of the attitude towards software patents could be confirmed. The negative tenor regarding the impact of patenting – beyond the obvious contradictions between fundamental opponents and adherents, or applicants of patents in the software sector – can however be adjusted. Many primary sector enterprises are very skeptical, not due to fundamental considerations, but because of a general insecurity about patentability, the danger of trivial patents, the costs and the perceived problems pertaining to an appropriate search, and the structural disadvantages which can arise for SMEs. Simultaneously, influenced by the negative experience that imitations of their own developments were introduced to the market by competitors, some firms have perceived advantages in patenting – although the implementation could and must be improved. In addition, it transpired that some of the enterprises that regard patenting with skepticism are still able to adapt to a broadening of patenting possibilities.

There are – by contrast with the results of the written survey – in the meantime also examples where pure software houses are beginning to patent strategically, that is, using patents not only as a protection against imitation, but also as a strategic asset in technology competition, and with clients. For start-up companies, in particular, holding a patent can be of enormous significance, for various reasons (image, capital market, self-confidence) (see below). At the same time, the growth in significance of software in the

---

[2]   The synoptical specification follows the general result derived from the written survey (Chapter 3, Section 3.7.5). The numbers refer to the lists provided in that chapter.

manufacturing industry led to an increase in software-related patents in the manufacturing sector which, however, at the moment makes the traditional enterprises in this area feel very insecure.

On the whole, the result that the enterprises which are actively involved in patenting stem from the secondary sector and as a rule are also internationally active, was definitely confirmed. The traditional practices of the secondary sector, as well as the pressures to adapt due to internationalization, are the most important drivers of patenting.

The impression of the written survey that the three specific characteristics of the software sector – sequentiality, interoperability and open source development – are influenced by patenting, is confirmed, in a somewhat weaker form. It is admittedly true that the declared patent opponents, in particular the companies with a large open source share, see disadvantages in all three dimensions. The greatest disadvantage, however, must consist in that under an increasingly more aggressive patent regime the existing practices of tacitly accepting a possible infringement lead to even greater uncertainties. The case studies made abundantly clear that there are numerous contractual, informal and tacit agreements to establish sequentiality and interoperability without the burdens of the patent regime. Moreover, the present regime has already made far-reaching co-operations possible between enterprises working in proprietary modes and those belonging to the open source community. The latter are frequently effective service providers for clients from industry; the former have a vested interest in flexible co-operation between both systems. This does not mean that open source developers do not feel unsure of themselves; it shows only that the existing patent protection permits numerous possibilities to establish interoperability and sequentiality and to pursue the development of open source further.

The desire for stronger support in patenting can be confirmed and will be discussed in the recommendations for action in more detail (see below). On the other hand, the desire for standardized, global regulations is limited to those enterprises which are already, or plan to be, internationally active. However, all enterprises which are not fervent adherents of the US model prefer to retain the status quo in Europe to a standardization along the lines of the US model. The explicit technical content of the patents is vehemently called for by all enterprises which have gathered experience from the secondary manufacturing sector. Retention of the technical content is also called for by the great majority of the firms examined which are not declared opponents of patents. However, the software houses per se have great problems with the definition of technical reference. They usually need an external lawyer to translate this dimension to their specific context. For the enterprises of this study willing to patent, it was not difficult to establish a technical reference. It would be problematic for some enterprises to abolish the precondition, as they see the danger therein that the large enterprises, very active in patenting and pure 'patent hunters' would tend to protect pure software code without the proof of technical transferability. The strong increase of such patenting activities could massively impair the technological freedom of action, not only in the primary, but also in the secondary sector.

The rejection of patenting business processes is practically a unanimous consensus; only smaller start-up companies which base their success on such a new idea would hope for additional security for their activities and market chances from this measure.

The firms can estimate the possible economic impacts of broad patenting only with great difficulty. The large secondary sector enterprises, and increasingly also the software houses in the primary sector, see therein partly a necessity to participate in the international technology race, which is also based on the portfolios of patents. The majority of the enterprises, however, see a worsening of the structural disadvantages in an extension of patenting, in particular for the SMEs, especially because of increased costs for searches.

The adaptions demanded by the firms which do not reject patenting out of hand or propagate a complete, coverall extension, refer mainly to precautions to prevent trivial patents and to improve search possibilities. With reference to the length of the protection period, individual opinions demand a reduction, which could then lead to easier interoperability with systems of older versions.

6.3 STATEMENT ON THE ADVANTAGES AND DISADVANTAGES OF SOFTWARE PATENTING

The literature overview listed and discussed a number of potential advantages and disadvantages of intellectual property rights.[3] In the following, the most important of these pros and cons are again cited and placed in the context of the results of the case studies and the survey.

6.3.1 Potential Advantages of Property Rights in the Software Area

Property rights:

- Widen the flow of knowledge through disclosures. This assertion was already refuted in the survey and is identified by the results of the case studies as absolutely untenable.

---

[3] See Chapter 2, Section 2.3.

- Promote incremental and sequential development work through disclosing new knowledge and thus increase variety and interoperability. This hypothesis could not be unambiguously tested by the existing data from the survey, but finds no support in the case examples at all.
- Extend the often very short period of the innovation leads. Whilst in the survey data no support for the theory could be found, the overwhelming majority of property rights users in the case studies oppose this argument, whereas exceptions, for example some of the start-up companies, must be mentioned.
- Steer innovation towards radical innovations, which cannot be tackled without patents. This hypothesis could not be tested with the survey data, the case studies of the patent-utilizing enterprises, however, underline as a rule that this assertion cannot be maintained.
- Make possible penetration price strategies, which can contribute to overcoming critical user numbers. This hypothesis could also not be tested on the grounds of the survey due to its dynamic dimension, but the case studies also did not provide a basis for confirmation.
- Raise the market transparency and reduce the transaction costs in the dynamic and confusing software market. This hypothesis deals with a subject which cannot be tested by means of a closed survey; in the case studies, on the other hand, this positive aspect of property rights in general and patents in particular could not be fundamentally confirmed.
- Secure the most crucial asset of enterprises – knowledge – with which SMEs and young enterprises can also protect themselves against the power of large firms in the market and against staff members who leave the enterprise and take their know-how with them. While no conclusive grounds to accept this hypothesis could be found on the basis of the survey, a number of case studies showed that this hypothesis is legitimate for start-up companies. The interviews showed that the enterprises also see the danger in the disclosure of an innovative idea in a patent document, that above all stronger competitors will assimilate and successfully market this idea.
- Facilitate the access to the capital market, especially for young enterprises. While no compelling reasons to adopt this hypothesis could be found in the survey, the case studies of the start-up companies showed that patents have a distinct significance for acquiring venture capital.

6.3.2 Potential Disadvantages of Property Rights in the Software Area

Property rights:

- Are not oriented to the idiosyncrasies of the sector (difficulties in determining the state of the art, complementary developments and so on).

Although the survey confirmed the idiosyncrasies, especially sequentiality and interoperability, of software development, the direct relationship to the suitability of property rights could not be unambiguously established. The case studies, however, make abundantly clear that there are difficulties in determining the state of the art, which are detrimental to an effective patent system.

- Hamper incremental and sequential development work through the ban on using protected algorithms.
- Thus reduce the variety and interoperability and harm in particular the open-source movement.
- Block under certain circumstances a multiplicity of applications and further developments.
- Slow down the speed of innovation in the entire software sector.
- Analogous to the survey, these negative implications, particularly of patents, could not be confirmed, but a number of enterprises still feared that this dimension could gain significance with increased software patenting.
- Lead to misallocation of resources, in that increased costs would occur through alternative designs for functional equivalents and interoperable applications and more resources will be invested in legal dealings instead of R&D. This hypothesis could not be proved in the survey with hard figures drawn from past experience, but was confirmed in the questions of attitude and expectations. A number of case studies show, however, that in many enterprises higher sums are already being invested in legal protection or pursuing property rights.
- Lead to long-term monopolies in combination with network effects. While the role of network effects in general and their interplay with property rights could not be elaborated in the survey, some of the case studies demonstrated that positive network effects – generated by a high number of users in interplay with property rights (copyright or patent protection) – not only promote the evolution of new products, but also form the basis for strong market positions.
- Create legal uncertainties. This dimension was questioned only as an expectation in the survey, but could be more concretely confirmed in the case studies. The great majority of the companies interviewed expressed their confusion about the criteria for awarding patents in the software area, and complained that it is exceedingly difficult to obtain an overview of awarded patents relevant for their enterprises in the software area.
- Place the rather more dynamic SMEs and young enterprises at a structural disadvantage. This dimension could only be recorded in the survey by means of the expectations expressed, but the case studies showed that this hypothesis cannot be fundamentally confirmed, for property rights can also protect this enterprise group against large firms.

This short overview of the reasons for and against intellectual property rights confirms our assumption that the complexity of IPR in the software area necessitates an adequate research methodology, that is, a combination of a broad survey and qualitative deep case studies. It has become clear that the case studies on the one hand confirm, supplement, but in part also call into question the survey results. As far as the potential advantages are concerned, it must be particularly pointed out that the case studies elaborated the positive implications of property rights, especially patents, for founding and establishing start-up companies. In addition, there are a number of firms which do not feel any special disadvantages from the patenting practices of other, usually large enterprises and are accordingly indifferent. With regard to disadvantages, it can be pointed out that the idiosyncrasy of software, in particular its dynamic character, places the effectiveness of the patent system under question, because grave difficulties arise when determining the state of the art. Concrete obstacles to development activities were recorded in the case studies in one case only – in the shape of a successfully contested patent. It is not foreseeable how the further dynamization of patenting will lead to further concrete obstructions. In addition, many enterprises expressed diffuse hold-ups, in that they conduct their own development activities under the shadow of potential patent infringements. Compared to the survey results, the general result from the analysis of the case studies is that on the whole the advantages and also the disadvantages of property rights, in particular of patents, have been toned down in the software sector.

6.4 RECOMMENDED ACTIONS

In conclusion, the recommended actions derived from the results of the representative survey and the legal expertise conducted in parallel to it, for which qualifications emerged from the case studies, will be further specified and new recommendations added.[4] As the empirical basis is limited to German companies, these recommendations also reflect the German situation. However, we firmly believe that they are also applicable to other national contexts in Europe. In addition, many consequences of these recommendations refer to the European level anyway.

6.4.1 Legal Framework and Procedure

As already mentioned, the demand for a standardized internationally harmonized law is still valid. A standardized European regulation would make

---

[4] Blind et al. (2003a) Chapter 6.

the activities of the internationally active firms much easier. However, it is important that the prevention of extending patenting should have priority over a global standardization. Europe should remain true to its more restrictive model and accept the frictions in international traffic. The opposition to an extension on the part of the enterprises justifies this, on the grounds alone of the obvious danger of a further dynamization of patenting in the software sector, which would increase the likelihood of trivial patents due to the increased numbers. The efficiency gains from standardization with the US model are relatively low, as the large enterprises which are already internationally active are also able to respond to US law and have already shown that they can adapt to various regimes. The costs of adaptation to a broader patenting regime which would have to be met by the majority of the firms in Germany appear much higher.

Regulations that would lead to extending the current patenting practice are rejected. The question whether 'software as such' should be banned from patenting appears of secondary importance against the background of the practices of the investigated enterprises. In all relevant cases the determination of the technical reference and novelty were key to the question of whether an invention should be patented or not. If patents are aspired to, then there was no problem in the case studies to present the technical character of the 'software as such'. A clear definition of the technical nature and a clear emphasis of the novelty and non-triviality of inventions appear therefore to be the essential challenges.

The results from the case studies are ambivalent regarding a novelty grace period, as called for in the survey. The support for a novelty grace period was relatively low in the interviews and was not demanded proactively by the enterprises themselves. As this concerns a discretionary ruling, which in the individual case benefits and does not harm the inventor, it is still to be supported.

The status quo makes it quite obviously possible to establish open source as the foundation of business models. At the same time, there are a number of examples in which firms of both modes co-operate. Whereas an extension of patenting would increase the difficulties of the open source developers, it would simultaneously be very problematical not to meet the need for protection of many market participants, through a more restrictive patenting policy or a general ban on patenting developments based on software. The study made clear that SMEs especially also suffer from neglecting the protection of their software-based developments and that there are also small enterprises which are able to secure their competitiveness by enforcing own patents. Thus, the major recommendation is that in principle the status quo in Germany is to be supported. But further development of open source must be observed very closely and in the case of increased obstruction of this mode, new thought must be given to this subject.[5]

Moreover, enterprises need clarity with relation to the patentability of software-related developments; more important than the quarrel about the course of the frontier line of patentability is to establish an exact frontier. Establishing this clear demarcation must be the urgent goal of the politicians and policy-makers. Enterprises are in a position to adjust to patenting norms as long as they can be implemented in clear instructions for action, which can also be understood by the developers. The requisite condition of technical reference is only further meaningful if it can be equally applied across the whole range of software-related developments and if it can be fully understood by software developers. An enumeration of technical areas, as proposed on the basis of the analysis of the relevant court decisions,[6] would certainly be easier for the enterprises to implement and should therefore be welcomed. It must, however, be guaranteed that the enumeration does not lead to a situation where patenting is regarded as generally permitted in the listed areas, with the effect of a further dynamization and increase of trivial patents. That means, for the explicitly listed technical areas it must also be guaranteed that all patenting criteria will continue to be very strictly examined.

A further conclusion from the investigation as regards establishing clarity is that the patent application specifications accepted by the patent office must be examined more stringently for comprehensibility and unambiguity. Not only the printed patent specifications, but also the legal documents drawn up in the course of collision negotiations are disassociated from the language used in the world of company managers and developers, and thus lie beyond their powers of comprehension. Several examples in the study make this obvious: this disassociation leads to frustration and to additional costs, and in many cases enterprises abandon their search activities entirely. Accordingly, the patent offices must insist more firmly on clarity in the patent specifications as a precondition for awarding patents. In addition, existing consulting institutions must also support enterprises in the interpretation of patent specifications.[7]

From the case studies it became apparent that the greatest problems of patenting concern establishing interoperability. Patents on generic developments and on interfaces which are important for many applications tend to

---

[5]   This is in the general interest; also in a very direct sense as many state institutions are in the process of switching over to open source software.

[6]   See Part C in Blind et al. (2003b).

[7]   See Section 6.4.2 below on the problems of enterprise-specific legal advice by consulting organizations.

lead to high costs in the system or to hindering complementary developments. It is not, however, practical to make the generic character of a software-based invention a test criterion in the patent offices. However, legal possibilities should be created in order to force the utilization of patent-protected generic software in certain cases. It should be investigated whether the §24 of Patent Law (PatG) – in agreement with valid international undertakings – should be supplemented accordingly. If an enterprise has patented generic software and refuses to grant a license to a potential licensee under 'reasonable and customary business' conditions (§24 PatG), then legal possibilities should be created to make licensing compulsory. As foreseen in §24 PatG, public interest must be involved in the licensing, for which appropriate criteria would have to be created (such as a monopoly detrimental to the market, hindering the development of complementary and alternative markets). Whether the software has generic character and is important for many applications could be established via opposition proceedings. As soon as a previously determined number of companies have claimed this convincingly and a certain potential market volume can credibly be proved, then the Federal Patent Court must investigate whether adequate public interest exists and compulsory licenses must be awarded accordingly.

6.4.2 Information and Support Infrastructure

A number of structural and pragmatic recommendations can be derived from these investigations. On the one hand, it is still obvious that lack of knowledge about the area of patenting contributes to uncertainty and all efforts to spread knowledge can only be supported. It was also shown that lack of knowledge does not correlate in linear fashion with the rejection of patenting in the software area. Therefore, broad and intelligent knowledge dissemination is needed in order to reduce uncertainty and leave the enterprises and developers in charge of future development. In addition, consulting should take up the importance of software patenting for start-up companies; in particular, consultancy institutions for start-up companies should be sensitized to the special problems of property rights in the software sector.

Furthermore, the exchange of knowledge about property rights in the software sector between enterprises as facilitated by institutions such as the German patent information centers need to be adjusted in order to meet the need and worries of SME. There is a real danger here – confirmed in individual case studies – that large firms with their specialists determine the discussion too much from their own perspective. In single cases it became apparent that smaller companies perceive the danger of large firms 'stealing ideas', and for this reason regard information events and knowledge exchange critically or avoid them. It would be a psychological relief if events were organized by public institutions, whose neutrality regarding the interests of the participants could reduce the inhibition threshold of the SMEs. In order to demolish such inhibition thresholds, it is also useful to organize information events during which concrete patents in certain technological fields are not explicitly discussed, but information on the general problems and possibilities of patenting is available, if possible through 'neutral' speakers, that is, explicitly not – or not mainly – representatives of large firms with fat patent portfolios.

A further form of state promotion consists in facilitating the formation of ultimately self-organized information and defense pools of enterprises. In one case, the bundling of resources led to a lawsuit being successfully brought against a patent. The costs and the expertise of a proceeding are easier to bear for whole groups of firms. State initiatives could support the self-organization of companies by offering anonymous marketplaces to forge contacts between similarly interested and affected enterprises. For instance, an Internet forum could be created, in which interested firms could report about their case and concerns whilst remaining anonymous. As soon as several enterprises with the same interests found each other, an interest pool could be formed which then continued to organize themselves and be active outside the forum.

The case studies reported moreover the firms' first experiences with the practice of depositing codes to secure own innovations. Such practices are interesting for software firms which do not want to participate in the patent system but at the same time, however, want a reliable consideration of their inventions in the examination of subsequent patent applications. Two variations are conceivable. Enterprises which want to secure the date of origin of their own code verifiably, but do not want to publish their codes, can deposit their code with a notary public. Such enterprises which do not shrink from, or even welcome, the disclosure of their own developments, can make use of existing services, which publish inventions in certain databases as an alternative to patents.[8] Both alternatives are cheap and practical means of defense against patent challenges in the future. It makes sense to propagate such practices also from the state side. In addition an official state body to deposit program code could be established, which could also serve to prevent the patenting of already 'objectively' known inventions in this area, but which can actually be investigated only with great difficulty.

The simplification, acceleration and reduction of costs for patent office and court procedures is a demand which all enterprises made. The practical problems, however, are once again graver for the SMEs, for which the costs of proceedings (especially nullity suits) seem prohibitive.

---

[8]   As for example the database RDISCLOSURE offered by STN (http://www.stn-international.de/stndatabases/databases/rdisclosure.html).

It must in addition be ensured that the patent offices conduct patent examinations according to valid criteria. In particular, the level of invention (the issue of trivial patents) was named by nearly all enterprises as the most decisive criterion. Further, it must be checked whether more software specialists can be employed in the patent offices. At the same time, the standardization of the interpretation of the patentability criteria in the patent offices must be a top priority. Many firms are very unsure whether their developments are patentable; moreover it is reported from experience that different examiners in the offices decide differently.

The sticking point of systematic patenting activities for the enterprises which do not aspire to patents themselves, but want to avoid infringements, is an effective patent search. The large firms in this study have optimized their search strategies and are in a position to search in different databases, for example with keyword strategies, and thus to create the necessary overview. The majority of the SMEs investigated in the study cannot perform such searches themselves, and as a rule their lawyers are also overtaxed in the complex area of software-related patents. To make searches easier by adding a classification 'software', which should additionally be quoted as horizontal class and secondary classification, if the software component is crucial, would be of enormous help. Furthermore, the establishment of adequate databases should also be considered, which are accessible for search strategies via key word searches in order to facilitate detecting relevant software patents.[9] Effective and reasonably cheap searches appear to be the best way to prevent the infringement of software patents. At the same time, the existing offers of support in searching, such as provided by the patent information centers, should be better brought to the firms' attention. Surely the market will provide a certain degree of assistance via the demand for specialized patent experts and attorneys in future here, too. However, it makes sense to reduce the costs for building up expertise in searching in enterprises and in the legal profession, which up to now only large firms could afford, by simplifying the search possibilities, and thus also reducing the expertise gap of the large firms.

The study has shown that up to now enterprises were not sufficiently informed about legal problems abroad, and enterprises which engaged in international activities should receive adequate advice. Obviously, the need for consultancy on the part of the enterprises has not yet been adequately communicated to the existing advisory institutions.[10] Guidelines and advice with

---

[9] At Fraunhofer ISI, in a pilot study for the OECD using a key word search with the two words 'software' and 'computer programs' in the World Patent Index database of the enterprise Derwent, it was shown that the share of software patents can be well established; see Schmoch (2003).

[10] Indeed, the onus is primarily on the enterprises to request the information on property rights problems from the existing consulting institutions, such as the Federal Agency for Foreign

a view to the export and internationalization efforts of SMEs and possible property right problems should be drawn up and proactively distributed. The chambers of commerce and business associations have an important function here, not only to demolish the obstacles, but also to point out the dangers.

This final point, however, draws attention to a general problem concerning giving advice to enterprises. The Legal Consulting Law links the permission to provide legal advice to enterprises to the condition that the advisor must be a registered lawyer. As a result, the institutions such as the chambers of commerce or the regional patent information centers can only give general information on the patent system or support in searches. As soon as a company has an enterprise-specific inquiry, the consulting by such bodies is no longer admissible. But as such institutions, because of their permanent, specialized consultancy activities, combine legal know-how with know-how about the market problems of enterprises, it would be very desirable if a change in the law also made legal consulting possible by qualified lawyers in these institutions.[11]

6.5 DESIDERATA OF RESEARCH FOR THE FURTHER DEVELOPMENT OF SOFTWARE PATENTING

In light of the experiences gathered in this study, it must be pointed out that fundamental and far-reaching changes in the patent system in this area require a deeper understanding of the economic and social impact of various patent regulations in the software area. The following in-depth studies and comparative analyses therefore seem urgently needed:

- In particular with regard to the long-term economic impact of patenting or non-patenting in the software area, further long-term studies would be necessary in future, which cannot be performed within the time and funding framework presently available. This applies all the more since also very up-to-date, comprehensive contributions in other countries (Académie des

Trade and Investment. According to information from, for example, the Federal Agency, this has not yet taken place. At the same time, these organizations should focus more strongly on this subject and raise awareness about it.

[11] In a similar sense, ifo Institut (1998), in a study on knowledge distribution and diffusion dynamics, call for the establishment of a general (unrelated to software) patent information service. This service should not only regularly place all relevant patent specifications proactively at firms' disposal ('invention reports') and regularly conduct workshops, in particular with SMEs, but in addition – in co-ordination with the patent legal profession – take on the task of supervising the property rights needs of inventions at the request of the inventor or other owners.

Technologies 2001; Smets-Solanes 2000)[12] do not supply additional empirical data or do not meet scientific demands (UK Patent Office 2001).[13]

- It appears very promising, by means of a comparative analysis among different patent regimes in the USA and in Europe, to analyze the medium-term effects on variety, competitiveness of all market participants (not just of those who patent) and on the dynamic of innovation development. Should patenting practices in Europe remain narrower than in the USA or become narrower again, then a comparison of the impacts in a few years would be the best method to arrive at a better understanding of the significance of patenting for the software sector. In that case, the thesis suggested by the present study, that the European regime is more advantageous in the long term, should be tested.

---

[12] Http://www.internet.gouv.fr/francais/textesref/avisacatec180701.htm (accessed 24 July 2001).
[13] See the consultations of the British Patent Office, http://www.patent.gov.uk/news/softpat.htm (accessed 30 June 2001).

Bibliography

Académie des Technologies (2001), *Avis de l'Académie des Technologies concernant la brevetabilité des inventions mises en oeuvre parordinateur*, http://www.internet. gouv.fr/francais/textesref/avisacatec180701.htm (24 July 2001).

Acs, Z.J. and D.B. Audretsch (1989), 'Patents as a measure of innovative activity', *Kyklos*, **42**, 171–80.

Allegrezza, S. and A. Guard-Rauchs (1999), 'The determinants of trademark deposits: an econometric investigation', *Economie Appliquée*, **52** (2), 51–68.

Arrow, K.J. (1962), 'Economic welfare and the allocation of resources for invention', in National Bureau of Economic Research (ed.), *The Rate and Direction of Inventive Activity: Economic and Social Factors*, Princeton, NJ: Princeton University Press.

Arundel, A. and I. Kabla (1998), 'What percentage of innovations are patented? Empirical estimates for European firms', *Research Policy*, **27**, 127–41.

Besen, S.M. and L.J. Raskind (1991), 'An introduction to the law and economics of intellectual property', *Journal of Economic Perspectives*, **5** (1), 3–27.

Bessen, J. (2001), *Open Source Software: Free Provision of Complex Public Goods*, working version April 2001, http://www.researchoninnovation.org/opensrc.pdf (25 April 2001).

Bessen, J. and E. Maskin (2000), *Sequential Innovation, Patents and Imitation*, MIT Working Paper, No. 1/2000, Cambridge: MIT.

Bessen, J. and R.M. Hunt (2004a), *A Reply to Hahn and Wallsten*, www.researchon-innovation.org/hahn.pdf.

Bessen, J. and R.M. Hunt (2004b), *An Emperical Look at Software Patents*, working paper No. 03-17/R, http://www.researchoninnovation.org/swpat.pdf, Philadelphia, PA: Federal Reserve Bank of Philadelphia.

Blind, K. (2003), 'The impact of patent rights on the propensity to standardise at standardisation development organisations: an international cross-section analysis', *Homo Oeconomicus*, **20** (1), 103–23.

Blind, K., J. Edler and M. Friedewald (2003a), *Geistige Eigentumsrechte in der Informationsgesellschaft: Eine Analyse der Rolle gewerblicher Schutzrechte bei Gründung und Markteintritt sowie für die Innovations- und Wettbewerbsfähigkeit von Softwareunternehmen anhand unternehmens- und softwaretypenbezogener Fallstudien*, final report to the Federal Ministry for Economics and Technology, Karlsruhe: Fraunhofer Institute Systems and Innovation Resarch (ISI).

Blind, K., J. Edler, R. Nack and J. Straus (2003b), *Software-Patente: Eine empirische Analyse aus ökonomischer und juristischer Perspektive*, Heidelberg: Physica-Verlag.

Blind, K., J. Edler, U. Schmoch, B. Andersen, J. Howells, I. Miles, J. Roberts, C. Hipp, L. Green, C. Herstatt and R. Evangelista (2003c), *Patents in the Service Industries*, final report, EC contract No ERBHPV2-CT-1999-06, Brussels: European Commission.

Blind, K., J. Edler, R. Frietsch and U. Schmoch (2004), *The Patent Upsurge in Germany: The Outcome of a Multi-Motive Game induced by Large Companies*, working paper presented at the 8th Schumpeter Conference in Milano, Karlsruhe: Fraunhofer Institute Systems and Innovation Research (ISI).

Blind, K. and H. Grupp (2000), *Gesamtwirtschaftlicher Nutzen der Normung. Volkswirtschaftlicher Nutzen: Zusammenhang zwischen Normung und technischem Wandel, ihr Einfluss auf die Gesamtwirtschaft und den Außenhandel der Bundesrepublik Deutschland*, Berlin: Deutschen Institut für Normung.

Boch, R. (1999), *Patentschutz und Innovation in Gegenwart und Geschichte*, Frankfurt am Main: Lang.

Brouwer, E. and A. Kleinknecht (1999), 'Innovative output and a firm's propensity to patent. An exploration of CIS micro data', *Research Policy*, **28**, 615–24.

Brügge, B., D. Harhoff, A. Picot, O. Creighton, M. Fiedler and J. Henkel (2004), *Open-Source-Software. Eine ökonomische und technische Analyse*, Berlin, Heidelberg and New York: Springer-Verlag.

Bugdahl, V. (1998), *Marken machen Märkte. Eine Anleitung zur erfolgreichen Markenpraxis*, München: C.H. Beck.

Church, J. and R. Ware (1998), 'Network industries, intellectual property rights and competition policy', in Anderson, R.D. and N.T. Gallini (eds), *Competition Policy and Intellectual Property Rights in the Knowledge-Based Economy*, Calgary: University of Calgary Press, pp. 227–86.

Cohen, W., R.R. Nelson and J. Walsh (2000), *Appropriability Conditions and Why Patent and Why They Do Not*, Washington, DC: National Bureau of Economic Research.

Commission of the European Communities (2000), *Patentability of Computer-implemented Inventions: Consultation Paper by the Services of the Directorate General for the Internal Market*, Brussels: Commission of the European Communities.

Commission of the European Communities (2002), *Proposal for a Directive of the European Parliament and of the Council on the Patentability of Computer-implemented Inventions*, Brussels: Commission of the European Communities.

Council of the European Union (2002), *Proposal for a Directive of the European Parliament and of the Council on the Patentability of Computer-implemented inventions – Common approach*, Brussels: Council of the European Union.

Council of the European Union (2004), *Proposal for a Directive of the European Parliament and of the Council on the Patentability of Computer-implemented Inventions – Political Agreement on the Council's Common Position*, Brussels: Council of the European Union.

Dam, K.W. (1995), 'Some economic considerations in the intellectual property protection of software', *Journal of Legal Studies*, **24**, 321–77.

Dasgupta, P. and J.E. Stiglitz (1980), 'Industrial structure and the nature of innovative activity', *Economic Journal*, **90**, 266–93.

Dempsey, B.J., D. Weiss, P. Jones and J. Greenberg (1999), *A Quantitative Profile of a Community of Open Source Linux Developers*, SILS Technical Report TR-1999-05.

Djellal, F. and F. Gallouj (2001), 'Patterns of innovation organisation in service firms: postal survey results and theoretical models', *Science and Public Policy*, **28**, 57–67.

Emery, S. (1996), 'Innovation and intellectual property protection: the software industry perspective', *Columbia Journal of World Business*, 31 January, 30–37.

Endres, A. (2000), '"Open Source" und die Zukunft der Software', *Informatik Spektrum*, 23 January, 316–21.

European Parliament (2003), *European Parliament Legislative Resolution on the Proposal for a Directive of the European Parliament and of the Council on the Patentability of Computer-implemented Inventions*, final report A5-0238/2003.

Eurostat (2000), *Statistics of Innovation in Europe*, Luxembourg: Eurostat.

Farrell, J. (1989), 'Standardization and intellectual property', *Jurimetrics Journal*, **30** (1), 35–50.

Farrell, J. (1995), 'Arguments for weaker intellectual property protection in network industries', in Kahin, B. and J. Abbate (eds), *Standards Policy for Information Infrastructure*, Cambridge, MA: MIT Press, pp. 368–77.

Farrell, J. and M.L. Katz (1998), 'The effects of antitrust and intellectual property law on compatibility and innovation', *The Antitrust Bulletin*, Fall – Winter 1998, 609–50.

Farrell, J. and Saloner G. (1985), 'Standardization, compatibility, and innovation', *RAND Journal of Economics*, **16**, 70–83.

Farrell, J. and Saloner G. (1992), 'Converters, compatibility, and the control of interfaces', *Journal of Industrial Economics*, March 1992, 9–36.

Free Software Foundation (1991), *Gnu General Public License*, version 2, http://www.gnu.org/copyleft/gpl.html.

Garfinkel, S.L., R.M. Stallman and M. Kapor (1996), 'Why patents are bad for software', in Ludlow, P. (ed.), *High Noon on the Electronic Front: Conceptual Issues in Cyberspace*, Cambridge, MA: MIT Press, pp. 35–46.

Gehring, R. (2000), *Berliner Ansatz zu Open Software Patents;* http://130.149.19.71:8080/Think-Ahead.ORG/Cyberlaw (15 March 2001).

Gerster, R. (1980), *Patentierte Profite. Zur Rolle der schweizerischen Patente in der Dritten Welt*, Basel: Z-Verlag.

Gerwinski, P. (2000), *Positionspapier 'Software-Patente'*, 16 May, Symposium Software Patents 18 May, Bonn: BMWi.

Gilbert, R. and C. Shapiro (1990), 'Optimal patent length and breadth', *RAND Journal of Economics*, **21**, 106–12.

Gould, D.M. and W.C. Gruben (1996), 'The role of intellectual property rights in economic growth', *Journal of Development Economics*, **48**, 323–50.

Graham, S. and D.C. Mowery (2003), 'Intellectual property protection in the US software industry', in Cohen, W. and S. Merrill (eds), *The Patent System in the Knowledge-based Economy*, Washington, DC: National Academies Press, pp. 219–58.

Gross, G. (2001), 'Leserbrief zu Albert Endres "Open Source und die Zukunft der Software"', *Informatik-Spektrum*, 24 February, 38–39.

Grossman, G. and E. Helpman (1991), *Innovation and Growth in the Global Economy*, Cambridge, MA: MIT Press.

Hahn, R.W. and S. Wallsten (2003), *A Review of Bessen and Hunt's Analysis of Software Patents*, American Enterprise Institute (ed.), http://www.reserachineurope.org/policy/hahn_wallsten.pdf.

Hall, C.D. (1986), 'Patents, licensing, and antitrust', *Research in Law and Economics*, **8**, 59–86.

Hart, R., P. Holmes and J. Reid (2000), *The Economic Impact of Patentability of Computer Programs*, report to the European Commission, London.

Heckel, P. (1996), 'Deunking the Software Patent Myth', in Ludlow, P. (ed.), *High Noon on the Electronic Front: Conceptual Issues in Cyber-Space*, Boston, MA: MIT Press, pp. 63–108.

Holmes, W.N. (2000), 'The evitability of software patents', *Computer*, **33** (3), 30–33.

Horns, A.H. (2000), *Der Patentschutz für software-bezogene Erfindungen im Verhältnis zur 'Open Source'-Software*, JurPC web document 223/2000.

ifo Institut (1998), *Wissensverbreitung und Diffusionsdynamik im Spannungsfeld zwischen innovierenden und imitierenden Unternehmen – Neue Ansätze für die Innovationspolitik*, report to the Federal Ministry for Economics and Labour, München: ifo Institut.

Jaffe, A.B. (1999), *The US Patent System in Transition: Policy Innovation and the Innovation Process*, Cambridge, MA: National Bureau of Economic Research.

Janz, N., S. Gottschalk, T. Hempell, B. Peters, G. Ebling and H. Niggemann (2001), *Innovationsverhalten der deutschen Wirtschaft: Indikatorenbericht zur Innovationserhebung 2000*, Mannheim: ZEW.

Jungmittag, A., K. Blind and H. Grupp (1999), 'Innovation, standardisation and the long-term production function. A cointegration analysis for Germany 1960–96', *Zeitschrift für Wirtschafts- und Sozialwissenschaften (ZWS)*, **119**, 205–22.

Kash, D.E. and W. Kingston (2001), 'Patents in a world of complex technologies', *Science and Public Policy*, **28** (1), 11–22.

Katz, M.L. and C. Shapiro (1985), 'Network externalities, competition, and compatibility', *American Economic Review*, **75**, 424–40.

Katz, M.L. and C. Shapiro (1986), 'Technology adoption in the presence of network externalities', *Journal of Political Economy*, **94**, 822–41.

Keely, L.C. and D. Quah (1998), *Technology in Growth*, working paper, London: Centre for Economic Policy Research.

Kitch, E.W. (1977), 'The nature and function of the patent system', *Journal of Law and Economics*, **20**, 265–90.

Klemperer, P. (1990), 'How broad should the scope of patent protection be?' *RAND Journal of Economics*, **21**, 113–30.

Kortum, S. and J. Lerner (1997), *Stronger Protection or Technological Revolution: What is Behind the Recent Surge in Patenting?* working paper 6204, Cambridge, MA: National Bureau of Economic Research.

Lea, G. (2000), *Software Patents: Will Europe Roll Over for the Multinationals?* The Register, http://.theregister.co.uk/content/1/13942.htm (12 October 2000).

Lee, J.-Y. and E. Mansfield (1996), 'International intellectual property rights protection and US foreign direct investment', *Review of Economics and Statistics*, **78** (2), 181–6.

Lerner, J. and J. Tirole (2000), *The Simple Economics of Open Source*, Cambridge, MA: National Bureau of Economic Research.

Levin, R.C., A. Klevorick, R.R. Nelson and S.G. Winter (1987), 'Appropriating the returns from industrial research and development', *Brookings Papers on Economic Activity*, **3**, 783–820.

Loury, G.C. (1979), 'Market structure and innovation', *Quarterly Journal of Economics*, **93**, 395–410.

Lutterbeck, B., R. Gehring and A.H. Horns (2000), *Sicherheit in der Informationstechnologie und Patentschutz für Software-Produkte – ein Widerspruch?* Report to the Federal Ministry for Economics and Technology (BMWi), Berlin.

Machlup, F. (1958), *An Economic Review of the Patent System*, study of the subcommittee on patents, trademarks, and copyrights of the committee on the judiciary US senate 85th Congress, Washington, DC: Government Printing Office.

Mansfield, E. (1986), 'Patents and innovation: an empirical study', *Management Science*, **32**, 173–81.

Maskus, K.E. (1998), 'The international regulation of intellectual property', *Weltwirt-schaftliches Archiv*, **134**, 186–208.

Maskus, K.E. and M. Penubarti (1998), 'How trade-related are intellectual property rights?' *Journal of International Economics*, **39**, 227–48.

Mazzoleni, R. and R.R. Nelson (1998), 'The benefits and costs of strong patent protections: a contribution to the current debate', *Research Policy*, **27**, 273–84.

McFetridge, D.G. and M. Rafiquzzaman (1986), 'The scope and duration of the patent right and the nature of research rivalry', *Research In Law and Economics*, **8**, 91–120.

Messerschmitt, D. G. and C. Szyperski (2001), *Industrial and Economic Properties of Software: Technology, Processes, and Value*, Berkeley, CA: University of California at Berkeley.

Murillo, G. (1998), *Institutional Development in the Software Industry: Intellectual Property Protection*, Ann Arbor, MI: UMI Dissertation Abstract.

Nalley, E.T. (2000), 'Intellectual property in the computer programs', *Business Horizons*, **43** (4), 43–51.

Nichols, K. (1999), 'The age of software patents', *Computer*, **32** (4), 25–31.

Nordhaus, W.D. (1969), *Invention, Growth, and Welfare. A Theoretical Treatment of Technological Change*, Cambridge, MA: MIT Press.

Nüttgens, M. and E. Tesei (2000a), *Open Source – Konzept, Communities und Institutionen*, Saarbrücken: Institut für Wirtschaftsinformatik (Iwi).

Nüttgens, M. and E. Tesei (2000b), *Open Source – Marktmodelle und Netzwerke*, Saarbrücken: Institut für Wirtschaftsinformatik (Iwi).

Nüttgens, M. and E. Tesei (2000c), *Open Source – Produktion, Organisation und Lizenzen*, Saarbrücken: Institut für Wirtschaftsinformatik (Iwi).

Ordover, J.A. (1991), 'A patent systems for both diffusion and exclusion', *Journal of Economic Perspectives*, **5** (1), 43–60.

Oz, E. (1998), 'Acceptable protection of software intellectual property: a survey of software developers and lawyers', *Information and Management*, **34**, 161–73.

O'Reilly, T. (2000), 'The Internet patent land grab', *Communication of the ACM*, **43** (6).

PbT Consultants (2001), *The Results of the European Commission Consultation Exercise on the Patentability of Computer Implemented Inventions*, Orston, Notts, UK: PbT Consultants Ltd.

Rammer, C. (2003), *Patente und Marken als Schutzmechanismen für Innovationen*, Bonn: Bundesministerium für Bildung und Forschung.

Rammer, C., T. Doherr, B. Peters and T. Schmidt (2004), *Innovationsreport: EDV-und Telekommunikationsdienstleister*, ZEW Branchenreport, Mannheim: ZEW.

Richardson, G.B. (1997), *Economic Analysis, Public Policy and the Software Industry*, DRUID Working Paper No 97/4, Denmark: DRUID.

Rivette, K.G. and D. Kline (2000), 'Wie sich aus Patenten mehr herausholen lässt', *Harvard Business Manager*, **4** (2000), 28–40.

Romer, P. (1990), 'Endogenous technological change', *Journal of Political Economy*, **98**, 71–102.

Samuelson, P., M. Denber and R.J. Glushko (1992), 'Developments on the intellectual property front', *Communications of the ACM*, **35**, 33–9.

Scherer, F.M. and D. Ross (1990), *Industrial Market Structure and Economic Performance*, Boston, MA: Houghton Mifflin Company.

Schmoch, U. (2003), *Definition of Software*, report for the OECD, Karlsruhe and Paris: OECD.

Shapiro, C. and H.R. Varian (1999), *Information Rules. A Strategic Guide to the Network Economy*, Boston, MA: Havard Business School Press.

Shy, O. and J.-F. Thisse (1999), 'A strategic approach to software protection', *Journal of Economics and Management Strategy*, **8** (2), 163–90.

Sietmann, R. (2001), 'Wettbewerb im Gerichtssaal. Der Kampf ums geistige Eigentum treibt das Patentwesen in die Zerreißprobe', *c't – Magazin für Computertechnik*, **17**, 170 ff.

Smarr, L. and S. Graham (2000), *Recommendations of the Panel on Open Source Software for High End Computing*, President's Information Technology Advisory Committee, 11 September.

Smets-Solanes, J.P. (2000), *Software Useright: Solving Inconsistencies of Software Patents*, 2nd Nordic European/USENIX Conference, Malmö, Schweden, 8–11 February.

Smets-Solanes, J.P. (2001), *Stimulating Competition and Innovation in the Information Society*, working document, http://www.pro-innovation.org (23 March 2001).

Smith, P.J. (1999), 'Are weak patent rights a barrier to US exports?' *Journal of International Economics*, **48**, 151–77.

Stahl, P., H.D. Rombach, M. Friedewald, R. Wucher, S. Hartkopf, K. Kohler, S. Kimpeler, P. Zoche, M. Broy and I. Krüger (2000), *Analyse und Evaluation der Software-Entwicklung in Deutschland. Eine Studie für das Bundesministerium für Bildung und Forschung,* Nürnberg: GfK Marktforschung, Karlsruhe: ISI, Kaiserslautern: IESE.

Stolpe, M. (2000), 'Protection against software piracy: a study of technology adoption for the enforcement of intellectual property rights', *Economics of Innovation and New Technology*, **9**, 25–52.

St Laurent, A. (2004), *Open Source and Free Software Licensing*, Sebastopol, CA: O'Reilly & Associates.

Takeyama, L.N. (1994), 'The welfare implications of unauthorized reproduction of intellectual property in the presence of demand network externalities', *Journal of Industrial Economics*, **42**, 155–66.

Thompson, M.A. and F.W. Rushing (1999), 'An empirical analysis of the impact of patent protection on economic growth: an extension,', *Journal of Economic Development*, **24** (1), 67–76.

Thumm, N. (2000a), *Intellectual Property Rights: National Systems and Harmonisation in Europe*, Heidelberg: Physica-Verlag.

Thumm, N. (2000b), *Neubeurteilung von Patenten als Schutzmittel*, IPTS Report, Sevilla, Spain: IPTS.

Thurow, L.C. (1997), 'Needed: a new System of intellectual property rights', *Harvard Business Review*, September–October, 95–103.

UK Patent Office (2001), *Software Patenting Consultation*, http:// www.patent.gov.uk/news/softpat.htm (30 June 2001).

Webb, R. (2001), *Software & Business Methods Patents: The UK Consultations*; lecture at a workshop of the Federal Ministry for Economics and Technology, Berlin, 10 July.

Appendices

ANNEX 1: HYPOTHESES CONCERNING THE IMPACTS OF PATENTS IN THE AREA OF SOFTWARE- AND COMPUTER-RELATED INVENTIONS

Part A: Initial Assumption: the Type and Nature of the Developed Software Product Influence the Significance of Property Rights

H1: software which is a partial component of other software relies decisively on interoperability. Interoperability is strongly influenced by formal and informal protective mechanisms (questions 2a, 15–18, 35).

H2: so-called embedded software, which is integrated in hardware or other technical systems, is indirectly protected by the formal and informal protective mechanisms applicable to hardware, so that patents in the area of software- and computer-related inventions are of less importance by comparison with independent (stand-alone) software (questions 2a, 2b, 24).

H3: due to sequential innovation cycles, patents on operating systems and components of operating systems can lead rather to a slowing down of technical progress than patents on application software, which is developed in parallel for various areas of application (questions 3, 34, 35).

H4: for bespoke software the necessary protection can be achieved by bilateral contracts between producer and client. Patents lose (some of) their meaning (questions 4, 24).

H5: very high numbers of units produced tend to lead to positive network externalities or to a *de facto* standard. Because of the high number of units, combined with lower unit costs and the *de facto* monopoly (lock-in), the development costs can be reappropriated, so that no temporary monopoly protection by patents is necessary (questions 4, 24).

H6: hardware manufacturers have an advantage in the patenting of software because of their size and due to established patent activities (experience, fixed costs) (questions 2b, 20, 23, 24).

Part B: Initial Assumption: Enterprises' Propensity to Innovate Depends among other Aspects also on Protection Possibilities

H7a: less innovative enterprises utilize the existing protective mechanisms more effectively than more innovative ones, because the former can thus maintain a temporary monopoly longer (questions 5, 6, 24, 38).

H7b: enterprises that invest much in development have greater incentives to utilize property rights intensively (questions 5, 7, 24, 37).

H8a: pioneering enterprises that introduce market novelties have a 'first-mover advantage' and are therefore not so forced to rely on patents (question 5, sub-question 'yes', 24).

H8b: property rights secure the amortization of high development costs on the part of pioneering companies. These firms support and make more use of patents (question 5, sub-question 'yes', 24).

H9: software is characterized by comparatively short product development times and lifetimes, or short operating life for clients. Formal protection strategies like patents are thereby less important and are employed less (questions 7, 8, 24).

H10: the development of different types of software products (question 3) depends very much on the input of other developers or firms. The interoperability of the various components and the sequentiality of the innovation process are of great significance in the software area. Both are hampered by extended patenting possibilities (questions 3, 9, 15–18, 35).

H11: a large part of the external input is open source code. Firms that utilize open source code as input for their own developments are hindered by patents in the software sector and are therefore especially afraid of negative impacts of a broader patenting (questions 9, 34, 35).

H12: the innovation process in software development is characterized by incremental improvements, which to a large extent fall back on or have recourse to already existing own or foreign code (questions 9, 10).

H13a: the effect of patents in the area of software- and computer-related inventions on the innovation activity of enterprises which reuse their own code to a great extent is positive, because additional incentives for development investments are created (questions 9, 10, 34).

H13b: the effect of patents in the area of software- and computer-related inventions on the innovation activity of other firms which reuse their own code to a large extent is negative, because complete product lines can thus be protected and monopolies which are difficult to contest are created thereby (questions 9, 10 and 32).

H14: open source/shareware/freeware is more meaningful the more it is used as a development tool (question 11).

H15: open source/freeware/shareware are characterized by particular features which are especially conducive to the development of software (open, dynamic system, high compatibility and so on), which are not met by proprietary software to the same degree (questions 12, 34, 35).

Part C: Initial Assumption: Enterprises Have a Number of Motives to Disclose Their Software Developments or Deliver Free of Charge, Which Would Be Impaired by the Strengthening/ Reinforcement of Formal Property Rights

H16: enterprises disclose the source codes of their different software products under certain conditions, or deliver their software free of charge, so that formal protection mechanisms are not necessary. By extending patenting in the field of software- and computer-related inventions, counter-productive effects for the economy as a whole could be triggered off if know-how diffusion is restricted (questions 13–15, 19, 34, 35).

H17: the disclosure of code has a number of important strategic motives and thus the innovation dynamic is accelerated (question 15).

H18: by disclosing code, enterprises try to establish their products and programs as standard software. Patenting involves extensive licensing negotiations which in turn lead to higher costs for formal standardization (questions 15, 35).

H19: the interoperability of products is a special feature of the software sector and facilitates wide product variety, low costs (network effects) and a greater innovation dynamic in software development. Patenting limits interoperability (questions 15–18, 34, 35).

H20: firms have many motives to pass on their software free of charge, so that formal protection mechanisms are of low significance (questions 19, 24).

Part D: Initial Assumption: the Product Range, Internal Organization and Regional Distribution of the Business Activity of Companies Influence how Strongly Firms Utilize Different Formal and Informal Protection Strategies or Respectively are Affected by Them

H21: firms with their own patent offices not only possess more knowledge, but they tend also for reasons of organizational theory and strategy to agree with permitting patenting of 'software as such' (according to the US pattern) (questions 20, 21, 23, 24, 33).

H22: the self-estimation of degree of knowledge about patents and copyrights correlates positively with the utilization of formal protection strategies, the assessment of the suitability of stronger methods of protection and the positive evaluation of the effect of patents in the area of software- and computer-related inventions (questions 23, 24, 34, 35).

H23: due to the idiosyncrasies of the software field, patenting does not play a large role; there is neither a broad awareness nor any perception of need. The need for protection is met by other strategic tools. In the manufacturing industry also, in relation to other protection strategies, the patent activities in the software sector are rather underdeveloped (questions 20–24, 28).

H24: patents on software- and computer-related inventions, compared with general business activities, are relatively more important in the USA than in Germany and the rest of Europe (questions 26, 27).

H25: patents have a very broad strategic significance, which extends beyond the mere protection from imitation. This strategic meaning correlates positively with enterprise size or market structure and with activities abroad (questions 27, 37, 38).

H26a: in the area of software- and computer-related inventions the significance of the reasons which stand in the way of a patent depends on the various types of software products (questions 2–4, 28).

H26b: the secondary branch allot a different meaning to the reasons which speak against patenting in the area of software- and computer-related inventions than do the primary branch, as their patenting activities in this area follow the example of their general patenting activities in the traditional product field (questions 2–4, 28).

H27: small and medium-sized enterprises conduct fewer searches in patent databases for cost reasons (questions 2, 37).

H28: a significant function of patents in the manufacturing industry is to reveal information. This information function does not play a role in the software sector, as the information about new developments runs through other channels here or is available via other mechanisms (question 30).

H29: legal actions in the area of software- and computer-related patents are still very rare in Europe. German firms are also very rarely the plaintiffs. The number of legal proceedings correlates with activity abroad and company size, or market structure (questions 31, 37, 38).

Part E: Initial Assumption: the Attitude towards a Desirable Patent System and Consequences of Patenting for One's Own Enterprise Depends on the Previous Activities, Specific Resources, Size, Type of Software, Utilization of Open Source, Innovation Dynamic, Company Size, Market Structure, and Activity Abroad

H30: the introduction of a novelty grace period is supported by firms that are involved in the open source movement, because they thus can file a patent application for their new developments despite the imminent disclosure (questions 13, 33).

H31: patent protection facilitates market entry for young software enterprises, as it offers them easier access to the capital market and gives them time to expand their production capacities (questions 27, 35).

H32: patent protection increases the incentive for direct investments from abroad, because the foreign investors can better appropriate the profits from their investments in software development (question 35).

H33: although it makes sense from the perspective of the individual company to patent more, in order to block competitors, this leads to serious impairment of innovation dynamics for the sector as a whole (questions 27, 35).

H34: the interoperability of products and systems will decrease as a result of stronger patent protection (question 35).

H35a: the development efforts in the area of open source will not be increased or strengthened by patents in the area of software- and computer-related inventions, because other motivations dominate here (questions 13, 35).

H35b: patents in the area of software- and computer-related inventions can hinder the open source movement, or reduce their efforts, because as a result of easier patenting the alternative incentives for software programmers increase (questions 13, 35).

H36: the possibility to patent 'software as such' has positive effects on the dynamics and growth of the software sector, because the incentives for spending on development activities increase and simultaneously more information about new developments is released (questions 34, 35).

H37: through more efficient portfolio management, large enterprises can establish an efficient portfolio balance in software development projects, so that they are less dependent on a temporary monopoly generated by patents (questions 37, 24).

H38: the tendency to patent increases with the relative share of activities abroad (questions 37, 24).

H39: SMEs have neither the awareness nor the resources to make effective use of patenting (questions 37, 24).

H40: enterprises conduct software development in co-operation. Property rights have here under certain circumstances a reverse meaning: on the one hand, they increase the legal security and create clarity in co-operation agreements; on the other hand, however, they erect entry barriers, if firms without a property rights portfolio are refused access to co-operations. Further, they are then unnecessary if a controlled exchange of code and know-how takes place in existing co-operations (question 39).

H41: the more established enterprises are in the market, the more knowledge they possess about the problems with property rights and the more inclined they are to utilize them actively and to allocate resources for this purpose (questions 20–24, 40).

H42: in software development, very young firms or individual businesses (micro firms) play a disproportionately large role (questions 1, 13, 40). This points to low market entry barriers and dynamic market development. Supposed negative effects of an extension of patent protection (patents for 'software as such') would be because they hamper the development of new firms (question 40 in connection with hypotheses 11, 15, 35).

ANNEX 2: QUESTIONNAIRE

Please give us your e-mail address:

1. **Please give your position in the company:**

   entrepreneur ☐
   member of the managing board/manager ☐
   chief technology officer/head of the ☐
   development department
   head of software development department ☐
   head of legal/patent department ☐
   independent software developer ☐
   if your position is not mentioned, please add: ☐

A   A description of your company's products

2a. **Please estimate the shares of turnover which your company reaches with the following types of internally developed or own software:**

   software as independent final product _____ %
   software which creates utility to the customer only in connection _____ %
   with existing third party software
   software development for customizing existing software _____ %
   embedded software _____ %

   Sum   100   %

2b. **Do you (also) develop and produce hardware which functions in connection with own and/or foreign software?**

   yes ☐   no ☐

3. **Please estimate the share of turnover in your company for ...**

   ... systems-related software _____ %
   ... tools for the development of software _____ %
   ... libraries of programs _____ %
   ... software applications for business management _____ %
   ... finance and retail software _____ %
   ... technical application software (e.g. CAD) _____ %
   ... software for automatic control engineering _____ %
   ... software for multimedia and Internet applications _____ %
   ... office automation and graphic charts (e.g. office products, DTP) _____ %
   ... computer games _____ %
   ... other software _____ _____ %

   Sum   100   %

4. **Which share of turnover does your company have for software products which are produced ...**

    ... as real individual software   [   ] %
    ... as small-lot production for specific customers [   ] %
    ... as standardized mass production   [   ] %

                                    Sum   100   %

B   **Innovation activities in your company**

5. **Did you develop new software products in the year 2000?**

    yes ☐   if yes: only new for your own company   ☐
                              novelty for the market   ☐
    no ☐

6. **Please estimate the share of turnover your company reached in the year 2000 with products novel to your company**

                        5 % ☐
                     6–10 % ☐
                    11–20 % ☐
                    21–30 % ☐
                    31–40 % ☐
                    41–50 % ☐
                  over 50 % ☐
                do not know ☐
                  no answer ☐
    not applicable as we limit ☐

7. **How long – on average – are the development times of your internally developed software?**

    [   ] months

8. **How many months does it take on average until your customers ...**

    ... replace a program by an improved version   [   ] months
    ... replace a program by a completely new program [   ] months

9. **Please estimate the share of software from the following sources in the development of your software in the year 2000. Please assess also the change of importance of these sources:**

	share in 2000	change in the next 2 years		
		increases	constant	decreases
open source	[ ] %	☐	☐	☐
shareware/freeware	[ ] %	☐	☐	☐
acquisition of standard software (incl. libraries)	[ ] %	☐	☐	☐

software developed by other companies on your behalf [   ] %   ⬜ ⬜ ⬜

imitation of the functions of competitive products [   ] %   ⬜ ⬜ ⬜

internal development [   ] %   ⬜ ⬜ ⬜

Sum   100   %

10. For all software products: how large is the average share of code-recycling of internally developed software?

5 % ⬜
6–10 % ⬜
11–20 % ⬜
21–30 % ⬜
31– 40 % ⬜
41–50 % ⬜
over 50 % ⬜
do not know ⬜
no answer ⬜

11. If you use open source or freeware/shareware: what purposes do you use them for? *(Multiple answers possible)*

	open source	freeware/shareware
as tools for development	⬜	⬜
as Internet software	⬜	⬜
as components of final products	⬜	⬜
others [ ]	⬜	⬜

12. Why do you use open source and freeware/shareware for the production of new software?

	open source					freeware/shareware				
	very low importance				very high importance	very low importance				very high importance
high quality	⬜	⬜	⬜	⬜	⬜	⬜	⬜	⬜	⬜	⬜
high safety	⬜	⬜	⬜	⬜	⬜	⬜	⬜	⬜	⬜	⬜
good adaptability	⬜	⬜	⬜	⬜	⬜	⬜	⬜	⬜	⬜	⬜
high topicality	⬜	⬜	⬜	⬜	⬜	⬜	⬜	⬜	⬜	⬜
low costs	⬜	⬜	⬜	⬜	⬜	⬜	⬜	⬜	⬜	⬜
high compatibility	⬜	⬜	⬜	⬜	⬜	⬜	⬜	⬜	⬜	⬜
others	⬜	⬜	⬜	⬜	⬜	⬜	⬜	⬜	⬜	⬜

[   ]

C Ways to deal with own software developments

13. Please indicate to which extent and under which conditions you release the source codes of your software products:

	yes, generally	yes, often	occasionally	in individual cases	never
free of charge to the general public	☐	☐	☐	☐	☐
for a fee to the general public	☐	☐	☐	☐	☐
to specific customers against payment	☐	☐	☐	☐	☐

14. For which type of software do you publish the source codes? *(Multiple answers possible)*

systems-related software	☐
software applications for business management	☐
technical application software	☐
software for multimedia and Internet applications	☐
software for other commercial applications [＿＿＿＿＿＿]	☐

15. If you disclose the source code, what is the importance of the following motives:

	very low				very high
securing the interoperability of my product with others	☐	☐	☐	☐	☐
establishing own development as a standard	☐	☐	☐	☐	☐
free access to other source codes	☐	☐	☐	☐	☐
to allow further development of my product by third parties	☐	☐	☐	☐	☐
to facilitate the development of comple-mentary products by third parties	☐	☐	☐	☐	☐
to foster ideas for complementary products by customers and suppliers	☐	☐	☐	☐	☐
quality signaling and transparency for customers	☐	☐	☐	☐	☐
expansion and improvement of co-operation opportunities	☐	☐	☐	☐	☐
fast market penetration	☐	☐	☐	☐	☐
license revenues	☐	☐	☐	☐	☐
improvement of own systems software by third parties	☐	☐	☐	☐	☐

16. How important is the interoperability of your software with the software of ...

	very low				very high
... your clients	☐	☐	☐	☐	☐
... your suppliers	☐	☐	☐	☐	☐
... the suppliers of competitive products	☐	☐	☐	☐	☐
... the suppliers of complementary products	☐	☐	☐	☐	☐

17. How do you secure the interoperability of your software with the software of your clients and suppliers? *(Multiple answers possible)*

	clients	suppliers
disclosure of the source code	☐	☐
disclosure of the interfaces	☐	☐
use of standardized sector-wide architectures	☐	☐
orientation towards the *de facto* standard of the market leader	☐	☐
get own solution accepted as *de facto* standard	☐	☐
co-operation for reciprocal use	☐	☐
others	☐	☐
interoperability undesirable or not necessary	☐	☐

18. How do you secure the interoperability of your software with the software of other suppliers? *(Multiple answers possible)*

	direct competitive products	complementary products
disclosure of the source code	☐	☐
disclosure of the interfaces	☐	☐
use of standardized sector-wide architectures	☐	☐
orientation towards the *de facto* standard of the market leader	☐	☐
get own solution accepted as *de facto* standard	☐	☐
co-operation for reciprocal use	☐	☐
others	☐	☐
interoperability undesirable or not necessary	☐	☐

19. Do you give your software products away free of charge?

yes,	yes, often	occasionally	in individual cases	never
☐	☐	☐	☐	☐

D   Experiences with intellectual property rights

20. Does your company have a department or unit which is in charge of intellectual property rights?

yes ☐   planned ☐   no ☐

21. Information about this department/unit:

When was this department/unit set up (year)? ☐

How many people (will) work in this ☐

What does this department cost per year? ☐ Euro

22. Why does such a department not exist? *(Multiple answers possible)*

use of external consultation (e.g. patent attorney) if required ☐

costs too high ☐

no demand ☐

patents have been no issue up to now ☐

other reasons ☐

23. How do you estimate the know-how for the acquisition and prosecution of intellectual property rights in your company?

	non-existent				very good
concerning patents	☐	☐	☐	☐	☐
concerning copyrights	☐	☐	☐	☐	☐

24. Do you use the following strategies for the protection of your software and computer-related developments?   **If yes, please give the respective importance**

	no	yes	very low				very high
patents	☐	☐	☐	☐	☐	☐	☐
patented designs, registered utility models	☐	☐	☐	☐	☐	☐	☐
trade marks	☐	☐	☐	☐	☐	☐	☐
prosecution of copyrights	☐	☐	☐	☐	☐	☐	☐
know-how contracts	☐	☐	☐	☐	☐	☐	☐
secrecy pledge (e.g. labor contracts) or incentives for employees	☐	☐	☐	☐	☐	☐	☐
protection against copying through hardware components (dongle, PLA etc.)	☐	☐	☐	☐	☐	☐	☐
protection against imitation or decompiling through software	☐	☐	☐	☐	☐	☐	☐
customer relations management	☐	☐	☐	☐	☐	☐	☐
lead-time advantages	☐	☐	☐	☐	☐	☐	☐
others ☐	☐	☐	☐	☐	☐	☐	☐

25. If you use patents, how many patents does your company own concerning software and computer-related developments?

number ☐   do not know ☐

26. Please indicate the importance of patenting of software and computer-related developments in the following regions for your company:

	very low				very high
in the home country	☐	☐	☐	☐	☐

	very low				
in other European countries	☐	☐	☐	☐	☐
in the USA	☐	☐	☐	☐	☐
in Japan	☐	☐	☐	☐	☐
in other regions	☐	☐	☐	☐	☐

27. How important are the following motives for your company to patent software and computer-related developments:

	very low				very high
protection of own development from imitation	☐	☐	☐	☐	☐
expansion of market lead	☐	☐	☐	☐	☐
impeding the software development of competitors	☐	☐	☐	☐	☐
high importance of patent protection					
in other European countries	☐	☐	☐	☐	☐
in the USA	☐	☐	☐	☐	☐
in Japan	☐	☐	☐	☐	☐
increase your company's value	☐	☐	☐	☐	☐
improved access to financial resources	☐	☐	☐	☐	☐
cross-licensing	☐	☐	☐	☐	☐
access to patent pools	☐	☐	☐	☐	☐
generation of licensing income	☐	☐	☐	☐	☐
others [＿＿＿＿＿＿＿＿＿]	☐	☐	☐	☐	☐

28. How important are the following motives for your company *not to* patent software and computer-related developments:

	very low				very high
low protection of patents	☐	☐	☐	☐	☐
patent infringements not verifiable	☐	☐	☐	☐	☐
long procedures until the issue of a patent	☐	☐	☐	☐	☐
costs of patent application, persecution and acceptance too high	☐	☐	☐	☐	☐
in view of the global medium Internet patent protection is not attractive because of the restricted domain of protection and resulting acceptance problems	☐	☐	☐	☐	☐
innovativeness of own products too low	☐	☐	☐	☐	☐
avoidance of the disclosure of product specifications	☐	☐	☐	☐	☐
not relevant	☐	☐	☐	☐	☐
insufficient knowledge about patent protection	☐	☐	☐	☐	☐
impediment of innovative dynamics in the sector	☐	☐	☐	☐	☐
bad image of patents/fear of damaged image in the case of aggressive persecution of patent rights	☐	☐	☐	☐	☐
doubts about the patentability or the acceptance of patents	☐	☐	☐	☐	☐

29. Does your company conduct searches in patent databases?

yes, regularly ▢   yes, from case to case ▢   no ▢   do not know ▢

30. If you conduct searches, how important are the following motives for the searches:

	very low				very high
covering against patent infringements	▢	▢	▢	▢	▢
gain information about the recent state of the development as input for own developments	▢	▢	▢	▢	▢
analysis of competitors	▢	▢	▢	▢	▢
identification of possible suppliers	▢	▢	▢	▢	▢
identification of possible co-operation partners	▢	▢	▢	▢	▢
other reasons [ ]	▢	▢	▢	▢	▢

31. Has your company ever been involved in a lawsuit concerning intellectual property rights?

no ▢   yes ▢   if yes:

	in patent law		**in copyright law**	
	in Europe	in the USA	in Europe	in the USA
as defendant	▢	▢	▢	▢
as plaintiff	▢	▢	▢	▢
do not know	▢	▢	▢	▢

32. Because of suspected intellectual property rights of competitors during software development...

	never	sometimes	often
... a project was impeded, went up in price or was prolonged	▢	▢	▢
... a project was cancelled	▢	▢	▢
... a project was not started	▢	▢	▢
... other measures were taken [ ]	▢	▢	▢

E   Your personal judgment

33. Which alternative legal settlement of Intellectual Property Rights for software- and computer-related inventions do you consider as being appropriate?

	not appropriate	ambivalent	appropriate	do not know
software should be excluded – to a great extent – from patenting	▢	▢	▢	▢
retaining the status quo: limited patent-ability (technical relation necessary)	▢	▢	▢	▢
keeping to current practise, but shortened patent protection period	▢	▢	▢	▢
general patentability for 'software as such' (similar to the US system)	▢	▢	▢	▢
extend patenting to software-related bus-iness methods (business methods patents)	▢	▢	▢	▢
introduction of a grace period for software and computer-related patents?	▢	▢	▢	▢

	strong decrease	decrease	no consequence	growth	strong growth
disclosure of the patent document on application day	☐	☐	☐	☐	
more deregulation, respectively more support with patenting	☐	☐	☐	☐	
globally unique, binding and enforceable patent law	☐	☐	☐	☐	
support for private initiatives to enforce and follow-up (patent search services etc.)	☐	☐	☐	☐	

further suggestions [   ]

34. Which consequences would it have *for your company* if it were legally possible to patent 'software as such'?

	strong decrease	decrease	no consequence	growth	strong growth
competitiveness					
in home country	☐	☐	☐	☐	☐
in Europe	☐	☐	☐	☐	☐
in the USA	☐	☐	☐	☐	☐
in South East Asia	☐	☐	☐	☐	☐
turnover	☐	☐	☐	☐	☐
number of employees	☐	☐	☐	☐	☐
number of co-operations with other companies	☐	☐	☐	☐	☐
quality of products	☐	☐	☐	☐	☐
variety of products	☐	☐	☐	☐	☐
development of open source software	☐	☐	☐	☐	☐
dynamic of innovation activities	☐	☐	☐	☐	☐
legal security	☐	☐	☐	☐	☐
cost for patent search and patent-related legal issues	☐	☐	☐	☐	☐
other [ ]	☐	☐	☐	☐	☐

35. Which consequence would it have *for your sector in your country* if it were legally possible to patent 'software as such'?

	strong decrease	decrease	no consequence	growth	strong growth
competitiveness					
in Europe	☐	☐	☐	☐	☐
in the USA	☐	☐	☐	☐	☐
in South East Asia	☐	☐	☐	☐	☐
turnover	☐	☐	☐	☐	☐
number of employees	☐	☐	☐	☐	☐
degree of competitiveness	☐	☐	☐	☐	☐
number of companies	☐	☐	☐	☐	☐

	strong decrease	decrease	no consequence	growth	strong growth
quality of products	☐	☐	☐	☐	☐
variety of products	☐	☐	☐	☐	☐
variety of components/reusables	☐	☐	☐	☐	☐
dynamic of innovation activities	☐	☐	☐	☐	☐
individual incentives to develop open source software	☐	☐	☐	☐	☐
interoperability of products or infrastructures	☐	☐	☐	☐	☐
legal security	☐	☐	☐	☐	☐
cost of formal software standardization (e.g. CEN, ISO)	☐	☐	☐	☐	☐
foreign direct investment in the home country	☐	☐	☐	☐	☐
other _____	☐	☐	☐	☐	☐

F Information on your company

36. Is your company part of a company group?

☐ yes, we are part of a company group.
☐ no, we are independent.

37. Please give the following indicators for your company in the year 2000:

turnover	_____	Euro
exports	_____	Euro
expenses for the development of new software	_____	Euro
number of employees	_____	persons
number of employees devoted to the development of new software (without maintenance and administration)	_____	persons
expenses for the development of new software	_____	Euro

38. How many competitors does your company have?

none ☐   one ☐   2–5 ☐   more than 5 ☐

39. How often does your company co-operate with other companies in order to develop new software?

	never				always
clients	☐	☐	☐	☐	☐
suppliers	☐	☐	☐	☐	☐
competitors	☐	☐	☐	☐	☐
other _____	☐	☐	☐	☐	☐

40. When was your company established?

_____

Index